Integrating Social and Environmental Archaeologies: Reconsidering Deposition

Edited by

James Morris
Mark Maltby

BAR International Series 2077
2010

Published in 2016 by
BAR Publishing, Oxford

BAR International Series 2077

Integrating Social and Environmental Archaeologies: Reconsidering Deposition

ISBN 978 1 4073 0638 4

© The editors and contributors severally and the Publisher 2010

The authors' moral rights under the 1988 UK Copyright,
Designs and Patents Act are hereby expressly asserted.

All rights reserved. No part of this work may be copied, reproduced, stored,
sold, distributed, scanned, saved in any form of digital format or transmitted
in any form digitally, without the written permission of the Publisher.

BAR Publishing is the trading name of British Archaeological Reports (Oxford) Ltd.
British Archaeological Reports was first incorporated in 1974 to publish the BAR
Series, International and British. In 1992 Hadrian Books Ltd became part of the BAR
group. This volume was originally published by Archaeopress in conjunction with
British Archaeological Reports (Oxford) Ltd / Hadrian Books Ltd, the Series principal
publisher, in 2010. This present volume is published by BAR Publishing, 2016.

Printed in England

BAR titles are available from:

        BAR Publishing
        122 Banbury Rd, Oxford, OX2 7BP, UK
EMAIL   info@barpublishing.com
PHONE +44 (0)1865 310431
FAX   +44 (0)1865 316916
        www.barpublishing.com

Contents

1. Introduction: Integrating social and Environmental Archaeologies 1
M. Maltby and J. Morris

2. The use of archaeological and zooarchaeological data in the interpretation 5
of Dún Ailinne, an Iron Age royal site in Co. Kildare, Ireland.
P. Crabtree, S. A. Johnston and D. V. Campana

3. Associated bone groups: beyond the Iron Age 12
J. Morris

4. Pits and wells 24
M. Maltby

5. New light on an old rite: reanalysis of an Iron Age burial group from 33
Blewburton Hill, Oxfordshire.
R. Bendrey, S. Leach and K. Clark

6. Structured Deposition or Casual Disposal of Human Remains? A Case Study 45
of Four Iron Age Sites from southern England.
A. Russell

7. Bone modification and the conceptual relationship between humans and 66
animals in Iron Age Wessex
R. Madgwick

8. More ritual rubbish? Exploring the taphonomic history, context formation 83
processes and 'specialness' of deposits including human and animal bone
in Iron Age pits.
C. Randall

9. The politics of the everyday: exploring 'midden' space in Late Bronze 103
Age Wiltshire
K. Waddington

List of Figures

2.1	Map of Ireland showing the location of Dún Ailinne and the other Irish royal sites.	5
2.2	Plan of the 1968-75 excavations at Dún Ailinne showing the locations of the Iron Age structures.	6
2.3	Kill-patterns for the cattle recovered from the Flame Phase deposits at Dún Ailinne.	7
2.4	Fragment of cattle metatarsal that has been sawn at both ends.	8
2.5	A bone needle and a possible spindle whorl from Dún Ailinne.	9
2.6	A bone object, made from a split rib, that may have been used for basketry or matting.	9
3.1	Percentage of sites per region and period with ABGs present.	13
3.2	Total percentage NISP for the most common species per period from southern England sites included in this study.	15
3.3	Total percentages of ABGs from each period for southern England.	15
3.4	Total percentage NISP for the most common species per period from Yorkshire sites included in this study.	16
3.5	Total percentage of ABGs from each period for Yorkshire.	17
3.6	Mortality profiles of complete ABGs per species.	18
3.7	Mortality profiles of partial ABG per species.	19
3.8	Percentage of complete ABGs present for the main species per period.	20
5.1	Map showing location of Blewburton Hill, Oxfordshire.	33
5.2	Blewburton Hill, Cutting F under excavation.	33
5.3	Section through defensive ditch around the Blewburton Hill Iron Age hillfort.	34
5.4	Hindleg of horse and human skull in filling of Blewburton Hill main ditch, Cutting F.	34
5.5	Dog skeleton in filling of Blewburton Hill main ditch, Cutting F.	34
5.6	Miscellaneous Iron Age small finds from Blewburton Hill.	35
5.7	Blewburton Hill human: eburnation is present on the left trapezium, indicating osteoarthritis.	36
5.8	Blewburton Hill human: degenerative disc disease is indicated by general degeneration of the surfaces of the cervical vertebrae bodies.	36
5.9	Blewburton Hill horse: new bone formation has bridged the interosseus border between the left metacarpal ii and metacarpal iii	37
5.10	Blewburton Hill horse: anterior view of left anterior proximal phalanx with periosteal reaction.	37
5.11	Blewburton Hill dog: left metacarpals II and III.	38
5.12	Blewburton Hill dog: right metatarsal IV.	38
6.1	Proportions of species in features with human remains, without human remains and with ABGs at Battlesbury Bowl.	49

6.2 Proportions of species in features with human remains, without human remains and with ABGs at Suddern Farm. 49

6.3 Proportions of species in features with human remains, without human remains and with ABGs at Houghton Down. 50

6.4 Proportions of species in features with human remains, without human remains and with ABGs at Nettlebank Copse. 51

6.5 Inter-site comparison of species proportions, from NISP counts, in features with human bone present. 52

6.6 Comparison of species proportions from the sites of study using total site NISPs. 52

6.7 Percentage of bones with taphonomic and butchery evidence at Battlesbury Bowl in features with and without human bone. 53

6.8 Percentage of bones with taphonomic and butchery evidence at Suddern Farm in features with and without human bone. 53

6.9 Percentage of bones with taphonomic and butchery evidence at Houghton Down in features with and without human bone. 54

6.10 Percentage of bones with taphonomic and butchery evidence at Nettlebank Copse in features with and without human bone. 54

6.11 Types of human deposits as a percentage of the total number per site. 55

6.12 The percentage of human deposits with gnawing, erosion and butchery marks present. 56

7.1 Pit 923, from Danebury showing the mass of material in various states of articulation. 67

7.2 The percentage of disarticulated human and faunal remains in different weathering stages. 72

7.3 The percentage of disarticulated human and faunal remains in different gnawing stages. 72

7.4 The percentage of disarticulated human and faunal remains affected by abrasion, trampling and longitudinal/spiral fracturing. 73

7.5 The percentage of animal bones in uniform features and mixed features in different weathering stages. 73

7.6 The percentage of animal bones from uniform features and mixed features in each gnawing stage. 74

7.7 The percentage of animal bones from uniform features and mixed features that are affected by trampling and abrasion. 74

7.8 The percentage of animal bones from uniform features and mixed features that are affected by longitudinal and spiral fracturing. 75

8.1 Location of Cadbury Castle, South Cadbury, Somerset. 85

8.2 Fluxgate gradiometer survey of the west end of Sigwells carried out in 1993. 86

8.3 Distribution of weathered, gnawed and burnt bone by feature types by percentage of total fragments for that feature type. 90

8.4 Histogram showing the incidence of animal bone fragments in layers in pits. 91

8.5 Comparison of total bone number recovered by the number of excavated litres per context. 92

8.6 Distribution of pottery sherd numbers within each pit third for total Iron Age. 93

8.7 Distribution of bone fragments within each pit third for total Iron Age. 93

8.8 Distribution of small/special finds within each third for total Iron Age.	93
8.9 Distribution of ABGs within each pit third.	93
8.10 Distribution of human remains within each pit third.	93
8.11 The presence of shell in shell-tempered pottery from a selection of contexts from three pits arranged by pit thirds.	95
8.12 Mean percentage of weathered identified bone by depth in pit thirds.	96
8.13 Mean percentage of bone portion for identified bone by depth in pit thirds.	96
8.14 Histogram showing the proportions of bone recovered by hand and via soil samples by volume of excavated context for a selection of five pits.	96
8.15 Comparison of burnt, weathered and gnawed bone as a percentage of the total bone fragment count in the main bone assemblages for Trench 14 pits by pit third.	97
8.16 Comparison of burnt, weathered and gnawed bone as a percentage of the total bone fragment count in the >6mm soil sample residue assemblages for Trench 14 pits by pit third.	97
8.17 Mean percentage of burnt bone in pit thirds middle Iron Age	97
8.18 Mean percentage of burnt bone in pit thirds late Iron Age.	97
8.19 Comparison of Magnetic Susceptibility by depth using pit thirds for five pits.	97
8.20 Comparison of pH values by depth using pit thirds for five pits.	97
9.1 Location plan showing a selection of excavated midden sites in southern Britain and distribution of the excavated sites in Wiltshire.	105
9.2 All Cannings Cross sits within the gently sloping valley floor, framed to the north by Clifford's Hill and Rybury hillfort.	108
9.3 Plan of an area excavated by Cunnington at All Cannings Cross showing the position of various features.	109
9.4 Sketch of a section at All Cannings Cross showing a sequence of dark humic soils and chalk platforms and plan of platform H showing associated pits.	109
9.5 Planning one of the irregular chalk platforms or floors at All Cannings Cross, during the recent excavations carried out by John Barrett and Dave McOmish.	110
9.6 View from the top of the mound at East Chisenbury, with All Cannings Cross in the distance to the north.	111
9.7 Grave digging at the cemetery of Potterne, August 2005, animal bone and pottery collected from the spoil heap of the grave and the section of the grave, showing a deep sequence of deposits and a laid stone surface running horizontally through the section.	111
9.8 A decorated pottery sherd with chalk inlay from trench B, context 22, at East Chisenbury.	113

List of Tables

2.1 A phase-by-phase summary of the animal bones recovered from the 1968-75 excavations at Dún Ailinne. — 6

2.2 Species ratios based on NISP for the Flame Phase deposits. — 8

3.1 Number of ABGs recorded per region and period. — 13

3.2 Percentage of complete, partial and unknown ABGs for the total assemblage (southern England and Yorkshire), per species. — 18

4.1 Summary of sequence of depositions in Greyhound Yard, Dorchester Shaft 13. — 26

4.2 Associated bone groups (ABG) in Greyhound Yard, Dorchester Shaft 13. — 27

4.3 Animal bones from Winchester Victoria Road pit F814. — 29

7.1 Stages for the identification of different levels of gnawing severity. — 70

8.1 The incidence of deposits in pit thirds in Hill's study. — 84

8.2 Taphonomic processes and other factors affecting animal bone assemblages. — 84

8.3 Sigwells fill types. — 88

8.4 Sigwells fill characters. — 89

8.5 NISP counts and percentages for domestic species and unidentified material by feature type for the Sigwells hand collected main assemblage. — 89

8.6 Details of all ABGs identified in the Sigwells site assemblage. — 91

8.7 Bone condition by species for pits. — 91

8.8 Mean percentages and numbers of fragments for various taphonomic indicators by fill type. — 95

1. Integrating social and environmental archaeologies

James Morris and Mark Maltby

Introduction

This volume developed from a session on the role that environmental archaeology can play in integrated investigations of 'ritual' deposits, at the Association of Environmental Archaeologists (AEA) conference in Exeter, 2006. The session drew together a wide range of speakers, all of whom had a particular take or example of the use of environmental evidence in the study of 'ritual'; with examples ranging from deposits in Iron Age Ireland to the activities that occurred on Bronze Age middens. Of the thirteen papers presented eight have been adapted and revised for publication in this volume.

Erecting barriers

Environmental archaeology has the potential to inform on a broad range of issues such as cuisine; diet; trade; ritual acts; the use of space; production and supply; status; acculturation; the development of technology and the structuring of societies, to name but a few. However, too often fellow archaeologists' views of the extent of environmental studies can be summarised in two questions; 'what was the diet?' and 'what was the local environment like?' Although practitioners of environmental archaeology may bemoan such narrow viewpoints, we are hardly blameless in allowing such opinions to continue, for we have in the past not been particularly active in advertising the range of information we can produce.

In the investigation of aspects such as 'ritual' behaviour such attitudes appear to be prevalent. Although much of the evidence discussed may be environmental in nature, it is telling that the specialist is rarely asked to comment on such deposits, beyond the identification of the material. A classic example is the recent Danebury environs project (Cunliffe 2000), within which many 'special animal deposits' were recovered. As these deposits were thought to be of a ritual significance in the reports they were discussed separately from the rest of the faunal material and it is perhaps telling that they were reported on by different authors. Of course there is no right or wrong way for such material to be reported upon, but it is interesting that environmental archaeologists are often not involved in the formation of broader interpretations of their data.

One of the reasons for this may well be the association of environmental archaeology with particular archaeological paradigms. The development of environmental archaeology into the widely practised discipline as it is today can be linked back to the scientific revolution in archaeology and the rise in processualism during the 1960's and 70's. The attitude to environmental remains can be seen in the first version of Science in Archaeology (Brothwell and Higgs 1963). In Reed's (1963) discussion of Osteo-Archaeology, the section on interpretation is separated into statistics; environment; census problems; domestication and hunting, butchery and food. Likewise Western's (1963) discussion of wood and charcoal concerns the evidence of past environments and the making of structures, tools and domestic equipment. The interpretation of environmental remains in both papers concerns functional economic aspects of human behaviour, whereas social issues are not addressed.

Environmental archaeology was greatly influenced by the emergence of the 'Palaeoeconomy' School at Cambridge under the leadership of Grahame Clark and Eric Higgs in the 1960's (Milner and Fuller 1999). The research conducted highlighted the contribution environmental studies could make to the procurement and consumption of food, as well as the growing field of taphonomic studies. With this, the wider archaeological community began to realise the value of environmental remains in the study of subsistence economies. However, regarding 'ritual' the 'palaeoeconomic' school took a hard line in stating that 'the soul leaves no skeleton' (Higgs and Jarman 1975). This corresponds to the general trend that archaeologists of the 1960's and 1970's were reluctant to investigate the role of ritual and religion (Renfrew 1994).

As archaeology began a period of philosophical change with the development of post-processual approaches in the 1980's, it could be argued that environmental archaeology lagged behind (see for example O'Conner 1991; Thomas 1990). The interpretation of Iron Age associated bone groups (see Morris, Chapter 3) highlights the divide that was occurring. In the 1980's new interpretations were being offered for these animal bone deposits, suggesting they were of a special ritual nature, possible representing sacrifices or acts of offering (Grant 1984; 1989; Méniel 1992; Wait 1985). Cunliffe (1992) developed these ideas to suggest that other environmental materials may also have been used in this manner. However, not all environmental specialists agreed. The animal remains section in the 1991 Danebury publication is very revealing, Grant (1991, 482) comments;

'*There is also, it must be added, an undercurrent of scepticism about these animal deposits, and some have argued, privately and publicly, though not necessarily in the press, that they represent nothing more than natural deaths of animals that died in circumstances that render them unfit for human consumption.*'

Later Hill (1995; 1996) suggested that there is a divide that appears to eliminate the ability of any archaeological evidence to illuminate the real world as soon as it is labelled ritual.

'It is perhaps because they feel any bone labelled 'ritual' cannot be used to reconstruct diet, herd management and other practical matters of the economy' (Hill 1996, 23).

It appears that at the time environmental studies had become separated from the wider field of archaeology, which is neither necessary nor helpful (O'Connor 1998). Milner and Fuller (1999), in discussing zooarchaeology, suggest that such specialists are often perceived to focus on methodological issues such as taphonomy, bone densities, fracture patterns, whereas the tendency of non-specialists was to see these matters as trivial. Also environmental archaeology is invariably linked to environmental determinism, which became an unpopular theory as it implies that cultural development is not determined by social, but in some part by environmental factors (O'Conner and Evans 2005, 7).

Knocking down the wall

In some part environmental archaeology may still be viewed as a separate 'processual' field by members of the archaeological community. They are perceived to be solely interested in issues such as climate; habitat; land use; agriculture; diet; food production and processing; living conditions; buildings; disease; economy; and especially taphonomy. Indeed some environmental specialists may secretly, or not so secretly in some cases, enjoy been given such a tag and flying in the face of alternative archaeological paradigms. All too often specialists in environmental and in some cases other forms of material culture, are viewed as fetishists, interested only in the material they study. Environmental archaeologists are not often perceived to be greatly interested in issues such as the social use of space; cognition; ritual; cuisine; and theoretical archaeology in general. However, it must be remembered that as archaeologists we all have the same goal, of exploring humanity's past. Perhaps the structure of modern archaeology does not help in this manner. Individuals are too often placed into specialist categories such as archaeobotanist, zooarchaeologist or geoarchaeologist, either due to the structure of commercial/government-funded archaeology, or for the purposes of academic teaching and research. It is through such separation of specialists and lack of communication on all sides that misconceptions are created and maintained.

What is therefore needed is better communication and understanding between the separate fields of archaeology. Environmental archaeologists will always have a concern with methodological issues as it is through our data that we study the past. But we must also ensure that we show the rest of the archaeological community just what we can do with such data.

Many recent studies are now starting to bridge the perceived gap between environmental and post-processual archaeologies. A great example was John Evans (2003) last book 'Environmental Archaeology and Social Order'. This argues that the environment is a means by which social relations can be explored, and combines environmental archaeology with concepts such as agency and phenomenology. Marciniak (2005) in his study of the faunal remains from Neolithic Central European communities focuses on the social context of animal use by recognising that animals were maintained and consumed in ways associated with their social relationships. Other environmental archaeologists are also starting to move away from purely economic interpretations and refocusing to look at the social meanings (Albarella 2001a; Fuller 2005; Morris 2005; O Day *et al.* 2004; Sykes 2007; Thomas 2007; van der Veen and Jones 2006).

By emphasing the social we are not arguing that the economic should be ignored rather that the social should also be included in our considerations. However, this should not be undertaken simply as a means of reconnecting with some other members of the archaeological community because it is in vogue. Rather, social aspects should be considered because it enables us all to further explore past human actions.

Integrating social and environmental archaeologies

It is hoped that the papers presented in this volume add to those already published in showing the virtues of considering the social in environmental archaeologies.

The papers are arranged in a broadly thematic order. The first three (Crabtree *et al*, Morris, Maltby) deal with the examination of faunal remains from differing archaeological sites. The second chapter (Crabtree *et al*) considers the interpretation of zooarchaeological data from the royal site in Co. Kildare, Ireland. It shows how the combination of faunal and archaeological data can help interpret the possible social actions which took place on the site. The third chapter (Morris) discusses the nature of a particular faunal deposit, associated bone groups, from two regions of England. It shows that such deposits were found throughout a number of archaeological periods and questions how we go about interpreting such faunal material. The fourth chapter (Maltby) also deals with associated bone groups, but this time from particular archaeological features, wells and shafts. It demonstrates how a greater involvement of environmental archaeologists can aid in the interpretation of such features and deposits.

Currently, one of the common calls for action, within environmental archaeology is for more integration, both between different specialists and the archaeological community as a whole (for example (Albarella 2001b;

Maltby 2006; Stallibrass and Thomas 2008). The next three papers are good examples of integrating information from both human and animal remains. The fifth chapter (Bendrey *et al*) discusses both the human and animal remains from a single deposit at Blewburton Hill, Oxfordshire, England. It shows not only the advantage of an integrated approach between different specialists, but also that such work can enhance our interpretations of deposits. Finally the paper also draws our attention to the potential of re-examining material from older excavations. The sixth and seventh chapters (Russell and Madgwick) both compare the evidence available from both human and animal remains for Iron Age deposits from southern England. As well as showing the advantages of integrated approaches to human and animal remains, both papers show how detailed statistical analysis can be utilised to consider broader social questions. Both papers can also be considered examples of the advantages offered when individuals have been trained in the study of both human and animal remains.

The final two papers (Randall and Waddington) draw together a wide range of not only environmental but all possible archaeological data to develop a picture of social actions. Chapter eight (Randall) examines the remains from the middle to late Iron Age site of Sigwells, Somerset, England. Although based mainly on the animal remains the paper draws in strands of evidence from other material types including the pottery, metalwork and human remains. This combined evidence is used to discuss the possible individuality of pit deposits and the need to develop more robust contextual analysis. The ninth chapter (Waddington) draws on a combination of environmental and other data to discuss the possible social actions taking place in the formation of extensive middens at the late Bronze Age sites of East Chisenbury and All Cannings Cross, Wiltshire, England. The paper demonstrates how environmental data and social theory can be combined to investigate human experience and actions.

The study of faunal remains does feature strongly in this volume, although a number of other material types are integrated into the analysis of many of the papers. The bias towards zooarchaeology is possibly due to the types of deposits currently being studied and utilised to explore social aspects of environmental remains. In particular a number of the papers concentrate on 'animal burials' referred to as associated bone groups. However social theory is not just being utilised to examine the 'unusual' faunal deposits as a number of the papers show (Crabtree *et al*, Russell, Madgwick, Waddington). It is hoped that the papers presented here show that the barriers discussed above do not need to be present, and we can move towards a truly social environmental archaeology.

Acknowledgments

In the preparation of this volume there are a number of individuals whom we would like to thank. Firstly we are grateful to Alan Outram for organising the AEA conference at Exeter, at which papers for this volume originated, and to all the participants and audience of the session for the stimulating debate. We would like to thank the contributors for their patience in the preparation of this volume and the reviewers for their comments. Finally, special thanks are due to Justine Biddle for all her hard work in helping to prepare this volume for publication.

Bibliography

Albarella, U. (ed.) (2001a) *Environmental Archaeology Meaning and Purpose.* Dordrecht, Kluwer Academic Publishers.

Albarella, U. (2001b) Exploring the real nature of environmental archaeology. An introduction. In. U. Albarella (ed.) *Environmental Archaeology Meaning and Purpose*, 3-13. Dordrecht, Kluwer Academic Publishers.

Brothwell, D. and Higgs, E. (1963) *Science in Archaeology. A comprehensive survey of progress and research.* London, Thames and Hudson.

Cunliffe, B. (1992) Pits, preconceptions and propitiation in the British Iron Age. *Oxford Journal of Archaeology* 11, 69-84.

Cunliffe, B. (2000) *The Danebury Environs Programme: The Prehistory of a Wessex Landscape. Volume 1, Introduction.* Oxford, English Heritage and Oxford University Committee for Archaeology. Monograph No 49.

Evans, J. G. (2003) *Environmental Archaeology and the Social Order.* London, Routledge.

Fuller, D. Q. (2005) Ceramics, seeds and culinary change in prehistoric India. *Antiquity* 79, 761-777.

Grant, A. (1984) Animal husbandry. In. B. Cunliffe (ed.) *Danebury: an Iron Age Hillfort in Hampshire. Volume 2. The Excavations 1969-1978: the Finds*, 496-548. London, Council for British Archaeology Research Report 52.

Grant, A. (1989) Animals and ritual in Early Britain: the visible and the invisible. In. P. Meniel (ed.) *Animal et Pratiques Religieuses: Les Manifestations Materielles. Anthropozoologica* Numero Special, 79-86.

Higgs, E. S. and Jarman, M. (1975) Palaeoeconomy. In. E. S. Higgs and M. Jarman (eds.) *Palaeoeconomy*, 1-7. Cambridge, Cambridge University Press.

Hill, J. D. (1995) *Ritual and Rubbish in the Iron Age of Wessex.* Oxford, British Archaeological Report British Series 242.

Hill, J. D. (1996) The identification of ritual deposits of animals. A general perspective from a specific study of 'special animal deposits' from the Southern English Iron Age. In. S. Anderson and K. Boyle (eds.) *Ritual Treatment of Human and Animal Remains. Proceedings of the First Meeting of the Osteoarchaeological Research Group held in Cambridge on 8th October 1994*, 17-32. Oxford, Oxbow.

Maltby, M. (2006) Integrating zooarchaeology: introduction. In. M. Maltby (ed.) *Integrating Zooarchaeology*, 1-4. Oxford, Oxbow.

Marciniak, A. (2005) *Placing Animals in the Neolithic*. London, UCL Press.

Méniel, P. (1992) *Les Sacrifices d'Animaux chez les Gaulois*. Paris, Editions Errance.

Milner, N. and Fuller, D. (1999) Contending with animal bones. *Archaeology Review from Cambridge* 16 (1), 1-12.

Morris, J. (2005) Red deer's role in social expression on the isles of Scotland. In. A. G. Pluskowski (ed.) *Just Skin and Bones. New Perspectives on Human-Animal Relations in the Historic Past*, 9-18. Oxford, British Archaeological Reports International Series 1410.

O'Conner, T. (1991) Science, evidential archaeology and the new scholasticism. *Scottish Archaeology Review* 8, 1-7.

O'Conner, T. and Evans, J. G. (2005) *Environmental Archaeology. Principles and Methods (2nd edition)*. Stroud, Sutton Publishing.

O'Connor, T. P. (1998) Environmental Archaeology: a matter of definition. *Environmental Archaeology* 2, 1-6.

O Day, S. J., Van Neer, W. and Ervynck, A. (eds.) (2004) *Behaviour Behind Bones. The zooarchaeology of Ritual, Religion, Status and Identity*. Oxford, Oxbow.

Reed, C. A. (1963) Osteo-Archaeology. In. D. Brothwell and E. Higgs (eds.) *Science in Archaeology. A comprehensive survey of progress and research*, 204-216. London, Thames and Hudson.

Renfrew, C. (1994) Towards a cognitive archaeology. In. C. Renfrew and E. Zubrow (eds.) *The Ancient Mind*, 1-12. Cambridge, Cambridge University Press.

Stallibrass, S. and Thomas, R. (2008) Food for thought: what's next on the menu? In. S. Stallibrass and R. Thomas (eds.) *Feeding the Roman Army. The Archaeology of Production and Supply in NW Europe*, 146-169. Oxford, Oxbow.

Sykes, N. (2007) Taking sides: the social life of venison in Medieval England. In. A. Pluskowski (ed.) *Breaking and Shaping Beastly Bodies.*, 149-160. Oxford, Oxbow.

Thomas, J. (1990) Silent running: the ills of environmental archaeology. *Scottish Archaeology Review* 7, 2-7.

Thomas, R. (2007) Chasing the ideal? Ritualism, pragmatism and the Late Medieval hunt in England. In. A. Pluskowski (ed.) *Breaking and Shaping Beastly Bodies*, 125-148. Oxford, Oxbow.

van der Veen, M. and Jones, G. (2006) A re-analysis of agricultural production and consumption: implications for understanding the British Iron Age. *Vegetation History and Archaeobotany* 15, 217-228.

Wait, G. (1985) *Ritual and Religion in Iron Age Britain*. Oxford, British Archaeological Report British Series 149.

Western, A. C. (1963) Wood and charcoal in archaeology. In. D. Brothwell and E. Higgs (eds.) *Science in Archaeology. A comprehensive survey of progress and research*, 150-158. London, Thames and Hudson.

Authors' Affiliations

James Morris
Museum of London Archaeology
Mortimer Wheeler House
46 Eagle Wharf Road
London
N1 7ED
UK

Mark Maltby
School of Conservation Science
Bournemouth University
Poole
Dorset
BH12 5BB
UK

2. The use of archaeological and zooarchaeological data in the interpretation of Dún Ailinne, an Iron Age royal site in Co. Kildare, Ireland.

Pam Crabtree, Susan A. Johnston and Douglas V. Campana

Abstract

Dún Ailinne, also known as Knockaulin Hill, in County Kildare is one of the Irish royal sites, identified in historical sources as the seat of the kings of Leinster. Excavations were conducted at the site from 1968 to 1975 under the direction of Professor Bernard Wailes of the University of Pennsylvania. The analysis of the archaeological remains and faunal materials from Dún Ailinne has recently been completed. This paper will show how archaeological data and faunal remains were critical in reconstructing the ways this ritual site was used during the Iron Age. The nature of the artefacts and structural remains at Dún Ailinne suggests that it was a ritual site, but the zooarchaeological data provide important additional evidence—that there was craft production at the site alongside ritual activity, and that there is a significant shift during the site's final phase when ritual feasting became a major focus.

Introduction

Dún Ailinne or Knockaulin Hill is located in County Kildare, Ireland, near the modern town of Kilcullen (Figure 2.1). Medieval Irish scholars identified Dún Ailinne with the pre-Christian kings of Leinster (Grabowski 1990). Other Irish royal sites include Tara, which has been associated with the kings of Meath (Newman 1997); Rathcroghan or Cruachain (Barton and Fenwick 2005), which has been associated with the kings of Connaught; and Navan or Emain Macha, which is traditionally associated with the kings of Ulster (Waterman 1997). On Knockaulin Hill, a bank and ditch encloses an area of 13 ha. This does not appear to have been a defensive fortification, since the bank is located outside the ditch, a pattern that is seen at the much earlier henge monuments in the British Isles (Wailes 1990). Radiocarbon dates for the Iron Age features at Dún Ailinne range from the third century BCE to the 4th century CE. Stylistic parallels for the metal objects found at the site are mostly first century BCE to first century CE (Wailes 2004: 239). All the royal sites are located on prominent hilltop locations with commanding views of the surrounding countryside, and they all include some type of timber structure at their centre (Johnston 2006).

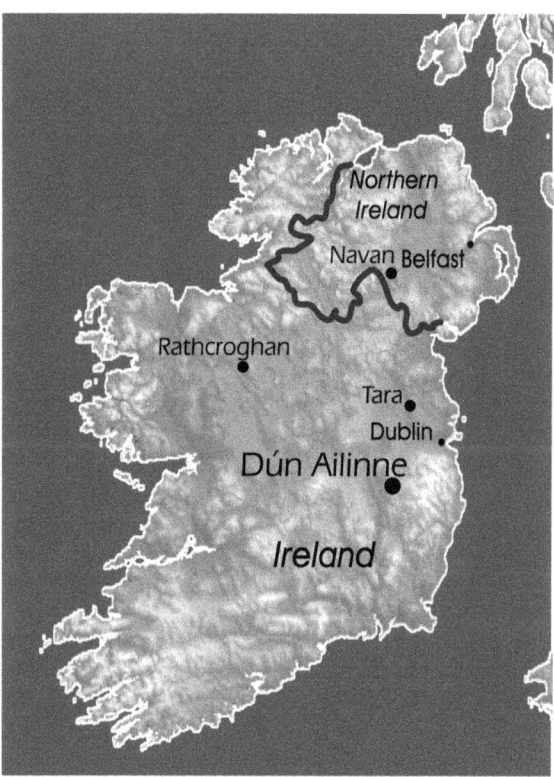

Figure 2.1 Map of Ireland showing the location of Dún Ailinne and the other Irish royal sites.

Excavations at Dún Ailinne

A major programme of excavation was carried out at Dún Ailinne between 1968 and 1975, under the direction of Prof. Bernard Wailes of the University of Pennsylvania (Wailes 1990; Johnston and Wailes 2007). Geophysical surveys indicated anomalies in the centre of the site, so the excavations were focused in that region. The excavations revealed a complex pattern of structural features and stratigraphic levels (Figure 2.2).

Three Iron Age timber structures were constructed at the site. The earliest structure, from the White Phase, would have held upright wooden posts. The White Phase structure was demolished and replaced by more complex Rose Phase structures that included a triple-walled, figure-of-eight timber structure with a funnel-shaped entrance. The Rose Phase structures in turn were demolished to make way for the Mauve phase constructions, which included a double-walled circular structure that surrounded an inner wooden building that is arguably a tower. When the Mauve Phase structures were demolished, a low mound of burnt material and animal bones accumulated (Flame Phase), suggesting that the site served as a location for feasting on a periodic basis long after the structural remains at the site were demolished. No features were recovered that could be associated with this phase. While Wailes' excavations revealed the complex architectural history of the Dún

Ailinne site, the question of the function or functions that this site may have served has been a matter of debate. Wailes (1990; 2004) has argued that the Dún Ailinne was a ritual site since the White, Rose, and Mauve Phase structures show no evidence for either residential or funerary use. But what kinds of activities were carried out at this ritual site?

Since the Irish medieval documents were written after Dún Ailinne was abandoned (see Grabowski 1990 for a complete review of the medieval historical record concerning Dún Ailinne), we have no direct historical evidence for the types of activities that may have been carried out at the site. In this paper, we will show how the analysis of the faunal remains and worked bone objects, when combined with the analysis of other artefact classes, have provided new evidence for some of the activities that may have been carried out at Dún Ailinne during the Iron Age.

Faunal Remains

The 1968-1975 excavations at Dún Ailinne yielded 18,755 mammal bones and unidentified fragments, making this faunal assemblage one of the very largest that has ever been recovered from a pre-Christian Iron Age site in Ireland. Preliminary analyses of the fauna were carried out by a number of different students between 1968 and 1983. In the early 1980s, one of us (Pam Crabtree) re-analyzed the entire Dún Ailinne faunal collection. The work was carried out using the comparative collections housed at the Museum Applied Science Center for Archaeology (MASCA) of the University Museum, University of Pennsylvania. Since the initial goal of the research was to determine whether ritual feasting took place at Dún Ailinne, the analysis focused on identification and quantification of the faunal remains. Dental eruption and wear, following Grant (1982) was used to determine the ages at death for cattle, sheep, and pigs.

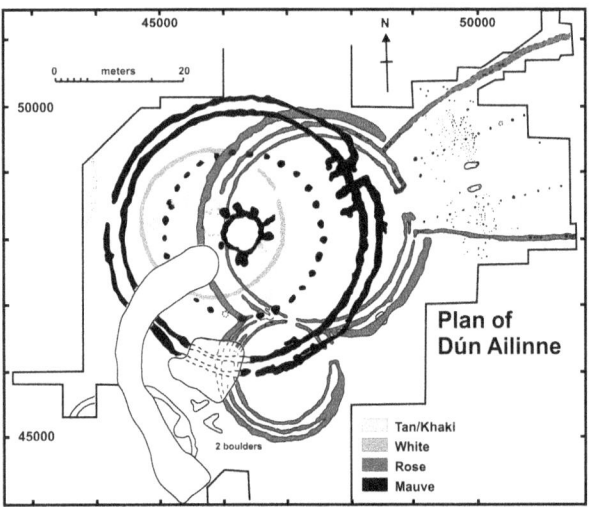

Figure 2.2 Plan of the 1968-75 excavations at Dún Ailinne showing the locations of the Iron Age structures.

Table 2.1 A phase-by-phase summary of the animal bones recovered from the 1968-75 excavations at Dún Ailinne.

	Cattle	Sheep	S/G	Pig	Horse	Dog	Red Deer	L. Ung.	S. Ar.	Unident.	Total
Flame	1075	11	162	711	46		2	773	446	2378	5604
Dun	91		9	72	3			35	65	119	394
U. Emerald	205	1	27	123	5			122	161	328	972
Crimson	54	1	5	29	2			17	40	179	327
L. Emerald	84		12	62	9	1		90	140	296	694
Later Iron Age	228	2	17	166	15			117	149	1232	1926
Harry	101		18	77	4		1	41	56	1309	1607
Jade	6		1	7	1			1	4	81	101
Niamh	3			18				2	5	55	83
Mauve	283	1	25	132	21			102	69	538	1171
Rose	491	3	44	355	17	2		165	190	2394	3504
White	27		8	23	1			12	53	135	259
Iron Age Gen.	32	1	7	45	1			16	47	73	222
Total Iron Age	**2680**	**20**	**335**	**1820**	**125**	**3**	**3**	**1493**	**1425**	**9117**	**16864**
Pre Iron Age	10			21	1				3	101	136
Unphased	127		19	92	4			73	92	1348	1755

Notes: S. Ar. includes fragments identified as small artiodactyl or "sheep-sized." L. Ung. includes fragments identified as large ungulate or "cattle-sized." S/G is used to designate indeterminate caprine (sheep/goat) fragments.

The mammal bones identified from the 1968-75 excavations are shown in Table 2.1. The material from the individual stratigraphic and structural phases was analyzed separately. The faunal remains from the Iron Age stratigraphic phases are listed in chronological order from youngest (Flame) to oldest (Lower Emerald). The later Iron Age category includes material that can be assigned to the Flame through Lower Emerald phases, but cannot be dated more closely. These data are followed by the fauna from the structural phases, listed from youngest (Harry) to oldest (White). The Iron Age General category includes a small number of bones which could not be assigned to a specific structural or stratigraphic phase. The largest faunal assemblage was recovered from the Flame Phase deposits in the low mound. This material accumulated after all the Iron Age structures had been dismantled. The Flame Phase material appears to represent the remains of periodic feasting at the site, and our discussion of the fauna will focus primarily on the Flame Phase remains.

The Flame Phase fauna is dominated by the remains of cattle (*Bos taurus*), pig (*Sus scrofa*), sheep (*Ovis aries*), and horse (*Equus caballus*). The only remains of wild animals are two bones of red deer (*Cervus elaphus*). Dog bones (*Canis familiaris*) are rare at Dún Ailinne, and there is no evidence for butchery marks on the three dog bones that were recovered from the site. In contrast, dog bones make up over 9% of the faunal remains from the Iron Age royal site at Tara (McCormick 2002), and a number of those bones revealed butchery traces. At Dún Ailinne, clear butchery traces were seen on cattle, sheep, pig, and horse bones only. Species ratios based on NISP counts (Table 2.2) show that cattle and pig bones made up the vast majority of the Flame Phase faunal assemblage; sheep and horses were relatively rare. Body part distributions (Crabtree 2007) show that all parts of the animal skeletons are represented, indicating that the animals were probably driven to the site on the hoof and then slaughtered on the spot.

Since the Dún Ailinne site is located on the top of a substantial hill, it would have been far easier to drive the animals to the top of the hill than to transport substantial quantities of dead meat up the steep slope. The ageing data for the Flame Phase cattle indicate that most of the cattle consumed at Dún Ailinne were either young calves or older adult cattle. The faunal remains from Dún Ailinne were highly fragmented, and only a small number of complete or near complete cattle mandibles were recovered from the site. Since so many of the cattle mandibles were fragmented, we chose to base our analyses of dental wear on individual teeth. We focused on the deciduous lower fourth premolar (dlp4) and the lower third molar (LM3). These teeth are

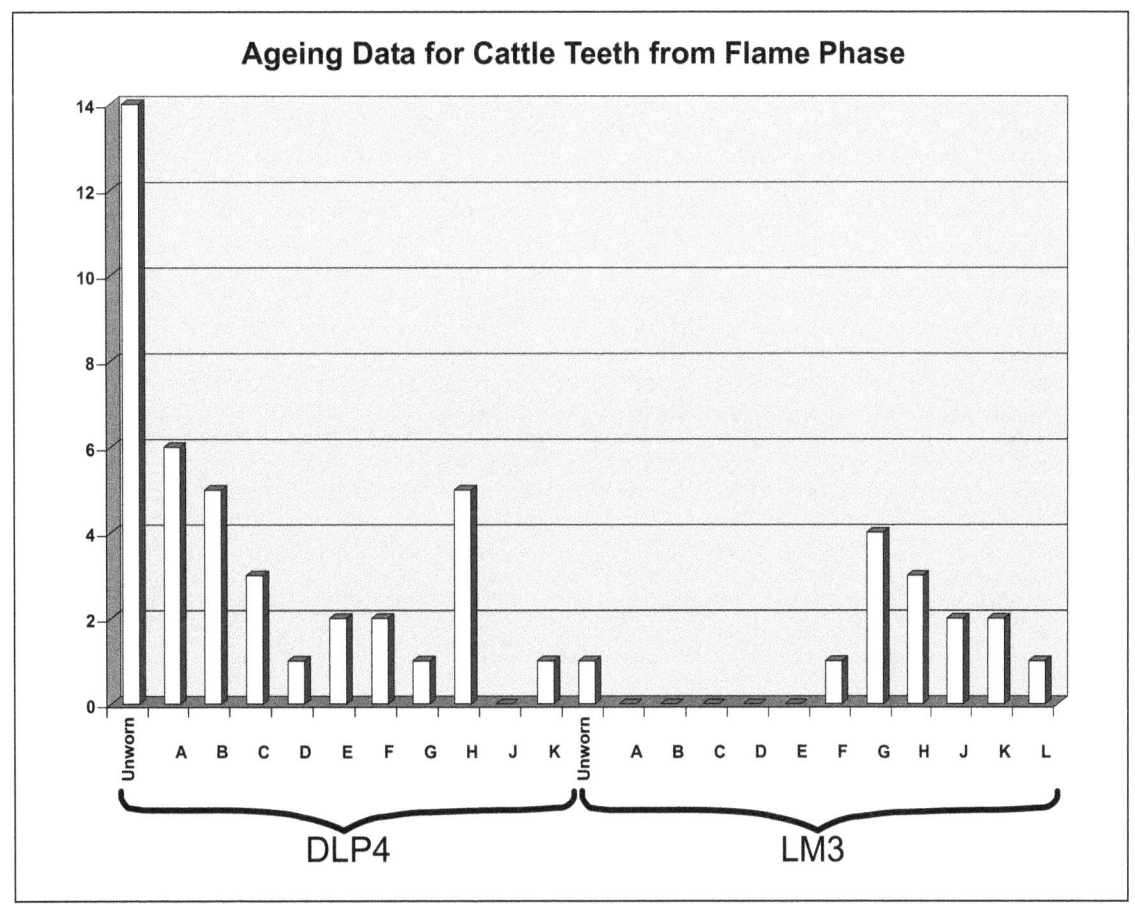

Figure 2.3 Kill-patterns for the cattle recovered from the Flame Phase deposits at Dún Ailinne. The stages illustrated follow Grant (1982).

Table 2.2 Species ratios based on NISP for the Flame Phase deposits.

Species	NISP	%NISP
Cattle	1075	53.6
Sheep/goat	173	8.6
Pig	711	35.5
Horse	46	2.3

morphologically distinctive, and the dlp4 is shed around the time that the LM3 begins to come into wear. The wear states for the cattle teeth were recorded following Grant (1982). The ageing data for the Flame Phase cattle from Dún Ailinne are shown in Figure 2.3. Most of the cattle that were consumed at Dún Ailinne were young calves, six months of age or younger. The rest of the animals were older adults, probably more than five years old when they were slaughtered. Few prime-age adults were used in feasting.

The unusual age distribution of the Dún Ailinne cattle raises some interesting questions about the relation of these ritual feasts to the broader Irish economy. Since dairying residues have recently been recovered from Neolithic and Iron Age ceramics in the British Isles (Copley *et al* 2003; Copley *et al* 2005), it is reasonable to assume that Iron Age cattle were raised, at least in part, for dairy production. If the slaughter of these young cattle caused their mothers to cease lactating, as McCormick (1991) has suggested, then these feasts would have been quite costly. They would have entailed the sacrifice of the calf and the loss of potential dairy products as well. The animals used in these feasts may well have been drawn from a wide area surrounding Dún Ailinne, and their cost may be a reflection of the power and wealth of the kings of Leinster.

Worked Bone Artifacts

While the faunal remains recovered from the Flame Phase deposits at Dún Ailinne reveal the components of ritual feasting, the worked bone objects highlight some of the other activities that may have been carried out at the site. Twenty-nine worked bone objects were recovered from the 1968-75 excavations at Dún Ailinne. An initial study of these objects (Crabtree 1982) focused primarily on the body parts from which they were made. In preparation for the final publication of the Dún Ailinne excavations (Johnston and Wailes 2007), we had the opportunity to re-examine the worked bone objects (Crabtree and Campana 2007). This new study has provided evidence for craft production activities that were carried out at Dún Ailinne.

Three fragments of worked bone were sectioned using a straight-toothed, short-bladed metal (presumably iron)

Figure 2.4 Fragment of cattle metatarsal that has been sawn at both ends. This object appears to be a blank for bone working.

saw. Since saws were not used for butchery in Ireland until the post-medieval period, these objects are clearly pieces of worked bone. They include the sawn-off distal end of a horse cannon bone, a 2 cm-long section of the shaft of a horse metapodial that is sawn on both ends, and a 9 cm-long section of a cattle metatarsal shaft that is sawn at both ends (Figure 2.4). Other than the obvious saw-marks, none of these fragments shows any evidence of further use. The sawn sections of metapodia appear to be unused blanks intended for further working into finished objects. The sawn distal end of the horse cannon bone is clearly a "waster," a left-over from bone working. The presence of this waste fragment suggests, along with the unmodified blanks, that bone-working was carried out on-site.

Two additional bone tools provide some evidence for textile manufacture (Figure 2.5). An unfused proximal epiphysis of a bovine femur was drilled from both sides, through the *fovea capitis*. There is no wear of any kind visible on this object; it may have served as a spindle whorl, although other interpretations are possible. A needle, possibly made from a pig fibula, provides even clearer evidence for textile working. The eye was carefully made from two intersecting drill holes. There is a small amount of rounding in the eye, indicating the object received some use. With an eye about 5 mm in length, this needle was probably too large to have been used in sewing, but may have served as a lacing or weaving needle.

Two wide, flat, spatulate implements (Figure 2.6) provide evidence for another craft activity at Dún Ailinne. The first was made from the exterior surface of a cattle-sized

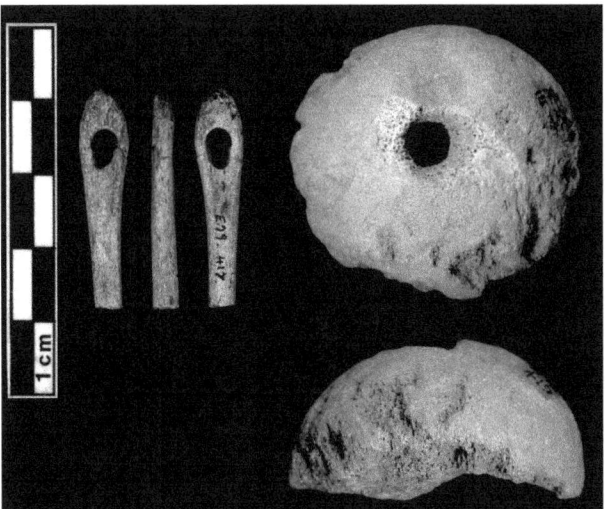

Figure 2.5 A bone needle and a possible spindle whorl from Dún Ailinne.

rib. The rib was split between thin inner and outer surfaces. The cancellous bone was then carefully removed, and the entire surface was worked to form a roughly elliptical outline with a very thin cross-section. The tip and the edges were intentionally rounded and smooth rather than sharp. The object had a light overall polish. The second implement was made from a large piece of mammal bone (possibly a rib as well). One face of this object has been flattened, resulting in a fairly sharp edge. There is no polish or evidence of use-wear on this specimen.

These objects generally resemble the tools made by a number of Native American groups for the sewing together of cattail mats (Ritzenthaler and Ritzenthaler 1983). These implements were made from split ribs in a roughly similar fashion, but they were perforated to carry the binding cord. The pattern of wear seen on the Native American tools is limited to a bit of polish on the surface, much like the wear seen on the first of the Dún Ailinne implements. Unfortunately, both the Dún Ailinne objects were broken, so it is uncertain whether they originally were perforated at one end. Even so, the formal resemblances suggest that they were utilised in broadly similar tasks, most probably for the making of mats, baskets, or perhaps as weaving tools.

The faunal evidence for craft production at Dún Ailinne does not stand in isolation. Recent analysis of the metal remains from the site indicates that small-scale bronze-working was also carried out there. This is in the form of slag (Hamilton 2007) and the presence of casting jets and a possible ingot among the bronze artifacts (Fisher 2007). In addition, a number of small glass fragments may indicate the presence of glass-working as well (Johnston and Wailes 2007). Iron needles, a bronze tracer, and stone spindle whorls or loom weights may also reflect this kind of activity.

Figure 2.6 A bone object, made from a split rib, that may have been used for basketry or matting.

Conclusions

Early medieval historical sources suggest that the Irish royal sites were "associated in particular with the inauguration and developing status of kingship" in Iron Age Ireland (Cooney and Grogan 1999: 188). These historical sources, however, provide little evidence for the range of activities that were carried out at Dún Ailinne and the other Irish royal sites and were in fact written well after the site was no longer being used. Stratigraphic study of the structures and features at Dún Ailinne, combined with detailed study of the unmodified faunal remains, indicates that the functions of the site changed through time. After the three elaborate timber structures were sequentially constructed and dismantled at the site, Dún Ailinne continued to serve as a locus for periodic ritual feasting. Beef and pork played a major role in these feasts, and smaller quantities of mutton and horseflesh were also consumed.

The worked bone objects indicate that feasting was only one of a number of activities that took place on Knockaulin Hill during the Iron Age. The bone tools and other worked bone items suggest that bone-working, matting or basketry, and possibly textile production were also carried out at the site. Archaeological evidence indicates that other crafts, including metal-working and possibly glass-working, were also carried out at Dún Ailinne. It is possible that, in addition to activities directly related to the emergence of kingly power, these

Irish royal sites may have also served as locations of periodic markets or craft fairs, similar to the Type A emporia described by Hodges (1981).

Prospect

The inverted bank and ditch surrounding the hilltop at Dún Ailinne enclosed an area of about 13 ha. The 1968-75 excavations at the site covered less than 10% of the enclosed area. In 2006, a new programme of resistivity and magnetometer survey began at the site under the leadership of one of us (Susan Johnston). During the summer of 2006, the joint American-Irish team surveyed 3 ha at the top of Knockaulin Hill and identified additional anomalies and features that may date to the Iron Age. Additional survey work is planned for the summer of 2007. This programme of remote sensing will serve as a guide to future excavations at Dún Ailinne, which may provide more evidence for the range of activities carried out at this Irish royal site.

Acknowledgements

The authors wish to thank the Irish Heritage Council and University Research Challenge Fund of New York University for support of the 2006 and 2007 field seasons at Dún Ailinne.

Bibliography

Barton, K. and Fenwick, J. (2005) Geophysical investigations at the ancient royal site of Rathcrogan, county Roscommon, Ireland. *Archaeological Prospection* 12, 3-18.

Cooney, G. and Grogan, E. (1999) *Irish Prehistory: A Social Perspective*. Dublin, Wordwell.

Copley, M. S., Berstan, R., Docherty, S., Mukherjee, A., Straker, V., Payne, S. and Evershed, R. P. (2003) The earliest direct evidence for dairying in prehistoric Britain. *Proceedings of the National Academy of Sciences* 100 (4), 1524-1529.

Copley, M. S., Berstan, R., Dudd, S. N., Aillaud, S., Mukherjee, A. J., Straker, V., Payne, S. and Evershed, R. (2005) Processing of milk products in pottery vessels through British prehistory. *Antiquity* 76, 895-908.

Crabtree, P. J. (1982) Worked bone from Dún Ailinne, Co. Kildare, Ireland. *MASCA Journal* 2 (1), 6-7.

Crabtree, P. J. (2007) Biological remains. In. S. A. Johnston and B. Wailes. *Excavations at Dún Ailinne, 1968-1975*, 156-169. Philadelphia, University of Pennsylvania Museum.

Crabtree, P. J., and Campana, D. V. (2007) Catalog of worked bone objects. In. S. A. Johnston and B. Wailes. *Excavations at Dún Ailinne, 1968-1975*, 125-131. Philadelphia, University of Pennsylvania Museum.

Fisher, G. C. (2007) Report on copper alloy objects. In. S. A. Johnston and B. Wailes. *Excavations at Dún Ailinne, 1968-1975*, 157-169. Philadelphia, University of Pennsylvania Museum.

Grabowski, K. (1990) The historical overview of Dún Ailinne. *Emania* 7, 32-36.

Grant, A. (1982) The use of tooth wear as a guide to the age of domestic ungulates. In. B. Wilson, C. Grigson, and S. Payne. *Ageing and Sexing Animal Bones from Archaeological Sites*, 91-108. Oxford, British Archaeological Reports British Series 109.

Hamilton, E. (2007) Report on the Slag from Dún Ailinne. In. S. A. Johnston and B. Wailes. *Excavations at Dún Ailinne, 1968-1975*, 145-152. Philadelphia, University of Pennsylvania Museum.

Hodges, R. (1981) *Dark Age Economics*. New York, St. Martin's Press.

Johnston, S. A. (2006) Revisiting the Irish royal sites. *Emania* 20, 53-59.

Johnston, S. A., and Wailes, B. (2007) *Excavations at Dún Ailinne, 1968-1975*. Philadelphia, University of Pennsylvania Museum.

McCormick, F. (1991) Evidence for dairying at Dún Ailinne? *Emania* 8, 57-59.

McCormick, F. (2002) The animal bones from Tara. *Discovery Programme Reports* 6, 103-116.

Newman, C. (1997) *Tara: An Archaeological Survey*. Dublin. Royal Irish Academy, Discovery Programme Monograph 2.

Ritzenthaler, R. E., and Ritzenthaler, P. (1983) *The Woodland Indians of the Western Great Lakes*. Garden City New York, Natural History Press.

Wailes, B. (1990) Dún Ailinne: a summary excavation report. *Emania* 7, 10-21.

Wailes, B. (2004) Irish Royal Sites. In. P. Bogucki and P. J. Crabtree (eds). *Ancient Europe 8000 B.C.-A.D.1000: Encyclopedia of the Barbarian World, Volume 2*, 239-240. New York, Charles Shribner and Sons.

Waterman, D. M. (1997) *Excavations at Navan Fort 1961-71*, completed and edited by C. J. Lynn. HMSO, Belfast.

Authors' affiliations

Pam Crabtree
Center for the Study of Human Origins
Anthropology Department
New York University
Rufus D. Smith Hall
25 Waverly Place
New York
10003
USA

Susan A. Johnston
Anthropology Department
George Washington University
2110 G Street Northwest

Washington DC
20052
USA

Douglas V. Campana
Anthropology Department
New York University
Rufus D. Smith Hall
25 Waverly Place
New York
10003
USA

Associated bone groups; beyond the Iron Age

James Morris

Abstract

As zooarchaeologists move away from the purely economic towards 'social zooarchaeological' interpretations, the consideration of articulated/associated faunal remains has become more common-place. This paper presents results from a research project which investigated the nature of these associated bone groups (ABGs). The majority of current work on these deposits has utilised Iron Age material, with ABGs becoming synonymous with certain Iron Age sites, particularly Danebury. This paper moves beyond the Iron Age and discusses their presence on sites from the Neolithic to the Medieval period. It utilises the results of a survey of published sources from southern England and Yorkshire and shows that ABGs are commonly recovered from other periods. Their composition is shown to differ between time periods and regions. Finally in light of the data presented it questions how we should view these deposits.

Introduction

During the last decade interest in what could be called 'social zooarchaeology' has developed and increased. The study of faunal remains, although still primarily concerned with economic/subsistence matters, is now utilised by archaeologists to look into socio-cultural areas, such as 'ritual' behaviour, as this volume and others show (Anderson and Boyle 1996; O'Day *et al.* 2004; Ryan and Crabtree 1995). Long recognised during archaeological excavations, articulated/associated faunal remains have become increasingly utilised in the interpretation of cultural aspects of society. These types of deposits have been subject to a number of descriptions, often heavily loaded with interpretation. Examples include 'animal burials' (Wheeler 1943, 115), 'butchery waste' (Maltby 1985), 'culled deposit' (Maltby 1981a), 'fall victim' (Maltby 1994), 'sacrificial offerings' (Ross 1968) and 'special animal deposit' (Grant 1984, 533; Wait 1985, 122).

One of the most influential pieces of work on the subject was Grant's (1984) study of the faunal material from the Iron Age hillfort of Danebury, Hampshire. A large number of articulated animal skeletons were encountered during the excavation, which Grant (1984) labelled as 'special animal deposits' and argued they resulted from a distinct type of ritual activity. Grant's work has been discussed and built upon by Hill's (1995) study into the nature of possible 'special' deposits within Iron Age pits from sites in Wessex. In order to be more objective in his analysis, Hill (1995, 27) utilised the term Articulated/Associated Animal Bone Group (ABG). This countered the problem of previous descriptions in that it removed the inherent assumption that the deposit is of a 'special' or 'ritual nature'.

Throughout this paper the term ABG is also utilised for the same reason. However, it is necessary to define what types of deposits have been recorded as ABGs. Previous studies such as those of Grant (1984; 1991) and Hill (1995) have included deposits of single bones in their examination of ABGs. This is because they were examining 'special animal deposits' within Iron Age features, which were defined by Grant (1984, 533) as consisting of three types; animal burials, skulls (plus horse mandibles) and articulated legs. However, the inclusion of individual elements, such as skulls or in some cases mandibles is inconsistent with the 'associated' nature of these deposits. It is this feature which distinguishes ABGs from the rest of the faunal material. Therefore, single bone deposits are not included in the analysis within this paper. This does not mean that skull deposits are discounted, but they will only be included if they are in association with other elements. For this study ABGs were defined as constituting three types of animal remains:

1. Remains that were deposited with some portion of the flesh or connective tissue still attached, causing them to remain in articulation.

2. Remains that became disarticulated post-deposition via taphonomic processes and were consequently recognized as constituting a single animal by the zooarchaeologist.

3. Disarticulated remains deposited in association, and subsequently identified as being from the same animal by the zooarchaeologist.

Data for this project were collected from southern England (Dorset, Hampshire and Wiltshire) and Yorkshire in northern England. The current results are derived from a systematic search of monographs, journals and English Heritage Ancient Monument Laboratory (AML) reports dating from 1945 onwards (a full list appears in Morris 2008b). This paper presents some of the results of this survey and aims to discuss the nature of ABGs from the above regions from c.4000BC to AD1550.

A common type of deposit

The majority of previous literature regarding ABGs has had a predominantly prehistoric focus, with deposits from the Iron Age receiving a large amount of attention, probably because of the well known work of Grant and Hill mentioned above. Although deposits from the

Table 3.1 Number of ABGs recorded per region and period.

Region	Neolithic	Bronze Age	Iron Age	Romano-British	Early Medieval	Later Medieval	Total
Southern England	54	61	746	820	78	104	1863
Yorkshire	1		38	88	14	58	199
Total	55	61	784	908	92	162	2062
Total %	2.67%	2.96%	38.02%	44.03%	4.46%	7.86%	

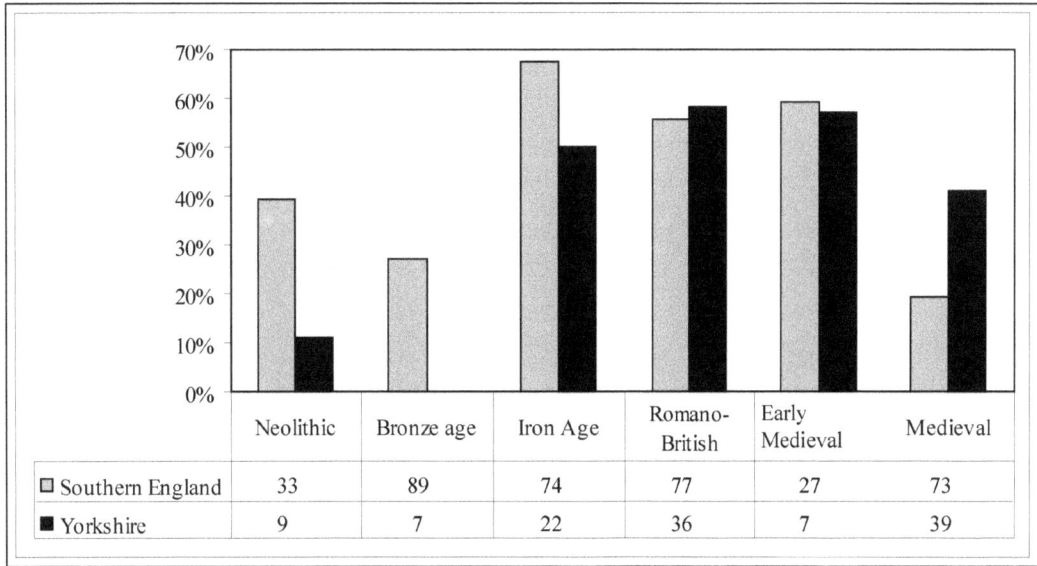

Figure 3.1 Percentage of sites per region and period with ABGs present.

Romano-British (Fulford 2001; Woodward and Woodward 2004) and early Medieval periods (Hamerow 2006) have also been discussed, a survey of the published literature would lead one to believe ABGs are an almost purely prehistoric phenomenon. However, this survey of excavation reports indicates this is not the case. Overall this project has recorded more ABGs from Romano-British sites than from any other period (Table 3.1).

In total, 2,062 ABGs were recorded in this study, the vast majority of which (90%) are from sites in southern England. This, however, is not an indication that they are more common in southern England. It is more likely a refection of the nature of the archaeological datasets from both regions. Simply, more data were available from southern England compared to Yorkshire and therefore more ABGs have been recorded. Overall the reports from 493 sites were examined for this study, 213 of which have ABGs recorded.

As already stated, the largest number of ABGs were recorded from Romano-British contexts which represents 44.0% of the total assemblage; those from Iron Age contexts constitute the second largest group (Table 3.1). Together, deposits from Iron Age and Romano-British contexts make up 82.0% of the ABGs recorded for this study. Surprisingly, ABGs from the Medieval period constitute a larger proportion of the assemblage, for both southern England and Yorkshire, than ABGs from the Neolithic and Bronze Age. In fact, a larger proportion of deposits were recorded from historic, as opposed to prehistoric contexts. Although a large proportion of the literature is concerned with prehistoric, ABGs, they appear to be just as common from historic contexts.

One of the problems with looking at just the total number of ABGs recorded per period is that the sample can be biased by large assemblages from individual sites. This is especially true for southern England where, for example, 62.8% of the Iron Age ABGs are recorded from seven sites (Morris 2008b). To negate this, we can use presence and absence data, which displays three interesting trends. Firstly, ABGs on Neolithic and Bronze Age sites are rarer in Yorkshire than southern England (Figure 3.1). However, this is more likely to simply reflect the small amount of faunal material that has been recorded from the area. Stallibrass (1995), in her review of animal remains from northern England, pointed out that although large quantities of animal bones may have been present at many sites, they were not collected or curated, as many sites were investigated in the nineteenth and early twentieth centuries. In addition, the underlying geology of many sites is not conducive for good bone survival.

Secondly, ABGs are more common on Medieval sites in Yorkshire compared to southern England (Figure 3.1). This is also indicated by the raw counts for Yorkshire, where, in contrast to southern England, the second largest assemblage is from the later Medieval period. There is always the possibility that the differences are due to publication or recording biases, with many pre-1980's excavations not reporting or recording ABGs. However, the majority of the southern England (94.2%) and Yorkshire (94.7%) reports were published from the

1980's onwards. The difference may be one of scale and detail of the excavations and reports, as the majority of Yorkshire later Medieval ABGs are recorded from the excellent York excavations, which produced large quantities of animal bones (O'Connor 1983; 1984a;b; Ryder 1970).

Finally, the presence and absence data indicate that a high proportion of Iron Age, Romano-British and early Medieval sites in both southern England and Yorkshire have ABGs present. Although the total number of ABG deposits is higher for the Romano-British period compared with the early Medieval period, a similar proportion of sites have them present. This indicates that although ABGs are found in greater concentrations in the Iron Age and Romano-British periods, they are still present on a high proportion of sites in later periods, albeit in smaller concentrations.

Constants and variables

One of the constants in the ABG data is the domination of domestic animals. Overall, 1,679 are from domestic animals which represent 81.4% of the total assemblage. There are slight variations between periods and regions, with the lowest percentage (85.5%) coming from later Medieval Yorkshire and the highest (100%) from Iron Age Yorkshire. Wild animals therefore rarely appear to be deposited as ABGs. This trend matches observations from the total faunal assemblages, with wild animals relatively rare in all periods, apart from some high status sites, particularly of Medieval date (Grant 1989; Hambleton 1999; Maltby 1981b; Pollard 2006; Sykes 2006). Although domestic animals consistently make up a large proportion of the ABG assemblages, there is substantial regional and chronological variation in the relative abundance of different domestic species represented.

Constants and variables; southern England

The majority of the southern England Neolithic ABGs are from cattle, which make up 53% of the assemblage. Pig and dog are the second and third most common species respectively. We must note that of the 55 Neolithic deposits, 26 (43%) are from Windmill Hill (Grigson 1999), 17 of which are cattle. However, cattle would still be the most common species if the Windmill Hill data were excluded. Cattle are also the most common species in the total faunal assemblage from the Neolithic. They make up 45.7% of the combined NISP count from the 13 sites included in this study (Figure 3.2), a percentage not very different from the ABGs (Figure 3.3).

Examination of the Bronze Age ABG data shows a different pattern with sheep/goat the most common species (45%), followed by cattle (36%) (Figure 3.3). This represents a large rise in the percentage of sheep/goat. In the Neolithic they represent just 7% of the assemblage with only four ABGs recorded from three different sites, Whitesheet Hill (Maltby 2004), Windmill Hill (Grigson 1999) and Marden enclosure (Harcourt 1969; 1971b). The increase in sheep/goat ABGs during the Bronze Age again mirrors the trends seen in the overall faunal material. In the combined NISP count from the 43 Bronze Age sites included in the study (most without ABGs present) sheep/goat make up 51.4% of the assemblage. In contrast sheep/goat represent only 12.8% of the combined Neolithic assemblages from 13 sites (Figure 3.2).

Therefore the pattern in the proportion of cattle and sheep/goat ABGs appears to follow the trend seen in the overall faunal data. The pig data shows a slightly different pattern. Pigs are the second most common species found as ABGs in the Neolithic. They are also the second most common species in the total faunal assemblage. However, whereas the percentages for cattle and sheep/goat are similar in the ABG and total faunal assemblages, pig make up a much higher proportion of the non-ABG faunal assemblage. The majority of pig ABGs are from early and middle Neolithic sites. None are present from late Neolithic sites examined in this study, despite the evidence that the late Neolithic sees a rise in the utilisation of pigs (Albarella and Serjeantson 2002). This is not clear in Figure 3.2, as the graph is only designed to show broader inter-period trends. The surprising lack of pig ABGs in the late Neolithic may reflect differences between site types of the early and late parts of the period and the limited size of the sample. The majority of the sites producing later Neolithic faunal assemblages in southern England are henge enclosures, but only two ABGs have been recorded from this site type, a dog and a sea eagle, both from Coneybury Henge (Maltby 1990). Durrington Walls (Harcourt 1971a) has produced one of the largest faunal samples from a henge enclosure, however no ABGs were recorded from that site. This may be a reflection of the original faunal analysis and report's limitations rather than a real absence. Recent excavations on the site indicate some pig ABGs are present (Parker-Pearson *et al.* 2007). Only one pig ABG is present in the Bronze Age sample, from the late Bronze Age settlement at Bell Street, Romsey, Hampshire (Coy 1993). The proportion of pig in the overall faunal assemblage also decreases in the Bronze Age (Figure 3.2).

Sheep/goat (35%) remain the most common ABG species in the Iron Age sample (Figure 3.3). They also remain the most common species (53%) found within the total faunal assemblage (Figure 3.2), which is dominated by the large datasets from Wessex chalk downland sites (Hambleton 2007). Cattle and pig respectively are the second and third most common animals represented in the total

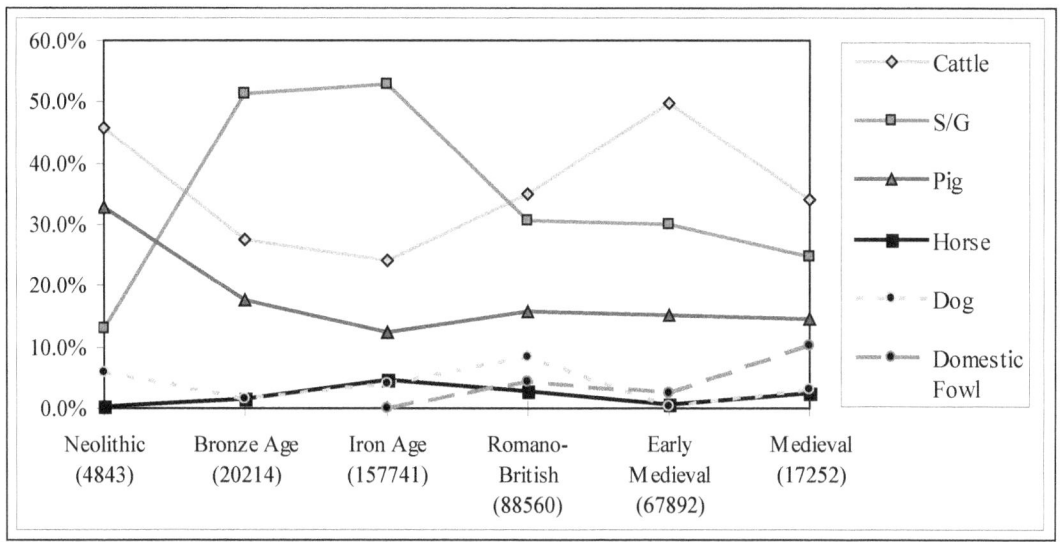

Figure 3.2 Total percentage NISP for the most common species per period from southern England sites included in this study. ABGs are included in the NISP counts. Total sample size in brackets.

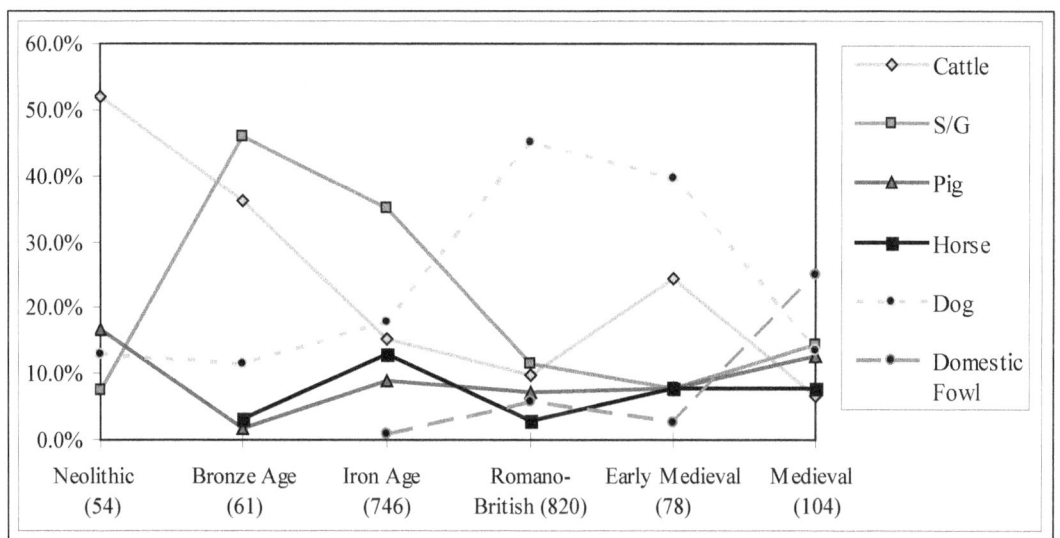

Figure 3.3 Total percentages of ABGs from each period for southern England. Number of ABGs per period in brackets.

faunal assemblage. However, the Iron Age is the first period when there are major differences between the total faunal and the ABG assemblages. Dog followed by cattle are the second and third most common ABG species.

The increase in dog ABGs continues into the Romano-British period, where they make up 45% of the assemblage. The proportion of sheep/goat drops sharply to 11.6%. Cattle remain the third most common species, although their proportion decreases from 15.1% to 9.6%. The proportion of horse ABGs reaches its highest level in the Iron Age sample (13%), but drops to its lowest level (2.2%) in the Romano-British assemblage. Significant changes occur to the ABG species representation in the transition from the Iron Age to the Romano-British period. However, these changes did not occur quickly. In the early Romano-British period, sheep/goat remain the most common species (Morris 2008a). The ABG results are in stark contrast to the species proportions in the total faunal assemblage in which cattle, sheep/goat and pig respectively are the three most common species.

The proportion of dog ABGs (39.7%) drops slightly in the early Medieval assemblage, although, they remain by far the most common species (Figure 3.3). There is a rise in the percentage of cattle ABGs, which had decreased in every period since the Neolithic, but in the early Medieval period cattle are the second most common species (24.4%). It is possible that the small sample from the early Medieval period may affect the results. For example, the majority of the dog ABGs are from the upper fill of pit 56 at Clifford Street, Southampton (Bourdillon 1990). The proportion of dog deposits drops significantly in the later Medieval period to 13.5%, although this still makes dogs the second most common ABG species. For the first time a bird species makes up a significant proportion of the assemblage with the rise of

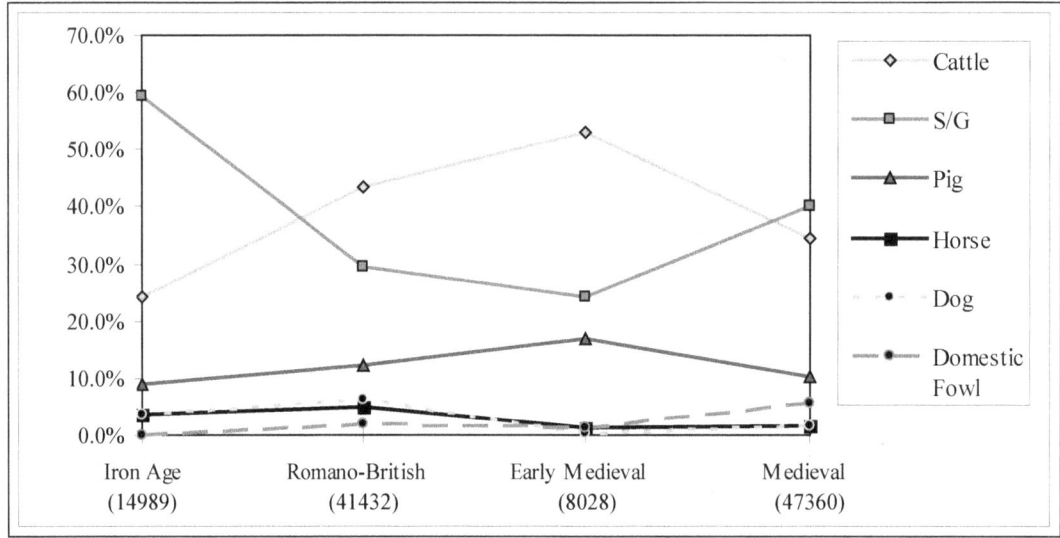

Figure 3.4 Total percentage NISP for the most common species per period from Yorkshire sites included in this study. ABGs are included in the NISP counts. Total sample size in brackets.

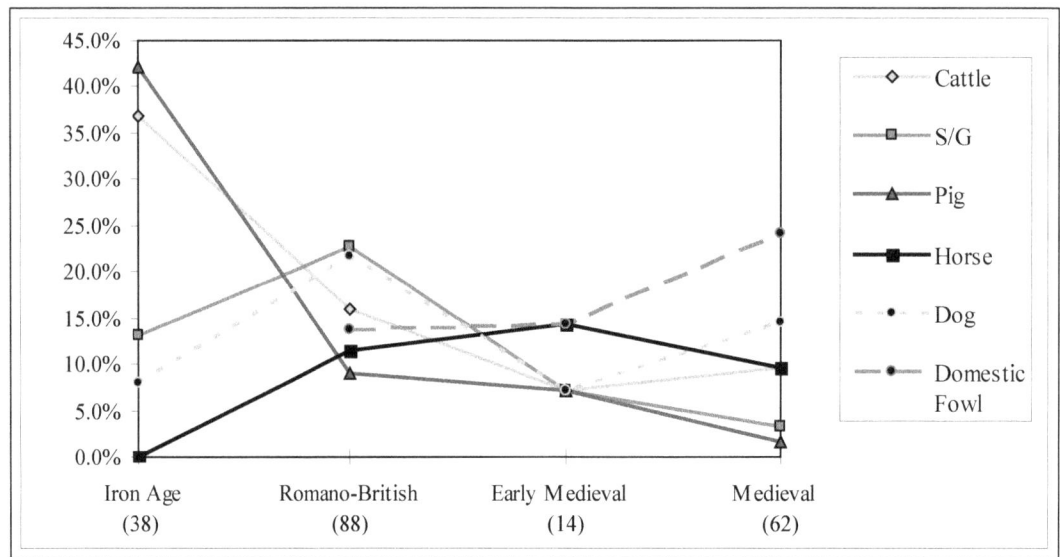

Figure 3.5 Total percentage of ABGs from each period for Yorkshire. Number of ABGs per period in brackets.

domestic fowl from 2.6% in the early Medieval period to 25% in the later Medieval. However, this is possibly due to the small and restricted sample with all but three domestic fowl ABGs being recorded from the manor of Faccombe Netherton, Hampshire (Sadler 1990).

Again the ABG species proportions from the early Medieval and later Medieval periods contrast with the overall faunal assemblage data. The proportion of cattle peaks in the early Medieval period and cattle, sheep/goat and pig remain the three most common species. There is a rise in the total number of domestic fowl in the later Medieval periods. This may be slightly exaggerated by the inclusion of ABGs in the overall faunal assemblage NISPs, as analysis of the faunal assemblages from sites with no ABGs present give the proportion of domestic fowl at 6.3% as opposed to the 10.2% from the overall faunal assemblage utilised in Figure 3.2.

Constants and variables; Yorkshire

The Yorkshire data record differs from the southern England one. Although sample size is an issue for the Yorkshire assemblage, it does show that regional differences need to be taken into account regarding ABGs.

Only one deposit consisting of a partial fox skeleton from Whitegrounds Barrow 1 (Riggott and Williams 1984) was recorded from the Neolithic. None were recorded from the Bronze Age Yorkshire dataset. However, this may be due to the small number of samples available for these periods. Fortunately a larger dataset is available from the Iron Age, with the majority of the ABGs consisting of either pig (42.1%) or cattle (36.8%) (Figure 3.5). This is in sharp contrast to the total faunal assemblage from the period, which has similar species percentages to the southern England data, with sheep/goat dominating (Figure 3.4). Pig remains therefore make up a much larger proportion of the ABG assemblage from Iron Age Yorkshire than in the southern England sample. Such a large difference is probably due partly to the small Yorkshire sample size and perhaps more significantly to the dominance of funerary sites. Of the 38 ABGs recorded, 16 come from five separate funerary sites. Four are from Stead's (1991) excavations around the Yorkshire Wolds area, north and west of Driffield, the other site is Grindale square barrow II, North Yorkshire (Manby 1980). However, even on settlement sites cattle ABGs are more common than those of sheep/goat at a ratio of 2:1, which is the complete opposite of the southern England results.

Another contrast is that no horse ABGs have been recorded from the Iron Age of Yorkshire, whereas a total of 97 were recorded from southern England. Horse remains are present in the total faunal assemblage, albeit in small numbers. Again, the difference may be due to the limited size of the sample and the high proportion of ABGs from funerary contexts. None of the horse ABGs from southern England were recovered from features that could be defined as funerary and only three of the horse ABGs from southern England are in association with articulated human remains, one from pit 113, Suddern Farm (Poole 2000b) and two from pit 5, Viables Farm (Maltby 1982).

The Romano-British period produced the largest ABG assemblage from Yorkshire. The species represented change dramatically compared with the Iron Age. The proportions of sheep/goat (22.7%) and dog (21.6%) rise. The percentage of cattle (15.9%) falls so it is only the third most common species, and the proportion of pig falls to only 9.1% (Figure 3.5). The decease in the number of pig ABGs could be due to an increase in the amount of data from settlement sites, as well as changes in the ABGs deposited within funerary settings. Domestic fowl and horse are also present in the Yorkshire assemblage for the first time in this period.

In contrast, the main change in the overall faunal assemblage from Yorkshire is a decrease in the proportion of sheep/goat with cattle becoming the most common species (Figure 3.4). This mirrors the change seen in southern England (Figure 3.2). However, the ABG assemblages show a very different species makeup. One of the main differences is that the Yorkshire sample does not display the dog-dominated pattern seen in the southern England data. This may be due to differences in the type of site and features excavated. Compared with southern England a limited number of faunal assemblages from urban contexts are available from Yorkshire. The majority of the dog ABGs from southern England are from pit/well deposits within Dorchester, Winchester and Silchester. Maltby (2010) discusses the evidence from 16 Romano-British towns, noting that dog ABGs are most often found within deep pits and wells. A large number of similar features from urban contexts have not been excavated in Yorkshire. However, to test this supposition we will have to wait for further Romano-British urban excavations to be carried out in Yorkshire, or extend the comparison by feature type to other regions.

Moving onto the early Medieval period, the ABG species proportions change again. Cat, domestic fowl and horse become the most common species, with cattle, sheep/goat, pig and dog being represented by only one deposit each. The change in species proportion is likely to be due to the very restricted ABG sample for this period, with over half, including all the cats, coming from the excavations at 16-22 Coppergate, York (O'Connor 1989). However, the trend does continue into the later Medieval period with domestic fowl and cat being the two most common ABG species respectively, followed by dog. The higher proportion of domestic fowl and dog deposits from later Medieval Yorkshire does correspond with the pattern for the same period in southern England (Figure 3.3). However, the high proportion of cat remains is different, with cat ABGs making up 22.6% of the assemblage from Yorkshire, but only 4.8% from Wessex. The high proportion of cat deposits from later Medieval Yorkshire may be due to the dominance of York data where excavation and particularly sieving standards were high. As with the southern England data, there is little correspondence between the ABG assemblage and the total faunal assemblage (Figure 3.4 and 3.5).

Composition; the changing nature of a deposit

As well as variation in species, these deposits also vary in form. Previous authors have also noticed such a trend. Grant (1984), Wait (1985), Maltby (1985) and Hill (1995, 57) all recorded different types of ABG deposits. This project took two different approaches. Firstly ABGs were defined simply as complete or partial, with complete not necessarily meaning all bones were present, but that all body areas are represented. The second approach was to record which body areas were present for each partial ABG. This has the advantage of using the data to define the types of ABG rather than trying to fit individual deposits into a specific category. The partial/complete results are presented in this paper.

As noted by Hill (1995, 59) the deposition of complete carcasses was rare in the Iron Age, and this appears to be the case for the other periods covered in this study. Overall, the majority of ABGs consist of non-complete skeletons of varying degrees (Table 3.2). However, this varies between species and periods.

The vast majority of the domestic mammal deposits recorded are incomplete. Cattle and horse are the domestic mammals that are most often found as partial ABGs. It is probably no coincidence that these are also the two largest mammals represented. This may simply be a refection of the practicality of depositing a complete

Table 3.2 Percentage of complete, partial and unknown ABGs for the total assemblage (southern England and Yorkshire), per species (Number of ABGs per species in brackets)

Species	Complete	Partial	Unknown
Cattle (303)	16	82	2
S/G (437)	20	77	3
Pig (181)	35	61	4
Horse (155)	8	92	1
Dog (593)	30	39	31
Cat (77)	35	57	8
Domestic Fowl (109)	56	42	2
Other Domestic Bird (9)	89	11	0
Wild Mammals (76)	59	32	9
Corvids (69)	9	72	19
Other Wild bird (50)	2	36	62
Total (2059)	**26**	**61**	**13**

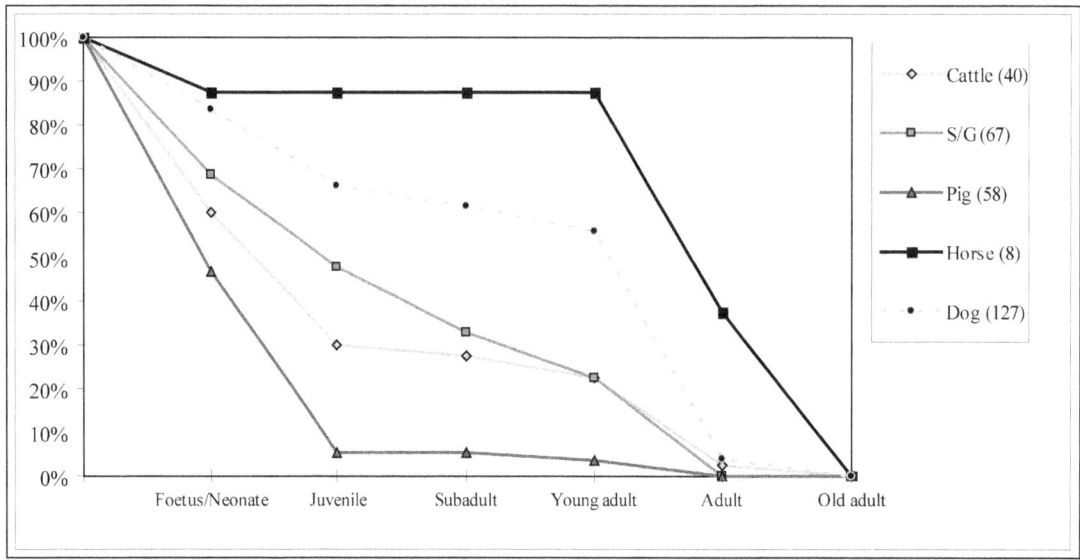

Figure 3.6 Mortality profiles of complete ABGs per species (combined results from all periods and regions with ageing data available).

cow or horse. The majority of complete cow ABGs encountered in this study have been from neonatal or juvenile individuals (Figure 3.6). In comparison, 42.4% of partial cattle ABGs are from adults (Figure 3.7). This pattern has been noted in a number of periods, in particular, the southern England Iron Age assemblage, where many of the ABGs have been interpreted as natural deaths (Morris 2008b).

Horse remains show a very different pattern with the majority of complete and partial ABGs coming from individuals that have reached maturity. This may be a reflection of the differences in status and utilisation of the two animals, with little evidence for the consumption of horsemeat in Britain and a low kill-off of immature animals. There are generally very few cases where bones of young horses have been found in non-ABG assemblages (e.g. Maltby 1981a; 2010).

A higher proportion of sheep/goat and pigs have been recorded as complete ABGs. There is little difference in the mortality profile of complete or partial sheep/goat. There is however a noticeable difference for pigs. Only 8.6% of the complete pig deposits are from individuals that lived beyond the juvenile stage of development (Figure 3.6). In comparison 18.8% of partial pigs are from individuals older than juvenile (Figure 3.7).

Surprisingly a higher proportion of complete pigs are recorded than dogs. However, the completeness of a large proportion of dog remains is unknown (Table 3.2) the majority of which are from Romano-British contexts. Their 'unknown' status is in a large part due to taphonomic factors, in particular post-depositional movement and mixing of multiple depositions within the deep pits/wells where they were often deposited. Maltby (1987; 1993, 326) has suggested that the majority of the dog ABGs (within this study recorded as unknown or partial) would have been originally deposited as complete skeletons. This would explain the even spread of dog elements in the partial ABGs and non-ABG faunal assemblages from many of the Romano-British sites.

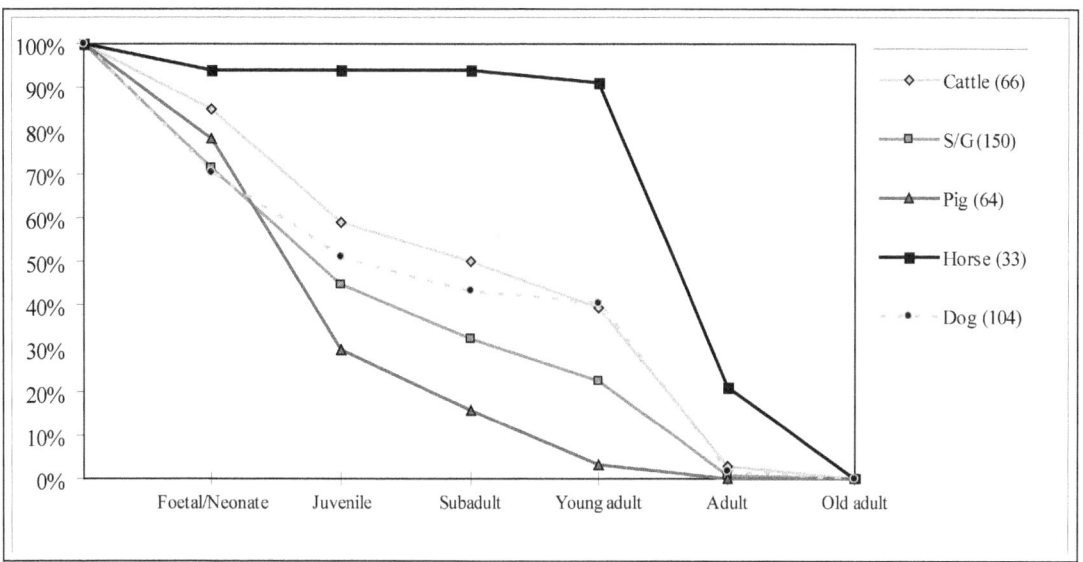

Figure 3.7 Mortality profiles of partial ABG per species (combined results from all periods and regions with ageing data available).

There also appears to be little overall age difference between complete and partial dog ABGs.

The majority of domestic bird ABGs recorded in this study consist of complete skeletons (Table 3.2). Complete domestic fowl have been recovered from sites in southern England and Yorkshire from the Romano-British period onwards. However, all the other poultry and raptors probably kept in captivity (goose, goshawk, peregrine falcon and sparrowhawk) are recorded from the Medieval site of Faccombe Netherton, Hampshire (Sadler 1990).

A higher proportion of the wild mammal ABGs recorded consists of complete skeletons. However, this is due to a small number of Iron Age and Romano-British sites affecting the data. No complete wild mammals are present in the Neolithic or Bronze Age assemblages. However, 76% and 65% of the wild mammals from Iron Age and Romano-British sites respectively are complete. However, both samples are heavily affected by individual sites in Hampshire. Thirteen of the 21 Iron Age wild mammal ABGs (excluding cat) are from a single deposit of 12 foxes and one red deer at Winklebury Camp (Jones 1977). In the Romano-British sample, 20 of the 24 complete wild mammals are from Oakridge Well (Maltby 1994). It is interesting to note that the Winklebury Camp red deer is the only one encountered in this study that consists of a complete skeleton. The majority of the complete wild mammals are from small carnivores, such as fox, stoat and weasel. There is little evidence of small carnivorous mammal consumption from the Neolithic onwards. Butchery marks are only present on one deposit. The lower front and hind limbs of a complete fox at the Iron Age site of Nettlebank Copse, Hampshire bears knife cuts, which are thought to indicate skinning of the animal (Poole 2000a). These ABGs may be complete because the carcasses have only been skinned and no further processing has taken place. This of course assumes that they are the result of human activity, some deposits have been interpreted as pitfall victims. Although the overall assemblage shows some species are more commonly found as complete skeletons, there is also much variation between the periods.

The Neolithic and Bronze Age assemblages have a very different pattern to those from the Iron Age and Romano-British periods. Sheep/goat have the highest proportion of complete ABGs in the Neolithic assemblage (Figure 3.8). However, this is due to the very small sample of four sheep/goat in total, two of which are complete. Seven complete sheep/goat ABGs are also present in the Bronze Age sample, the majority of which are from the Crab Farm enclosure, Dorset (Locker 1992). The highest proportion (32%) of complete cattle is also recorded from the Bronze Age. With the exception of the Down Farm Pond Barrow, Dorset (Legge 1991), all the complete cattle ABGs are from settlement sites (Legge 1991; Locker 1992; Maltby 1992).

During the Iron Age and Romano-British periods, domestic fowl are often found as complete ABGs. The Iron Age sample is small with only six recorded, three of which are complete. The number of domestic fowl ABGs increases in the Romano-British period to 58, with 21 complete. In this period there appears to be a specific pattern of deposition, with the majority recorded from funerary sites such as Poundbury, Dorchester (Buckland-Wright 1993) and Trentholme Drive, York (Fraser and Ryder 1968).

A relatively high proportion of the pig ABGs also consist of complete skeletons in the Iron Age and Romano-British periods (Figure 3.8). In this regard the Iron Age assemblage is dominated by the results from Danebury, from which over half the complete pigs are recorded. The majority of these were neonatal and dated to the middle

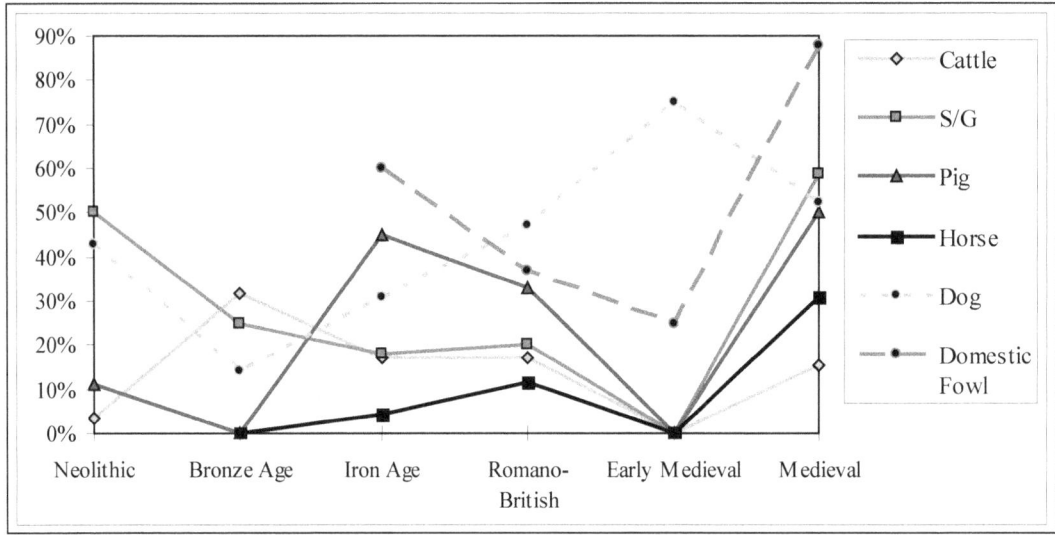

Figure 3.8 Percentage of complete ABGs present for the main species per period.

Iron Age. No one site dominates the Romano-British assemblage. Again, all the complete and partial pigs are from neonatal or juvenile individuals. Perhaps significantly, of the 22 complete pig deposits, all except two, one from Silchester (Grant 2000), and one from Portchester, Hampshire (Grant 1975) are from rural settlements.

A substantial proportion of dog ABGs in each period consist of complete skeletons, although it is not until the early Medieval period that the proportion of complete dogs is higher than for any other species. But overall more complete dogs were recorded than any other species. Also, as discussed, many of the partial dog ABGs may have originally been deposited as complete skeletons.

In the later Medieval sample domestic fowl are the most common ABG recorded as complete. However, as with the Iron Age and Romano-British wild mammal data, this is heavily affected by the data from a small number of sites. All the complete domestic fowl from southern England are from one site, Faccombe Netherton (Sadler 1990). A similar pattern is seen in the Yorkshire data where all the Medieval domestic fowl ABGs consist of complete skeletons, but all are recorded from two sites in York, The Bedern Foundry (Bond and O'Connor 1999) and 58-59, Skeldergate (O'Connor 1984b). In fact, only one domestic fowl from the Medieval ABG assemblage has been recorded as a partial skeleton. There is generally a high proportion of complete ABGs for most species in the Medieval period, with 59% of sheep/goat and 50% of pig consisting of complete deposits (Figure 3.8). However, as with the domestic birds, these figures are dominated by a restricted number of southern England sites.

Conclusions; Beyond the Iron Age

As discussed at the beginning of this paper, the majority of the literature utilising ABGs concerns prehistoric deposits. However, the results presented above have shown that such deposits are recovered from sites ranging from the Neolithic to Medieval periods. In fact they are more common on historic rather than prehistoric sites. As this study utilised only published sources, there are undoubtedly many more examples of ABGs present in 'grey literature' and the results presented here may be seen as just the minimum numbers. Although this paper has shown that such deposits have a long history, they are also extremely variable. They differ not only in the species which were deposited but also in the composition of the deposit. Some trends do exist within each period, but it could be argued that no two ABG deposits are exactly alike. At this point we must start to consider the implications for the interpretation of these deposits.

As discussed at the beginning of this paper, previous names for ABGs have been heavily loaded with interpretative descriptions such as 'sacrificial offerings' (Ross 1968). The utilisation of such descriptions is one of the main problems when it comes to interpreting ABG deposits and has led archaeologists to be stuck into circular arguments. In many cases the interpretation of the deposit has been defined by the current preconceptions of certain time periods which can be summarised as prehistoric ABGs are 'ritual' whereas historic ABGs are 'functional'. There has also been a trend towards more 'ritual' interpretations of Romano-British ABGs in the last decade (Morris 2008a; in press). This has resulted in the interpretation not been led by the evidence from the individual ABGs. It is therefore important to emphasise that the above discussion deals only with the physical make-up of the deposits rather than the preconceived metaphysical ideals applied to them.

This lack of separation between interpretation and description is also one of the main reasons the interpretation of these deposits is often stuck in a dichotomy between 'ritual' and 'functional'. It has also led to the interpretation of those ABGs thought to be part of a ritualised activity to rarely move beyond what could be called 'meta-level' ritual explanations. 'Ritual' as a term is an overarching generalisation made up of a number of different events. For example, sacrifice, feasting and offerings are all forms of ritual activity. Therefore by using the term 'ritual' as both an explanation and description the archaeologist is not theorising what actions may have resulted in the ABG, but are rather assigning it to a vague overarching category.

To try and move away from such problems, only the ABG composition data has been presented in this paper. Hopefully this has shown that the nature of ABGs is extremely variable. We must therefore question whether the blanket interpretations often applied are suitable. If the deposits are so variable, then they may have undergone a number of different human actions in their creation. We could also hypothesize that the actions may have different meanings. Taking such an approach would therefore lead us away from trying to interpret ABGs as a concept rather than interpreting individual deposits.

Therefore, although this paper offers no answers as to the actions and meanings behind ABGs, it hopefully demonstrates that they are not just Iron Age phenomena. Additionally, the variable nature of the deposits across all time periods suggests that we should start to view ABGs as individual deposits, incorporating not only zoological, but taphonomic (i.e. butchery, gnawing, weathering) and contextual information. Therefore the question we should be asking is not 'what do ABGs mean' but rather 'what does *this* ABG mean'.

Acknowledgements

As this paper is concerned with synthesising the results of others, I am indebted to the hard work and dedication of the zooarchaeological community. Polydora Baker and Andy Hammon provided much help with accessing the AML reports, Mark Maltby and Ellen Hambleton provided comments on the draft of this paper. However, any errors remain the author's responsibility. Justine Biddle provided much needed editing help, along with her continued support.

Bibliography

Albarella, U. and Serjeantson, D. (2002) A passion for pork: meat consumption at the British late Neolithic site of Durrington Walls. In. P. Miracle and N. Milner (eds.) *Consuming Passions and Patterns of Consumption*, 33-49. Cambridge, McDonald Institute for Archaeological Research.

Anderson, S. and Boyle, K. (eds.) (1996) *Ritual Treatment of Human and Animal Remains. Proceedings of the First Meeting of the Osteoarchaeological Research Group held in Cambridge on 8th October 1994*. Oxford, Oxbow.

Bond, J. M. and O'Connor, T. P. (1999) *Bones from Medieval Deposits at 16-22 Coppergate and Other Sites in York. The Archaeology of York 15/5*. York, Council for British Archaeology.

Bourdillon, J. (1990) Animal bones recovered by coarse water-sieved recovery from middle Saxon Southampton, Hampshire (SOU15, excavated in 1974). English Heritage, Ancient Monuments Laboratory Report 103/90.

Buckland-Wright, J. C. (1993) The animal bones. In. D. E. Farwell and T. L. Molleson (eds.) *Excavations at Poundbury 1966-80. Volume II: The Cemeteries*, 110-111. Dorchester, Dorset Natural History and Archaeology Society Monograph Series 11.

Coy, J. (1993) The assemblage from context 320 Bell Street. In. H. Rees (ed.) Late Bronze Age and Early Iron Age settlement in the Lower Test Valley. Evidence from excavations and finds, 1981-9. *Proceedings of the Hampshire Field Club and Archaeological Society* 49, 39-41.

Fraser, F. C. and Ryder, M. L. (1968) Animal bones. In. L. P. Wenham (ed.) *The Romano-British Cemetery at Trentholme Drive, York*, 104-109. London, HMSO.

Fulford, M. (2001) Links with the past: pervasive 'ritual' behaviour in Roman Britain. *Britannia* 32, 119-218.

Grant, A. (1975) The animal bones. In. B. Cunliffe (ed.) *Excavations at Porchester Castle. Volume 1: Roman*, 437-450. London, Report of the Research Committee Society of Antiquaries of London 32.

Grant, A. (1984) Animal husbandry. In. B. Cunliffe (ed.) *Danebury: an Iron Age Hillfort in Hampshire. Volume 2. The Excavations 1969-1978: the Finds*, 496-548. London, Council for British Archaeology Research Report 52.

Grant, A. (1989) Animals in Roman Britain. In. M. Todd (ed.) *Research on Roman Britain: 1960-1989*, 425-500. London, Britannia Monograph 11.

Grant, A. (1991) Animal husbandry. In. B. Cunliffe and C. Poole (eds.) *Danebury: an Iron Age Hillfort in Hampshire. Volume 5. The Excavations 1979-1988: the Finds*, 447-487. London, Council for British Archaeology Research Report 73.

Grant, A. (2000) Diet, economy and ritual evidence from the faunal remains. In. M. Fulford and J. Timby (eds.) *Late Iron Age and Roman Silchester: Excavations on the Site of the Forum-Basilica 1977, 1980-86*, 425-482. London, Britannia Monograph 15.

Grigson, C. (1999) The mammalian remains. In. A. Whittle, J. Pollard and C. Grigson (eds.) *The Harmony of Symbols. The Windmill Hill*

Causewayed Enclosure, 164-252. Oxford, Oxbow.

Hambleton, E. (1999) *Animal Husbandry Regimes in Iron Age Britain*. Oxford, British Archaeological Report British Series 282.

Hambleton, E. (2007) Review of Middle Bronze Age to Late Iron Age faunal Assemblages from southern Britain. English Heritage Report.

Hamerow, H. (2006) 'Special deposits' in Anglo-Saxon settlements. *Medieval Archaeology* 50, 1-30.

Harcourt, R. (1969) Animal bones from Marden. English Heritage, Ancient Monuments Laboratory Report 1555.

Harcourt, R. (1971a) Animal bones from Durrington Walls. In. G. J. Wainwright and I. H. Longworth (eds.) *Durrington Walls: Excavations 1966-1968*, 338-350. London, Reports of the Research Committee of the Society of Antiquaries of London 30.

Harcourt, R. (1971b) Animal bones from Marden. In. G. J. Wainwright, J. G. Evans and I. H. Longworth. The excavation of a Late Neolithic enclosure at Marden, Wiltshire. *The Antiquaries Journal* 51, 234-235.

Hill, J. D. (1995) *Ritual and Rubbish in the Iron Age of Wessex*. Oxford, British Archaeological Report British Series 242.

Jones, R. (1977) Animal bones. In. K. Smith. The excavation of Winklebury Camp, Basingstoke, Hampshire. *Proceedings of the Prehistoric Society* 43, 58-69.

Legge, A. J. (1991) The animal remains from six sites at Down Farm, Woodcutts. In. J. Barrett, R. Bradley and M. Hall (eds.) *Papers on the Prehistoric Archaeology of Cranborne Chase*, 54-100. Oxford, Oxbow Monograph 11.

Locker, A. (1992) Animal bone. In. M. Papworth (ed.) Excavation and survey of Bronze Age sites in the Badbury area, Kingston Lacy Estate. *Proceedings of the Dorset Natural History and Archaeological Society* 114, 56-57.

Maltby, M. (1981a) The animal bones. In. S. Davies. The excavations at Old Down Farm, Andover. Part 2 Prehistoric and Roman. *Proceedings of the Hampshire Field Club* 37, 147-153.

Maltby, M. (1981b) Iron Age, Romano-British and Anglo-Saxon animal husbandry: a review of the faunal evidence. In. M. Jones and G. Dimbleby (eds.) *The Environment of Man; the Iron Age to the Anglo-Saxon Period*, 155-204. Oxford, British Archaeological Report British Series 87.

Maltby, M. (1982) The animal bones. In. M. Millett and D. Russell. An Iron Age burial from Viables Farm, Basingstoke. *Archaeological Journal* 139, 75-81.

Maltby, M. (1985) The animal bones. In. P. Fasham (ed.) *The Prehistoric Settlement at Winnall Down, Winchester*, 97-125. Winchester, Hampshire Field Club Monograph 2.

Maltby, M. (1987) The Animal Bones from the Excavations at Owslebury, Hants. An Iron Age and Early Romano-British settlement. Ancient Monuments Laboratory Report 6/1987.

Maltby, M. (1990) Animal bones. In. J. Richards (ed.) *The Stonehenge Environs Project*, 207-208. London, English Heritage Archaeology Report 16.

Maltby, M. (1992) The animal bone. In. C. Gingell (ed.) *The Marlborough Downs: a Late Bronze Age Landscape and its Origins*, 137-142. Salisbury, Wiltshire Archaeological and Natural History Society Monograph 1.

Maltby, M. (1993) Animal bones. In. P. J. Woodward, S. M. Davies and A. H. Graham (eds.) *Excavations at the Old Methodist Chapel and Greyhound Yard, Dorchester, 1981-1984*, 314-340. Dorchester, Dorset Natural History and Archaeological Society Monograph Series 12.

Maltby, M. (1994) The animal bone from a Romano-British well at Oakridge II, Basingstoke, Hampshire. *Proceedings of the Hampshire Field Club and Archaeological Society* 49, 47-76.

Maltby, M. (2004) The animal bones. In. M. Rawlings, M. J. Allen and F. Healy. Investigation of the Whitesheet Down environs 1989-90: Neolithic causeway enclosure and Iron Age settlement. *Wiltshire Archaeological and Natural History Magazine* 97, 167-170.

Maltby, M. (2010) *Feeding a Roman Town: Environmental Evidence from Excavations in Winchester, 1972-1985*. Winchester, Archétype.

Manby, T. G. (1980) Excavation of barrows at Grindale and Boynton, East Yorkshire, 1972. *Yorkshire Archaeological Journal* 52, 19-48.

Morris, J. (2008a) Associated bone groups; one archaeologist's rubbish is another's ritual deposition. In. O. Davis, N. Sharples and K. Waddington (eds.) *Changing Perspectives on the First Millenium BC*, 83-98. Oxford, Oxbow.

Morris, J. (2008b) Re-examining Associated Bone Groups from Southern England and Yorkshire, c.4000BC to AD1550, Bournemouth University, PhD Thesis.

Morris, J. (in press) The composition and interpretation of associated bone groups from wessex. In. D. Campana, A. Choyke, P. Crabtree, S. Defrance and J. Lev-Tov (eds.) *Anthropological Approaches to Zooarchaeology: Colonialism, Complexity and Animal Transformations*, Oxford, Oxbow.

O'Connor, T. P. (1983) Report on bone spot-findings from 16-22 Coppegate, York. English Heritage, Ancient Monuments Laboratory Report 4100.

O'Connor, T. P. (1984a) Bones from Aldwark, York. English Heritage, Ancient Monuments Laboratory Report 4391.

O'Connor, T. P. (1984b) *Selected Groups of Bones from Skeldergate and Walmgate. The Archaeology of York 15/1*. York, Council for British Archaeology.

O'Connor, T. P. (1989) *Bones from Anglo-Scandinavian Levels at 16-22 Coppergate. The Archaeology of*

York 15/3. York, Council for British Archaeology.
O'Day, S. J., Neer, W. N. and Ervynck, A. (eds.) (2004) *Behaviour Behind Bones. The Zooarchaeology of Ritual, Religon, Status and Identity*. Oxford, Oxbow.
Parker-Pearson, M., Pollard, J., Richards, C., Thomas, J., Tilley, C., Welham, K., Allen, M., Bennett, W., Field, D., French, C., Linford, N., Payne, A., Robinson, D. and Ruggles, C. (2007) The Stonehenge Riverside Project Summary Interim Report on the 2006 Season. Sheffield, Sheffield University.
Pollard, J. (2006) A community of beings: animals and people in the Neolithic of southern Britain. In. D. Serjeantson and D. Field (eds.) *Animals in the Neolithic of Britian and Europe. Neolithic Studies Group Seminar Papers 7*, 135-148. Oxford, Oxbow Books.
Poole, C. (2000a) Special deposits. In. B. Cunliffe and C. Poole (eds.) *The Danebury Environs Programme. The Prehistory of a Wessex Landscape. Vol 2. Part 5. Nettlebank Copse, Wherwell, Hants, 1993*, Microfiche 9:E10-G14. Oxford, English Heritage and Oxford University Committee for Archaeology Monograph 49.
Poole, C. (2000b) Special deposits in pits. In. B. Cunliffe and C. Poole (eds.) *The Danebury Environs Programme. The Prehistory of a Wessex Landscape. Volume 2, Part 3. Suddern Farm, Middle Wallop, Hants, 1991 and 1996*, Microfiche 4:G5-5:C10. Oxford, English Heritage and Oxford University Committee for Archaeology Monograph 49.
Riggott, J. M. and Williams, I. C. (1984) Report on the animal bones. In. T. C. M. Brewster (ed.) *The Excavation of Whitegrounds Barrow, Burythorpe*, 18-19. Malton, East Riding Archaeological Research Committee.
Ross, A. (1968) Shafts, pits, wells - sanctuaries of the Belgic Britons? In. J. M. Coles and D. D. A. Simpson (eds.) *Studies in Ancient Europe*, 255-285. Leicester, Leicester University Press.
Ryan, K. and Crabtree, P. (eds.) (1995) *The Symbolic Role of Animals in Archaeology*. Philadelphia, University of Pennsylvania, MASCA Research Papers in Science and Archaeology 12.
Ryder, M. L. (1970) The animal remains from Petergate, York, 1957-58. *Yorkshire Archaeological Journal* 42, 418-428.
Sadler, P. (1990) Faunal remains. In. J. R. Fairbrother (ed.) *Faccombe Netherton. Excavations of a Saxon and Medieval Manorial Complex. Vol 2*, 462-508. London, British Museum Occasional Paper 74.
Stallibrass, S. (1995) Review of the vertebrate remains. In. J. P. Huntley and S. Stallibrass (eds.) *Plant and Vertebrate Remains from Archaeological Sites in Northern England: Data Reviews and Future Directions*, 84-198. Durham, Architectural and Archaeological Society of Durham and Northumberland Research Report 4.

Stead, I. M. (1991) *Iron Age Cemeteries in East Yorkshire*. London, English Heritage.
Sykes, N. (2006) The impact of Normans on hunting practices in England. In. C. M. Woolgar, D. Serjeantson and T. Waldron (eds.) *Food in Medieval England: Diet and Nutrition*, 162-175. Oxford, Oxford University Press.
Wait, G. (1985) *Ritual and Religion in Iron Age Britain*. Oxford, British Archaeological Report British Series 149.
Wheeler, R. E. M. (1943) *Maiden Castle, Dorset*. London, Report of the Research Committee of the Society of Antiquaries 12.
Woodward, P. and Woodward, A. (2004) Dedicating the town: urban foundation deposits in Roman Britain. *World Archaeology* 36 (1), 68-86.

Authors' Affiliations

James Morris
Museum of London Archaeology
Mortimer Wheeler House
46 Eagle Wharf Road
London
N1 7ED
UK

4. Zooarchaeology and the Interpretation of Depositions in Shafts

Mark Maltby

Abstract

Wells and other shafts are common depositories for animal bones and other environmental data. Interpretations of these depositions have varied greatly. This paper reviews the deposition of animal bone groups (ABGs) in two Romano-British shafts. When examined in detail, there are significant variations in the make-up of these ABGs, and it is argued that they should not be considered as one generic group. To understand such depositions, detailed records of the location and condition of all the finds are required. ABGs should not be considered in isolation and a much more holistic approach is required which should make use of environmental archaeological data.

Introduction

Wells and other shafts have been discovered on a wide range of British archaeological sites. In many instances their interpretation has attracted discussion about the motivations behind their construction, use and infilling. These interpretations have ranged from the exclusively functional (e.g. extraction of water; flint and other raw materials) to the purely ritual with various others combining elements of both. Environmental archaeologists have been involved in the analysis of many of these features. Bones of both humans and other animals have been frequently recovered and subjected to investigation by human osteoarchaeologists and zooarchaeologists. Less consistently, other environmental archaeologists have also been involved in examining a range of materials including soils, insects, wood and other macroscopic plant remains, pollen and snails. A wide range of other archaeological specialists have also been involved in the analysis of the non-environmental artefacts deposited in these features.

This paper is concerned with whether and how the contributions of environmental archaeologists, in particular zooarchaeologists, have been incorporated into the overall interpretations of wells and shafts. It examines to what extent, if at all, their interpretations have been influenced by the results of colleagues examining other materials from the same feature.

Problems of integrating environmental archaeology with other archaeological evidence in the interpretation of shafts are most clearly illustrated in the report of the Wilsford Shaft (Ashbee *et al* 1989). This shaft was originally thought to be an Early Bronze Age pond barrow located just 800m to the south of Stonehenge in Wiltshire. Excavations revealed that the depression represented the cone of a shaft that extended to a depth of 100 feet (30m) through the chalk subsoil. Subsequent clarification of the chronology has shown that the shaft was originally dug in the Neolithic and was in-filled at various times in the Bronze and Iron Age. Within the published report, Martin Bell emphasised a functional interpretation (use as a well; local environmental conditions), whereas Paul Ashbee emphasised the possible ritual motivations behind the construction of the shaft and subsequent depositions. Therefore material deposited in the shaft was interpreted differently by members of the same investigation team.

The larger animal bones from the shaft were examined by Caroline Grigson (1989). These included a number of associated animal bone groups (ABGs) (see Morris this volume for discussion on the general nature of this deposit type). Three groups of neonatal sheep/goat bones from near the base of the shaft were interpreted as remains of animals being bred near the site. Sheep head and foot bones found at a depth of c.44 feet (c.13.4m) were interpreted as either skinning or butchery waste or the ritual deposition of head and hooves. Two sets of sheep/goat thoracic vertebrae located at the base of the weathering cone were interpreted as butchery waste, based on the evidence of cut marks. In the upper cone amongst Iron Age material, Grigson noted the presence of small groups of horse bones and a cattle skull amongst disarticulated human remains. She described this as *"unusual human discard behaviour: whether or not this should be regarded as ritualistic is uncertain"* (Grigson 1989, 115). Disarticulated animal bones from the shaft were generally regarded as the product of *"ordinary domestic refuse"*.

Small vertebrate bones were examined by Yalden and Yalden (1989). The amphibian bones were interpreted as the victims of falls. Bones of swallows were interpreted as the remains of birds nesting in the upper part of the shaft. Therefore different associated bone groups were accorded different interpretations based on their species, completeness and other taphonomic evidence. The analyses from the Wilsford shaft therefore highlight many of the problems associated with interpreting animal remains from such features. The interpretations given are often variable and frequently dependent upon the individual author's preconceptions and favoured paradigms.

This paper will critically review interpretations of faunal remains studied by the author from two other shafts, both of Romano-British date. The validity of the original interpretations will be discussed in relation to general changes in the interpretation of wells and shafts. The sites in question are Greyhound Yard, Dorchester (Woodward et al 1993) and Victoria Road, Winchester (Qualmann et al 2010; Maltby 2010).

Greyhound Yard, Dorchester

Dorchester, Dorset was the *civitas* capital of the Durotriges during the Romano-British period. Extensive excavations tool place on the Greyhound Yard site in 1984, incorporating about a third of an *insula* situated to the south of the Forum (Woodward *et al* 1993). Amongst a complex sequence of building developments spanning the Romano-British period, a number of deep shafts were investigated, many producing a rich range of finds. These features included wells, which reached the depth of the water table. Other shafts, although up to five metres in depth, ended well above the water table. Most of these were originally interpreted as cess pits filled with a variety of refuse (*ibid*, 31-83). Subsequently, Woodward and Woodward (2003) have reinterpreted some of these shafts. By reconsidering the location and alignment of the pits, they argue cogently that some of these features were created as part of the original foundation and laying out of the town. They suggest *"that certain shafts...were dug to receive placed deposits of ritual significance"* (*ibid*, 70) and that evidence for repeated acts of deposition *"can be related to the possible enactment of urban foundation rituals, and their continuing celebration"* (*ibid*, 83). They based their arguments on the discovery of complete ceramic vessels, animal burials and rich small finds assemblages within the fills of these features.

Nineteen shafts were reinterpreted, of which three are illustrated and discussed in detail (Woodward *et al* 1993). This section will review the extent to which artefactual and environmental data were utilised in both the original interpretation and subsequent reinterpretation of some of these features. This critique will be restricted to those features described in most detail in Woodward and Woodward (2003)

The original interpretation of these features was partly based on the analyses of diverse specialists who worked on the materials recovered from the site. The excavation monograph is structured in a manner typical of such reports (Woodward *et al* 1993). The first chapters are concerned with a detailed description of the stratigraphic sequence arranged in chronological order and including a chapter on the Roman phases. This is followed by a chapter concerned with the description and interpretation of the small finds. This includes 20 separate reports created by a total of 14 specialists. The next chapter consists of the pottery evidence, which involved the work and reports of six specialists. The finds reports have heavy emphasis on typology and provide general assessments and comparisons between periods. However, they rarely discuss finds or assemblages from individual features.

The work of eight environmental archaeologists forms the framework of the penultimate chapter of the monograph. The analyses that include data from the shafts, however, are restricted to those on the mammal and bird bones (Maltby 1993), the fish bones (Hamilton-Dyer 1993), oysters (Winder 1993), the human remains (Rogers 2003), cess and dog coprolites (Allen 1993) and macroscopic plant remains (Jones and Straker 1993). However, constraints of rescue archaeology severely restricted sieving and other sampling for environmental data. Apart from the animal bones, which were retrieved during hand-excavation from all contexts, environmental data was collected and analysed from a very restricted range of contexts.

As in the case of the artefacts, the emphasis within the published animal bone reports was on general trends between periods rather than analysis of assemblages by feature, property or area. This was an editorial decision made for understandable reasons of keeping the monograph to a reasonable size with regard to publication costs. More details were made available in the form of microfiche, which consists of 24 appendices that includes catalogues of all the metalwork, worked stone, shale, glass and building materials. They also contain summary lists of the Samian, imported finewares and mortaria and various summary tables of the animal bones, marine mollusca and plant remains. However, records of all the other categories of pottery and detailed records of the faunal remains are only available in the archives held at the Dorset County Museum.

The final chapter in the monograph (Woodward 1993) is typical of most excavation reports in that it consists of a discussion, in which the excavation co-ordinator has the unenviable task of synthesising the disparate specialist reports and attempting to integrate these with the stratigraphic evidence.

Shaft 13 (Feature F2310)
This feature was the one which was highlighted as an example for evidence of *"repetitive and structured deposition"* (Woodward and Woodward 2003, 74). It consisted of 3.30m of early-mid 2nd Century fills from the lower part of a vertical shaft. The fills mainly consisted of layers of fine clayey loam containing dark organic deposits interspersed with layers of chalk rubble, limestone slabs and a wooden box (Woodward *et al* 1993, 47; Woodward and Woodward, 2003, 74). In the original report attention was drawn to the presence of several dog skeletons and neonatal puppies. The position of two of the adult dog skeletons led to the suggestion that they may have been tied together at the throat when deposited. It was also suggested that two other dogs had been decapitated. Although the significance of these dogs was described as uncertain, this shaft, like the others, was interpreted primarily as a cess-pit (Woodward *et al* 1993, 47).

Table 4.1 Summary of sequence of depositions in Greyhound Yard, Dorchester Shaft 13. Data adapted from Woodward and Woodward (2003, 75). 2313 also includes a wooden box cover, ABG = animal bone groups; s/g= sheep/goat; cw = coarse ware vessels

Context	Approx. Depth (m)	Fill	ABGs	Ceramics	Personal Items
2114		terracing/later infill			
2279		terracing/later infill			
2282		terracing/later infill			
2283		terracing/later infill			
2290	0.00-0.20	organic			
2312	0.20-0.60	chalk seal			
2313	0.60-0.90	loam	4 s/g; 3 dogs; puppy; 2 birds	3 whole cw; 2 half cw	
2328	0.90-1.10	organic			
2316	1.10-1.50	organic above chalk seal	4 dog; puppy; 2 s/g; pig; 2 birds		
2321	1.50-1.80	clayey loam	dog; puppy; rodent		pottery and glass counters
2334	1.80-2.20	organic above limestone	cat; dog		
2335	2.20-2.90	clayey loam	frog; s/g; puppy	2 whole cw; 1 half cw	
2362	2.90-3.30	chalk rubble			

The reinterpretation highlighted the evidence for structured deposition. Table 4.1 summarises the discussion originally presented by Woodward and Woodward (2003, 74-77). Their discussion is supported by a figure, which describes all the animal bone groups (ABGs), complete and half-complete pottery vessels and personal items as votive deposits (*ibid*, 75, Figure 3). This unfortunately oversimplifies the nature of these ABGs, giving the impression that they are all complete skeletons. Although the discussion of the finds makes it clear that, for example, the rodent and frogs probably were victims of falls and some of the remains are joints of meat rather than unbutchered skeletons (*ibid*, 75-77), the impression gained is that all the ABGs are of equal significance.

An examination of the original animal bone analysis demonstrates that this is not the case. Unfortunately space precluded the publication of the details of the ABGs in the text of the original excavation report, although summary data are available in the microfiche (Maltby 1993, mf6). A brief discussion of the faunal remains from this shaft supported by these tables was also produced as an English Heritage, Ancient Monuments Laboratory Report (Maltby 1990). That report did note that an unusually high proportion of the 1,754 animal bone elements in the shaft formed ABGs. Table 4.2 reproduces the summary details recorded in the original analysis. A total of 29 ABGs from 11 species contributed a total of 1,287 animal bone fragments. Undoubtedly, this pit received repeated depositions of a variety of species and the argument that these were of ritual significance, ignored in the original report, certainly deserves serious consideration. However, to obtain a more comprehensive understanding of the nature of these depositions, the completeness of the skeletons and taphonomic evidence also needs to be taken into consideration.

To examine these ABGs in the sequence of deposition, *2335* at the base of the shaft contained 4 ABGs along with two complete pots and substantial parts of a third. The frogs referred to by Woodward and Woodward (2003, 74) were in fact partial skeletons of a frog and toad (Table 4.2). The lack of sieving probably accounts for the absence of the remainder of the skeletons and the interpretation that these were pitfall victims is still the most feasible. The puppy remains consisted of just nine bones and without confirmation from sieving, it is unclear whether these were from a complete carcase or from the surviving remains of a partial skeleton that may have been redeposited. Probably of greater significance are the 76 bones of a sheep. The description of this as a sheep joint (*ibid*, 74) is inaccurate as the group consists of bones from most parts of the body of a neonatal lamb, which bears no evidence of butchery. Other bones of this skeleton may have been overlooked during excavation but this cannot be confirmed due to the lack of sieving. However, it is probable that this was a complete carcase that was deposited.

Context *2334*, which consisted mainly of clean chalk rubble and limestone slabs sealing *2335*, produced just two small ABGs. Four bones of an older dog and six bones of an immature cat, which appear to lie on top of a limestone slab, are unlikely to represent the surviving remains of complete carcases. It is possible that the dog

Table 4.2 Associated bone groups (ABG) in Greyhound Yard, Dorchester Shaft 13. Data adapted from Maltby (1990 Table 33). Dog excluding neonatal puppies; Pigeon = pigeon species; N = number of bones in ABGs

Species	2313 ABG	2313 N	2316 ABG	2316 N	2321 ABG	2321 N	2334 ABG	2334 N	2335 ABG	2335 N	Total ABG	Total N
Sheep	3	68	2	161					1	76	6	305
Goat	1	61									1	61
Pig			1	62							1	62
Dog	3	347	4	46	1	138	1	4			9	535
Puppy	1	26	1	104	1	13			1	9	4	152
Cat							1	6			1	6
Pigeon			1	4							1	4
Raven			1	84							1	84
Rook/Crow	1	30	1	20							2	50
Jackdaw	1	3									1	3
Frog									1	14	1	14
Toad									1	11	1	11
Total	10	535	11	481	2	151	2	10	4	110	29	1287

bones belonged to more complete skeletons recorded in fills above this context. However, both could also represent the redeposited remains of disturbed skeletons.

Context *2321* incorporated the largely complete skeleton of an immature male dog, which does appear to have been buried whole without prior disturbance. Thirteen neonatal puppy bones were also recorded, as well as a bag containing gaming counters. This was sealed by a dump of chalk and clay, above which a substantial organic deposit, *2316*, produced four dog partial ABGs totalling 46 bones, which are not necessarily from four different dogs as implied by the illustration of Woodward & Woodward (2004, 75). The bones are all from adult animals but could be from some of the more complete skeletons located above in *2313*. Over 100 bones from at least three neonatal puppies were also recovered in this context, not one as stated by Woodward and Woodward (*ibid*, 77). Two further fairly complete neonatal lamb skeletons were also found in *2316*, again neither showing any evidence of butchery and therefore should not be regarded as joints of meat. Similarly, the 62 bones of pig belonged to a neonatal mortality, which was also probably deposited as a complete unprocessed carcase. A fairly complete raven (84 bones) represents the disposal of a complete bird. Twenty bones of a rook/crow were also recovered. These mainly consisted of the larger bones of the skeleton but many of the smaller bones may have been overlooked during excavation. Four bones of a pigeon were also retrieved.

Context *2316* was sealed with a wooden box or cover, above which a thick loamy deposit, *2313*, contained several more ABGs as well as five complete or substantially complete coarse ware vessels (Table 4.1). Three complete dog skeletons were deposited, including the two believed to have been tied together (alternatively they could also have been deposited in a bag). Two of these dogs were adults; the third was from an immature animal. Twenty-six bones from at least two neonatal puppies were also retrieved (not one as illustrated in Woodward and Woodward 2004, 75). Four further sheep/goat ABGs were recovered. These are also all described as sheep joints by Woodward and Woodward (*ibid*, 77) but again this disguises the heterogeneity of the groups. Two of them consist solely of the skulls and mandibles of sub-adult sheep, both skulls having being split open to remove the brain prior to deposition. The third consists of 60 bones of another young lamb. Again all parts of the body are represented and this again probably represents the carcase of an unbutchered complete burial. The fourth group consists of a goat rather than a sheep. All 61 bones are from the head, all four feet and the tail. Knife cuts on both astragali, a calcaneus and the distal end of the tibia indicate that the hind feet had been dismembered (Maltby 1990). The bones represented are those often detached with the skin and it therefore appears that this ABG represents the deposition of a goatskin, or bones removed during processing the skin, rather than a joint of meat.

Two further corvid ABGs were recovered from *2313*. Thirty bones of a rook/crow probably represents the carcase of a complete bird; However, the other group consists of just three bones from a jackdaw, which more likely represents only a partial skeleton that has probably been redeposited.

Although Shaft 13 undoubtedly incorporates an unusually rich ABG assemblage, it is clear that the ABGs vary substantially in their make-up. Some of the material can be interpreted as well preserved primary butchery waste (sheep skulls); other ABGs represent victims of falls (amphibians; rodents) and one group is likely to have been incorporated in a skin (goat). Some of the smaller groups (cat; jackdaw; pigeon) seem unlikely to represent the deposition of complete skeletons and may have been parts of redeposited carcases. Most of the more complete skeletons are from neonatal or juvenile mortalities of a pig, four sheep and at least seven puppies. Although these could be regarded as sacrifices, the town is likely to have housed a substantial breeding population of dogs and natural peri-natal mortalities or the disposal of unwanted litters could both account for the presence of these skeletons. It has also been argued that some pigs may have been kept and bred in Dorchester (Maltby 1993; 1994), which could explain the presence of the neonatal pig. However, three of the sheep are also neonatal mortalities and it is more difficult to use the same argument to account for their presence, as it is less likely that breeding flocks would have been kept near the centre of the town. Similarly the raven and possibly both the rook/crow skeletons can be interpreted as birds that would be attracted to the town's rubbish heaps and they could have died or been killed as scavengers, as has been suggested in some reports (e.g. Maltby 1979; 1993). However, some Roman urban settlements have produced substantial numbers of raven skeletons in shafts (Maltby 2010), and Fulford (2001) and Woodward and Woodward (2004) have plausibly argued that these depositions might represent the continuation of Iron Age ritual practices. Similarly, the presence of several skeletons of dogs of various ages (in addition to neonatal puppies) can be interpreted in different ways. They could be simply representative of the mortality rates of dogs resident in the town, whose bodies were deposited in suitable open shafts. However, although dog ABGs occur commonly in other pits and shafts in Dorchester, it is true that they are present in large numbers in some features including Shafts 13 and 6 (Maltby 1993; Woodward and Woodward 2004) and this may be ritually significant, particularly as two of the dogs do appear to have been decapitated before deposition, either tied together or within a bag. However, even these, it could be argued, simply represent evidence for the disposal of animals not required for processing. Some of the dog ABGs in the lower fills of Shaft 13 are small and could indicate redeposition of dog skeletons originally deposited above ground.

Another aspect partially overlooked by Woodward and Woodward (2004), is that these ABGs, complete pots and small finds were not found in isolation within any of the shafts considered. Within Shaft 13, there were over 500 animal bones not assigned to ABGs (Maltby 1990). Although many of these came from layers above the ABGs, substantial numbers were found in the same contexts. The identified material included cattle (NISP 96), sheep/goat (83), pig (59), domestic fowl (28), duck (6), jackdaw (5), rook/crow (4), pigeon (5), roe deer (1), hare (1) and horse (1). Therefore most of the species represented as ABGs (with the notable exceptions of dog and raven) were also present amongst disarticulated material. Butchery marks were found on around 100 fragments and at least 89 of the bones were damaged by gnawing prior to their final deposition. There were also a few fish bones (Hamilton-Dyer 1993) and marine mollusca (Winder 1993). In addition to the fairly complete small finds, there were also fragments of glass vessels, shale armlets, a copper bracelet and brooch.

There were substantial numbers of small pottery sherds. It should not be overlooked that many of the ABGs were found amongst cess deposits and dog coprolites were also identified (Allen 1993). It seems therefore that substantial amounts of the material deposited in the shaft (including some of the ABGs) were derived from middens or other dumps. If the ABGs and complete pots do represent acts of ritual deposition, they were accompanied with, or at least interspersed with, substantial amounts of previously discarded material and excrement. Concretions on some of the bones of several ABGs indicate that they had lain within cess deposits. Therefore the depositional processes involved in the accumulation of material in Shaft 13 are complex and cannot be easily separated into ritual and non-ritual categories.

Victoria Road, Winchester

The second Romano-British example is from excavations of another *civitas* capital in southern England, Winchester, Hampshire. Excavations of the northern suburb in the 1970s unearthed cemeteries and occupation deposits of an adjacent suburb that developed in the later Roman period (Qualmann *et al* 2010). Several shafts and wells were discovered. The one where there is the best evidence for possible ritual deposits is pit F814, which was created and in-filled in the middle of the fourth century AD (Maltby 2010). The shaft was 3.8m deep but did not reach the water table. There were only two fills. The lower fill (context *3262*) of silty clay extended to within 0.7m of the top and contained around 2,500 of the 2,819 animal bones recovered from the pit by hand and in sieved samples (Table 4.3).

At least 925 bones were in ABGs but again these differ in their composition. Sieving produced large numbers of amphibian bones, mainly of frogs, and it must be assumed that many more were not recovered. These were found mainly in the lowest part of the pit and represent a period when frogs, which were probably colonising the area, were prone to being victims of falls. The numbers imply that the pit must have lain open at one point for some considerable time. The major group of complete ABGs consisted of over 300 bones belonging to a minimum of eight dogs. Unfortunately, the bones of these burials were not separated and it was not possible to assign all the bones to individuals. Nor is it clear from the excavation records whether the skeletons were originally found in groups or admixed together, although one photograph of the pit during excavation shows that at least one of the dogs formed a discrete burial. All but one of the dogs were adult, the other was immature. No neonatal puppies were found in this pit (but are present in some of the other shafts – Maltby, 2010). There is no evidence of butchery or gnawing on any of their bones. Two small groups of associated cat bones were found in *3262*. A pair of femora and a tibia from an immature animal formed the first group; eight ribs from an adult cat

Table 4.3 Animal bones from Winchester Victoria Road pit F814. Data adapted from Maltby (2010). * unsieved counts probably include some bones from ABGs

Species	NISP Unsieved ABG	NISP Unsieved Other	NISP Sieved ABGs	NISP Sieved Other	Total NISP	MNI of ABG
Cattle		658		3	661	
Sheep/Goat		273	5	2	280	1
Pig		73		2	75	
Horse		17			17	
Dog	330	4		1	335	8
Cat	11				11	2
Mouse				2	2	
Rodent		2		2	4	
Frog			201		201	
Toad			10		10	
Frog/Toad			281		281	
Domestic Fowl*		33	62	1	96	1(+)
Duck		3			3	
Raven	25				25	1
Sea Eagle		1			1	
Large Mammal		493		13	506	
Medium Mammal		197		23	220	
Unid. Mammal		71		19	90	
Unid. Bird				1	1	
Total	366	1825	559	69	2819	13 (+)

formed the second. No evidence of butchery was found and it is therefore probable that these represent only partial skeletons, perhaps of carcases that were originally deposited elsewhere. The only ABG of the major food species consisted of the complete skull, mandibles, and hyoids of an adult hornless sheep recovered from a soil sample selected for sieving. Although the skull was not split open, it may still represent the deposition of primary processing waste. The presence of several pairs of sheep metapodials in the same context also raises the possibility that sheepskins, or bones (feet and heads) removed from sheepskins after processing, were deposited.

An adult raven ABG in *3262* was represented by 26 bones from all parts of the body, indicating the deposition of a complete bird. A sieved sample produced 62 bones from an immature domestic fowl. There is no evidence that this chicken was processed and it seems likely that the complete carcase was deposited. At least six probable pairs of domestic fowl bones were recorded amongst the hand-collected material. Although these could not be assigned to ABGs, it is probable that other domestic fowl ABGs were deposited.

Excluding amphibians, at least thirteen partial or complete animal burials were deposited in pit F814 (Table 4.3). Apart from the sheep and the chickens, all the ABGs in this pit were from animals rarely processed for meat. Again it is the dogs and the raven skeletons that represent the best cases for ritual deposition, using the same arguments outlined above for the ABGs in Shaft 13 at Dorchester. If the dogs were deposited together (although there is no conclusive evidence that they were),

the probability of eight dogs all dying of natural causes at about the same time and deposited in the same context seems remote, although an epidemic of, for example, canine distemper cannot be ruled out. It is more likely, however, that these dogs were deliberately killed. It is plausible that this was ritually motivated but the possibility that there may have been a purge on stray dogs in an attempt to control their numbers also needs consideration. The abundance of gnawed bones in all deposits (this pit included) testifies that many dogs had free access to processing waste in the town. If their numbers became too large, they may have been deemed a health hazard, particularly in areas where a lot of rubbish was dumped. The numbers of dog ABGs increase significantly in the Romano-British period in southern England, particularly in towns (Morris 2008, 187) and this might imply that stray dogs had become more of a problem within densely occupied areas. Such an explanation could also account for the presence of the raven, perhaps also a victim of the same purge of scavenging animals.

However, other finds lend support to the possibility of ritual deposition. As in Shaft 13 at Dorchester, complete pottery vessels were found in the lower layer of the pit. These include ten complete or near complete colour-coated beakers, a glass vessel and stone roofing tiles (Rees *et al* 2008). Another unusual find was the humerus of a white-tailed eagle. A skull of the same species was found in a Roman well in Droitwich, where a ritual interpretation was attributed (Baxter 1993). However, Mulkeen and O'Connor (1997) note that white-tailed eagles could also have been attracted to urban sites as scavengers.

However, more mundane finds were also deposited in this pit. There were many more small sherds of pottery than complete vessels and over 1,900 animal bone fragments not assigned to ABGs were also recorded (Table 4.3). Cattle dominated this assemblage, their numbers enhanced by evidence for the large-scale disposal of certain parts of their carcases. At least 24 cattle were represented by the area of the skull situated at the junction of the horn core. Butchery marks showed that the horns had been systematically removed. Although other parts of the body were less well represented, 11 cattle were represented by metatarsals, ten by tibiae, and nine each by metacarpals and mandibles.

Another unusual feature about the cattle assemblage was the large number (21) of complete metacarpals and metatarsals. These have been rarely encountered elsewhere in Roman Winchester because these bones were systematically broken open for marrow. The metapodials from F814 also included an unusually high proportion of male specimens, whereas those of cows were usually much more common in other deposits in the area. Since the shape of the surviving horn cores also indicated that steers were commonly represented in F814, it is feasible that these metapodials and adjoining phalanges were associated with some of the skulls. It seems possible that cattle hides were being processed in the vicinity. A substantial part of the assemblage could therefore be the waste from tanning and horn-working specialists. Raw material for these specialist activities may have relied on sources of stock not usually as well represented in the rest of the assemblages.

Sheep/goat elements were moderately frequent, and at least 12 were represented by mandibles and radii. Pig and horse were very poorly represented. Small numbers of duck and rodent bones were also found (Table 4.3). Over 270 of the identified bones had been butchered and at least 212 of the identified fragments from the hand-excavated sample had been damaged by gnawing, indicating a high incidence of secondary deposition.

The faunal assemblage from pit F814 is the most likely candidate to justify the label of a 'special deposit' as defined by Grant (1984) of any of the faunal assemblages from shafts in the Winchester excavations. However, although a case can be made to argue that there was a ritual significance to at least some of the ABGs, particularly in that they were associated with a number of complete artefacts and a bone of a rare species of bird, they were also associated with waste from specialist processing and other discarded material, much of which appears to have been redeposited in the pit. The presence of concretions on many of the bones again indicates that cess was also amongst the material deposited. Unfortunately the sequence of deposition of various components of the faunal and artefact assemblages in this substantial deposit cannot now be ascertained.

Conclusions

The two case studies have demonstrated that animal depositions in shafts are often complex and not easily categorised as ritual or non-ritual. Indeed, these terms are inadequately vague labels as Morris (2008, 349; Waddington, this volume) have pointed out. As is demonstrated in a number of papers in this volume, detailed contextual analysis is required to better understand the taphonomic history of different depositions. Many interpretations of these depositions are handicapped by the lack of an adequate sieving programme. The Winchester case study demonstrated that sieving significantly increased the numbers of amphibians recovered, providing some information about the history of infilling, and providing additional ABGs. However, in many cases it is impossible to be certain whether partial ABGs, particularly of smaller mammals and birds, represent all the bones deposited or just a biased selection of the larger bones of a more complete carcase. This information is crucial in determining whether the internment was primary or secondary.

The inadequacies of environmental sampling within shafts in general are also apparent. Depositions of plants may have potentially had as much symbolic significance as depositions of animals. Admittedly, their potential survival is more limited, but, particularly where waterlogged conditions prevail, possible depositions should be recognised. Similarly, mineralised material might survive in cess deposits. In addition, much more rigorous and detailed scientific examination of each individual fill is required, to gain a fuller understanding of their depositional history (Randall, this volume). Of course, there are significant cost implications. In many cases, developer funding restricts the excavation of deep shafts to the upper fills, although, as these and other studies have demonstrated, it is often the lowest fills that provide the largest number of ABGs, complete artefacts and other significant finds. In addition, it is important to know whether a shaft reached the water table and functioned originally as a well.

It is also abundantly clear that successful interpretation of the nature of ABGs relies on them being recognised at source. Excavation teams need some personnel who have received training in animal bone identification, in order to recognise the completeness or otherwise of such deposits, particularly in deposits rich in bones containing multiple ABGs. Some ABGs may represent loosely associated rather than articulated groups and this is important information to record. Interpretation of the Winchester shaft, in particular, is handicapped by the failure to adequately separate out different ABGs, accurately record their location within the fills, and determine their spatial relationship with the specialist processing waste and the complete pottery vessels.

The studies have also demonstrated that ABGs vary enormously in their composition. Within a single feature, ABGs can represent several different types of deposition event. They should not be treated as a single category and they should not be studied in isolation from other faunal remains deposited within the same feature. They need to be recorded fully. Ancillary data such as butchery marks, gnawing damage, surface condition, evidence for weathering, erosion and burning and fragmentation patterns need to be recorded and it is just as important to explicitly note the absence of these taphonomic indicators as well as their presence.

As Fulford (2001) and Woodward and Woodward (2004) have demonstrated, understanding deposition in shafts needs a holistic approach that incorporates the study of different find categories. Here we are faced with the problems, as demonstrated at Greyhound Yard, Dorchester, that these find categories are studied by a large number of different independent specialists, who produce separate reports often in isolation from studies of other materials from the same features. To reconstruct an overall interpretation from these disparate sources is a difficult task but one which needs to be tackled (preferably in consultation with the specialists), if we are to advance our understanding of deposition in shafts. Environmental archaeologists have an important part to play in improving these interpretations.

Acknowledgements

I would like to thank James Morris for constructive comments on the first draft of this paper.

References

Allen, M. J. (1993) Mineralised coprolites and cess. In. P. J. Woodward, S. M. Davies & A. H. Graham (eds.) *Excavations at the Old Methodist Chapel and Greyhound Yard, Dorchester, 1981-1984*, 348-349. Dorchester, Dorset Natural History and Archaeological Society Monograph Series 12.

Ashbee, P. Bell, M. and Proudfoot, E. (1989) *Wilsford Shaft: Excavations 1960-2*. London, English Heritage Monograph Report 11.

Baxter, I. (1993) An eagle, *Haliaeetus albicilla* (L), skull from Roman Leicester, England, with some speculations concerning the palaeoecology of the Soar Valley. *Circaea*, 10, 31-37.

Fulford, M. (2001) Links with the past: pervasive 'ritual' behaviour in Roman Britain. *Britannia*, 32, 119-218.

Grant, A. (1984) Animal husbandry. In. B. Cunliffe (ed.) *Danebury: an Iron Age Hillfort in Hampshire. Volume 2. The Excavations 1969-1978: the Finds*, 102-119. London, Council for British Archaeology Research Report 52.

Grigson, C. (1989) Large mammals. In P. Ashbee, M. Bell, and E. Proudfoot. *Wilsford Shaft: Excavations 1960-2*, 106-121. London, English Heritage Monograph Report 11.

Hamilton-Dyer, S. (1993) Fish remains. In. P. J. Woodward, S. M. Davies and A. H. Graham (eds.) *Excavations at the Old Methodist Chapel and Greyhound Yard, Dorchester, 1981-1984*, 345-346. Dorchester, Dorset Natural History and Archaeological Society Monograph Series 12.

Jones, J. and Straker, V. (1993) Macroscopic plant remains. In. P. J. Woodward, S. M. Davies and A. H. Graham (eds.) *Excavations at the Old Methodist Chapel and Greyhound Yard, Dorchester, 1981-1984*, 349-350. Dorchester, Dorset Natural History and Archaeological Society Monograph Series 12.

Maltby, M. (1979) *Faunal Studies on Urban Sites: the Animal Bones from Exeter 1971-1975*. Exeter Archaeological Reports 2. Sheffield, University of Sheffield.

Maltby, M. (1990) The Animal Bones from the Romano-British Deposits at the Greyhound Yard and Methodist Chapel Sites in Dorchester, Dorset. English Heritage, Ancient Monuments Laboratory Report 9/90.

Maltby, M. (1993) Animal bones. In. P. J. Woodward, S. M. Davies and A. H. Graham (eds.) *Excavations at the Old Methodist Chapel and Greyhound Yard, Dorchester, 1981-1984*, 314-340. Dorchester, Dorset Natural History and Archaeological Society Monograph Series 12.

Maltby, M. (1994) The meat supply in Roman Dorchester and Winchester. In A. R. Hall and H. K. Kenward (eds.) *Urban-rural Connexions: Perspectives from Environmental Archaeology*, 85-102. Symposia of the Association for Environmental Archaeology 12. Oxford, Oxbow Monograph 47.

Maltby, M. (2010) *Feeding a Roman Town: Environmental Evidence from Excavations in Winchester, 1972-1985*. Winchester, Archétype.

Morris, J. (2008) Re-examining Associated Bone Groups from Southern England and Yorkshire, c.4000BC to AD1550. Bournemouth University, PhD Thesis.

Mulkeen, S. and O'Connor, T. (1997) Raptors in towns: towards an ecological model. *International Journal of Osteoarchaeology*, 7, 440-449.

Qualmann, K. Rees, H and Scobie, G. D. (2010) Introduction to Roman Winchester. In M. Maltby. *Feeding a Roman Town: Environmental Evidence from Excavations in Winchester, 1972-1985*, 4-9. Winchester, Archétype.

Rees, H., Crummy, N., Ottaway, P. J. and Dunn, G. (2008) *Artefacts and Society in Roman and Medieval Winchester. Small Finds from the Suburbs and Defences, 1971-1986*. Winchester, Archétype.

Rogers, J. (1993) Human remains. In. P. J. Woodward, S. M. Davies and A. H. Graham (eds.) *Excavations at the Old Methodist Chapel and Greyhound Yard, Dorchester, 1981-1984*, 314-315. Dorchester, Dorset Natural History and Archaeological Society Monograph Series 12.

Winder, J. 1993. Oyster and other marine mollusc shells. In. P. J. Woodward, S. M. Davies and A. H. Graham (eds.) *Excavations at the Old Methodist Chapel and Greyhound Yard, Dorchester, 1981-1984*, 347-349. Dorchester, Dorset Natural History and Archaeological Society Monograph Series 12.

Woodward, P. J. (1993) Discussion. In. P. J. Woodward, S. M. Davies and A. H. Graham (eds.) *Excavations at the Old Methodist Chapel and Greyhound Yard, Dorchester, 1981-1984*, 351-382. Dorchester, Dorset Natural History and Archaeological Society Monograph Series 12.

Woodward, P. J., Davies, S. M. and Graham, A.H. (eds.) (1993) *Excavations at the Old Methodist Chapel and Greyhound Yard, Dorchester, 1981-1984*. Dorchester, Dorset Natural History and Archaeological Society Monograph Series 12.

Woodward, P. and Woodward, A. (2004) Dedicating the town: urban foundation deposits in Roman Britain. *World Archaeology*, 36, 68-86.

Yalden, P. E. and Yalden, D. W. (1989) Small vertebrates. In P. Ashbee, M. Bell, and E. Proudfoot. *Wilsford Shaft: Excavations 1960-2*, 103-106. London, English Heritage Monograph Report 11.

Authors' Affiliations

Mark Maltby
School of Conservation Science
Bournemouth University
Poole
Dorset
BH12 5BB
UK

5. New light on an old rite: reanalysis of an Iron Age burial group from Blewburton Hill, Oxfordshire

Robin Bendrey, Stephany Leach and Kate Clark

Abstract

In the late 1940s the skeletons of a human, a horse and a dog were found in association at the base of the defensive ditch of the Iron Age hillfort at Blewburton Hill, Oxfordshire. This article presents reanalyses of these skeletons employing up-to-date methods and approaches. The importance of reanalysis of finds from older excavations is stressed, especially where hypotheses are based on small numbers of archaeological finds. Without returning to source data, out-of-date information and interpretations can remain fixed and unchallenged in the literature. This paper forwards fresh data, and suggests a more complex meaning and set of associations than previously assigned to this deposit.

Introduction

The burial of a man, a horse and a dog skeleton in the defensive ditch of the Iron Age hillfort at Blewburton Hill, Oxfordshire (Figure 5.1), is reported by Collins (1952). The three skeletons were excavated from the base of the ditch, from Cutting F (Figures 5.2 and 5.3).

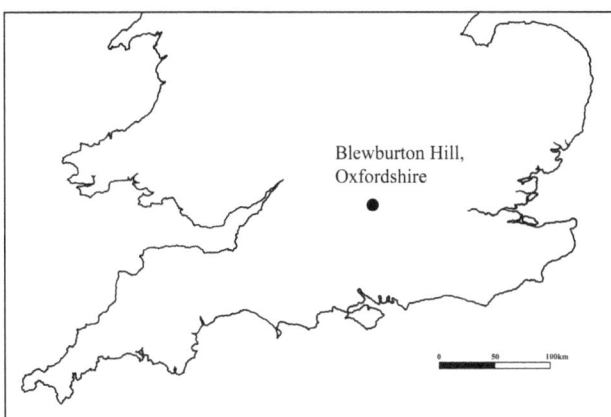

Figure 5.1 Map showing location of Blewburton Hill, Oxfordshire.

The site at Blewburton Hill, Oxfordshire was originally excavated between 1947 and 1953 (Collins 1947; 1952; Collins and Collins 1959). It was later re-excavated in 1967 (Harding 1967; 1976). Harding (1976, 145-6) suggests the following dates for the structural sequence: a seventh-sixth century BC date for the construction of the stockaded camp; a sixth-fifth century date for its replacement by the first hillfort; refortification with the dump rampart, and re-occupation of the site, at the end of the second or start of the first century BC, continuing until abandonment of the site before the end of the first century BC. Precise dating of the three skeletons is uncertain, but it might be expected that they post-date the construction of the dump rampart, at which time the ditch was probably redug to make it deeper and wider (Harding 1976, 135). This paper presents key findings from the reanalysis of these skeletons by the current authors.

Figure 5.2 Blewburton Hill, Cutting F under excavation: view looking west, from the rampart (defensive ditch in the foreground). This cutting, 6 ft. wide and 280 ft. long, was laid out to give a complete transverse section of the Iron Age defences and the lynchets at Blewburton Hill. Copyright Reading Museum Service (Reading Borough Council). All rights reserved.

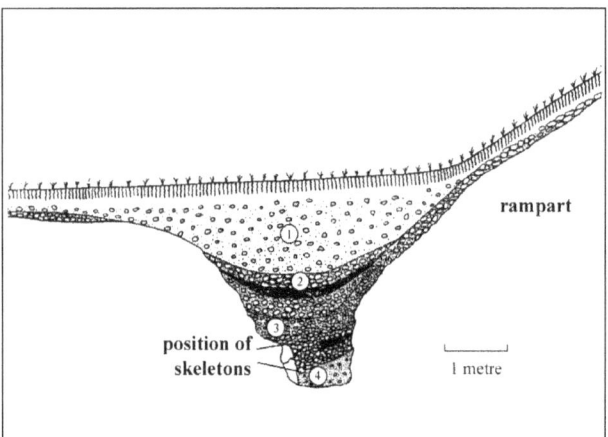

Figure 5.3 Section through defensive ditch around the Blewburton Hill Iron Age hillfort (Cutting F), showing location of the associated skeletons, adapted from Collins (1952, figure 3). The rampart is on the eastern side of the ditch. Numbers denote: dark brown earth with small rounded chalk pebbles [1]; dirty chalk rubble [2]; small rounded chalk fragments with some earth [3]; khaki 'earth' with some chalk fragments [4] [details from Collins (1952, figure 3)].

Figure 5.4 Hindleg of horse and human skull in filling of Blewburton Hill main ditch, Cutting F (1948). Copyright Reading Museum Service (Reading Borough Council). All rights reserved.

The deposit

The three skeletons were found in association at the base of the defensive ditch around the Iron Age hillfort (Figures 5.3-5.5). According to Collins' description the first traces of the skeletons were found at about 8 foot (ft) down in the ditch, at which point the ditch narrowed significantly (Figure 5.3). The following description is summarised from Collins' (1952) more lengthy published notes.

The horse was laid on its left side; the spine parallel with the southern wall of, and legs stretched across, the cutting. The head and neck of the horse rested on the outer (western) face of the ditch, with the head twisted back over the withers. The human was positioned with one leg over and the other under the horse's hindquarters, the spine parallel with that of the horse, and the body between the horse's front and hind legs. The skull had been displaced from the end of the spine and pushed down into the rib cage of the horse. The juxtaposition of the human skull with the left hind leg of the horse can be seen in Figure 5.4.

The dog skeleton was located at the base of the ditch, a further 1 ft. below the horse and human (Figure 5.5). The mandible of the human was found during the final clearing down of the outer face of the ditch, some two foot from the skull. Associated finds include an iron pin or rivet, a burnished black pot, an iron adze, and over 100 Bunter quartzite pebbles (Figure 5.6). Fragments of the pot were found with the hind legs of the horse and with the dog, indicating that the three skeletons were deposited

Figure 5.5 Dog skeleton in filling of Blewburton Hill main ditch, Cutting F (1948). Copyright Reading Museum Service (Reading Borough Council). All rights reserved.

at the same time. Also, Collins (1952, 31) suggests that a possible turf-line at about 2 ft. above the base of the ditch was in existence before the skeletons were buried. Collins' interpretation of the combined deposit was as follows;

"The displacement of the lower jaw and of the skull may have been due to the general settling of the ditch filling after the decay of the flesh, but might have been due to mutilation before burial. The man's general posture is clear, with one leg over and the other under the horse's

hind quarters and his body occupying the space between the horse's fore and hind legs. Can this be explained by saying that the man had been cast into the ditch riding the horse, with his feet tied together under its belly? If the man had then slewed round under the horse's belly one could thus account for the position of his legs over and under the hind quarters." (Collins 1952, 31).

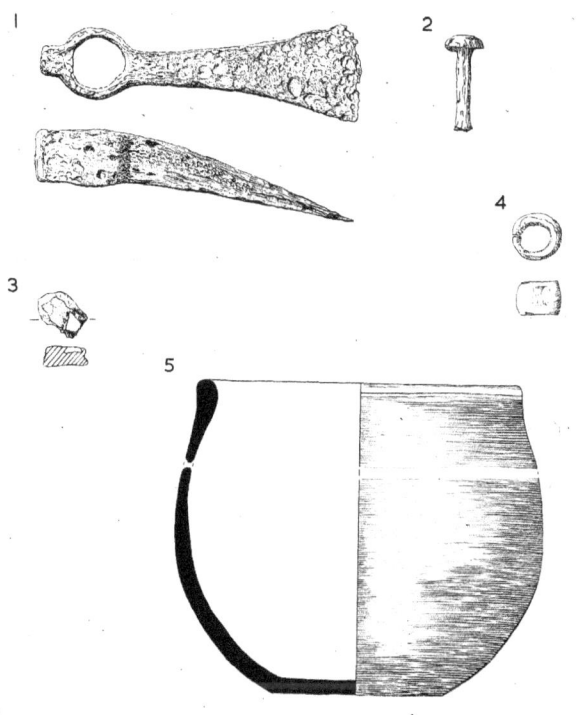

Figure 5.6 **Miscellaneous Iron Age small finds from Blewburton Hill, including objects (nos. 1, 2, 5) associated with the skeletons in the ditch: an iron adze (1), an iron pin or rivet (2), and a burnished black pot (5). Copyright Reading Museum Service (Reading Borough Council). All rights reserved.**

Reanalysis of the skeletons

The human remains

There are a minimum number of two individuals represented in the human skeletal assemblage, based on the presence of two left femora. The skeletal remains appear to represent one individual, plus one extra, robust femur.

The evidence suggests that the main individual buried in the pit was tall, elderly and probably female. The skeletal remains were quite fragmented and pale, and the bones were light and porous. No evidence of weathering or animal activity was noted and, as most of the elements of the skeleton were present, this suggests lack of exposure of the body, protection from scavenging animals and deposition soon after death.

Age and sex indicators

Degenerative changes of the auricular surface indicate that this individual was over the age of 50 years at death (Lovejoy et al 1985). Pubic symphysis (Katz and Suchey 1986) and sternal rib (Loth and Iscan 1989) age indicators are not present, as they did not survive the burial environment. The presence of ossified cartilage is in accord with the interpretation that this individual had reached a mature age at death.

The skeleton had been previously described as male (Collins 1952, 30-31), perhaps due to slight development of the supra-orbital ridges. The reanalysis, however, does not concur with this interpretation. The pubic bone is not present, but the auricular surface height, preauricular sulcus and postauricular space exhibit definite female characteristics (Buikstra and Ubelaker 1994, 16-19). The mastoids and glabella profile also exhibit female characteristics, but the supra-orbital ridge exhibits a slightly pronounced profile, perhaps more indicative of male cranial characteristics (Buikstra and Ubelaker 1994, 19-20). This can, however, also occur in elderly females. Joint surface dimensions either produced a female or intermediate classification (Chamberlain 1994, 11). Stature estimates based on maximum long bone lengths indicate a height of 165 – 169cm (5'5" - 5'6") (Trotter 1970). This would be tall for a woman of this period (Roberts and Cox 2003, 103).

Health and activity indicators

Musculoskeletal stress markers (Hawkey and Merbs 1995) suggest this individual led a physically active life. Osteoarthritis (indicated by the presence of eburnation) was present in the bones of the left wrist (Figure 5.7), foot (right distal first metatarsal) and vertebral column (11th thoracic vertebra) and degenerative disc disease was indicated by general degeneration of the surfaces of the cervical vertebrae bodies and prolific marginal osteophytes (Figure 5.8). Large carious cavities were present in the second mandibular molars. The maxilla was almost edentulous; only two very worn central incisors were present.

The horse

The horse is identified as female, on the basis of small, vestigial canines and the shape of the pelvis (Sisson and Grossman 1966, 104-112) and is complete, except for the absence of the right hind limb (femur to phalanges). No cut marks were observed on the right pelvis to indicate the removal of this limb. The animal is described as 'complete' in the original publication, with the additional comment that

"the discovery of a non-cloven hoof on the right hind leg of the creature revealed it as a horse" (Collins 1952, 30).

Figure 5.7 Blewburton Hill human: eburnation is present on the left trapezium, indicating osteoarthritis. Copyright Reading Museum Service (Reading Borough Council). All rights reserved.

Figure 5.8 Blewburton Hill human: degenerative disc disease is indicated by general degeneration of the surfaces of the cervical vertebrae bodies. Copyright Reading Museum Service (Reading Borough Council). All rights reserved.

It is possible that since excavation the missing hindlimb has been separated from the rest of the skeleton (perhaps removed for display, teaching or research purposes), but attempts to locate this limb have been unsuccessful and the absence of this limb prior to burial cannot be confirmed.

The post-cranial skeleton is fully fused, indicating an age in excess of 5 years (Silver 1969, 285). Examination of the lower incisors indicates an age at death of 6 years (Cornevin and Lesbre 1894). Estimates of size from measurements of the bones suggest a height at the withers of 1.11 to 1.18 metres, or approximately 11 to 11.2 hands [using the factors of Kiesewalter (1888) to reconstruct the stature]. This is towards the lower end of the size range recorded for Iron Age horses (Grant 1984a, 521; Maltby 1981).

Pathology and other skeletal changes

There is evidence for bitting damage to the lower second premolars in the form of a parallel-sided band of enamel exposed on the anterior edge of each tooth, indicating that the horse was harnessed with a bit, either for riding or driving. Bendrey (2007a) argues that such bands of enamel exposure on the 'front', or anterior, edge of equid lower second premolars derive from a bit coming into contact with this side of the tooth and wearing away a strip of cementum to expose the enamel beneath (more severe bitting damage can also expose areas of dentine). Another non-specific indicator of work is the fusion of the left lateral facets of the fifth and sixth lumbar vertebrae. In a study of ankylosing lesions in the spine of 245 equid skeletons, Stecher and Goss (1961) identified that the lateral joints of lumbar vertebrae transverse processes were only fused in domestic equids and not wild ones, suggesting that it is related to increased stresses on the skeleton associated with riding or traction. Abnormality in the cranium is limited to a malformed upper third incisor and slight periodontal disease around the upper cheek teeth.

A number of bony changes identified in the lower limbs are of note.

New bone deposition has bridged the interosseus border between the third metacarpal and the medial splint bone (second metacarpal) in the left fore limb (Figure 5.9); the other metapodials in this horse remain unattached. The ossification of the interosseous ligaments between the metapodials in horses, a condition known as splints, occurs as a response to the repeated movements of the bones, causing damage to the connecting ligaments and periosteum of the bones, ultimately leading to their ossification (Bertone 2002). This bony change is known to be, in part, age-related, and that in the metacarpals fusion progresses normally with ageing, although it can also occur due to trauma to a joint (Bertone 2002). Bendrey (2007b) presents a comparative study of splints in a small population of Przewalski's horses (unworked zoo animals). This study suggests the expression of splints appears to be generally, but not always, bilateral. Although the splint in the Blewburton Hill animal may have been caused by trauma to this limb, once the inflammation and proliferative periostitis were resolved and the joint stabilised, the limb would probably have been sound (Bertone 2002).

Also in the left forelimb, there is a periosteal reaction across the anterior and medial portions of the proximal diaphysis of the first phalanx - resolving medially but still active at death anteriorly (Figure 5.10). Possibly associated with this is a small patch of faint periosteal reaction on the medial border of the distal part of the third metacarpal diaphysis. This periostitis may be the result of a traumatic injury and/or bacterial ingress through a penetrating wound (Baxter and Turner 2002, 428). In a case where bacterial infection did not occur through a break in the skin, haematogenous infection might have occurred, which could suggest a case of septicaemia (bacterial infection of the blood stream) (Baker and Brothwell 1980, 64; Baxter and Turner 2002, 428).

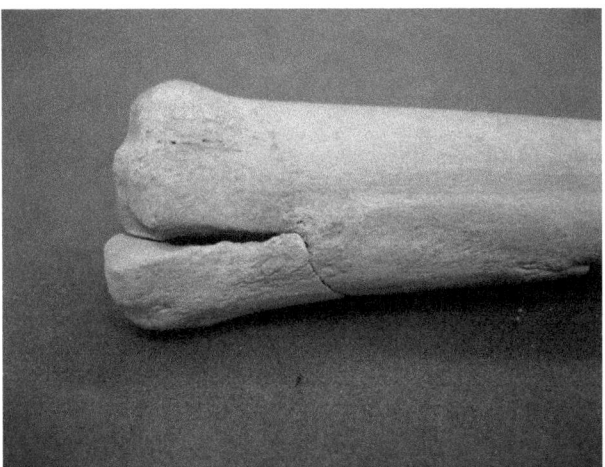

Figure 5.9 Blewburton Hill horse: new bone formation has bridged the interosseus border between the left metacarpal ii and metacarpal iii (medial view). Copyright Reading Museum Service (Reading Borough Council). All rights reserved.

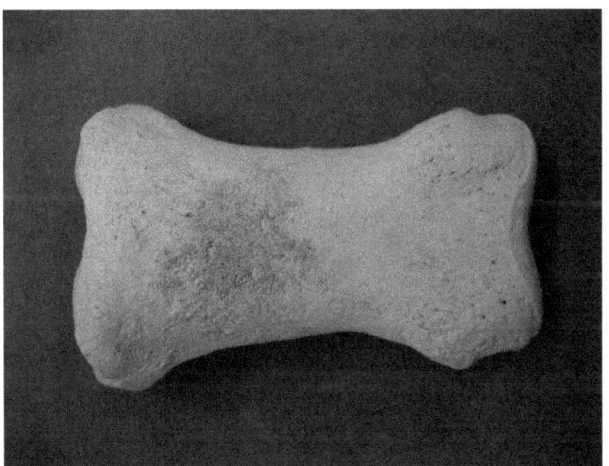

Figure 5.10 Blewburton Hill horse: anterior view of left anterior proximal phalanx with periosteal reaction. Copyright Reading Museum Service (Reading Borough Council). All rights reserved.

The dog

The dog, buried as an intact carcass, is male and skeletally mature. However, apart from early osteophyte development on the cranial face of the sacrum and on a caudal vertebra, there are no significant age-related arthropathies denoting senescence. Furthermore, although teeth are notoriously unreliable for estimating the age of dogs, this animal's dentition does not exhibit the level of wear normally associated with elderly dogs. On balance, therefore, it is likely that this dog was older than three years, but was not an elderly animal.

The dog stood approximately 49 cms at the shoulder (Harcourt 1974), which places it fairly centrally within the range of Iron Age dogs, and in stature and skeletal robusticity correlates closely with the modern labrador type. Similarly, the skull resembles the size and morphology of a modern labrador.

Pathology

The pathological lesions manifest in the skeletal remains give some insight into the life history of the dog, and its condition at time of death.

There is evidence of two significant head injuries, both of which were survived but caused a degree of distortion. There is a depressed fracture of the right maxilla, involving the whole bone superior to the infra-orbital foramen. Although this fracture is visible only at the margins, the internal area of the lesion having been lost, it is clear that full healing has taken place. In the posterior portion of the cranium there is a marked asymmetry probably caused by another, fully healed, depression fracture of the right parietal bone. The right side of the sagittal crest has subsequently become thickened, and the right parietal bone shortened, and the asymmetry extends to the occipital bone which is distorted on the right. The lack of any sign of marginal healing suggests that this injury was sustained in early life.

Oral pathology is restricted to the maxillae, where the right second premolar has been lost and the alveolus filled, and the left first premolar has been broken at jaw level. An infection surrounding the left canine has caused some resorption and proliferation of the alveolar bone.

Several traumatic lesions are visible in the axial and appendicular skeleton:

The thirteenth thoracic and first lumbar vertebrae have suffered an injury, probably a blow to the back, which has distorted the neural spines. The left radius exhibits an infection mid-shaft which is possibly a result of an infected fracture site now healed, and there is also some bony proliferation on the right ulna adjacent to this radial lesion. It is likely that the ulna has acted as a 'splint' to retain the radial fracture in reduced position.

The left forefoot is significantly affected by an infection following an unreduced fracture of the second metacarpal (Figure 5.11), the infection having spread from the first to the fourth metacarpals. The right hindfoot has also suffered a fracture of the fourth metatarsal followed by infection (Figure 5.12). The right femur exhibits some ossification of the insertion of the muscle, which adducts the thigh and rotates the limb laterally, probably due to repeated strain on this tendon.

Finally, there appears to be a proliferative and infective bony lesion at the tip of the baculum.

Figure 5.11 Blewburton Hill dog: left metacarpals II and III. Copyright Reading Museum Service (Reading Borough Council). All rights reserved.

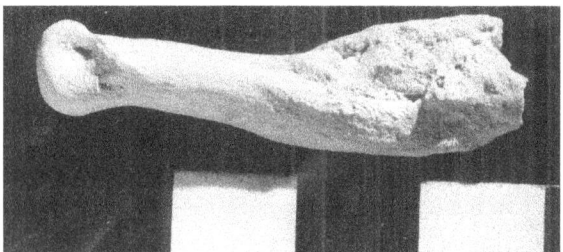

Figure 5.12 Blewburton Hill dog: right metatarsal IV. Copyright Reading Museum Service (Reading Borough Council). All rights reserved.

Discussion

Humans

There is only minimal evidence for burial rites or mortuary behaviour throughout most of the Iron Age in the archaeological record; only in the latest pre-conquest phase do human remains occur with any frequency in the burial record (Cunliffe 1991; 1995b; Haselgrove 1999; Hill 1995; Wait 1985; Whimster 1981).

Discussions of Iron Age activities concern the deposition of human remains in storage pits, ditches and postholes (Craig *et al* 2005; Cunliffe 1991; 1992; 1995a; 1995b; Cunliffe and Poole 1991; Green 2001; Hill 1995; Wait 1985; Whimster 1981). Some storage pits, following disuse, became repositories of structured deposits, including the deposition of human and animal remains, both in an articulated and disarticulated condition or as isolated body parts or skeletal elements most notably the skull, mostly occurring in southern Britain but also noted in other areas (Cunliffe 1991; Hill 1995). This practice occurred mostly during the second half of the first millennium BC, although evidence would indicate that these activities were not a common or frequent occurrence and human remains recovered from these contexts represent only a minority of the total Iron Age population (Cunliffe 1995a; Hill 1995; Whimster 1981). It is now widely accepted that these deposits do not represent casual disposal of human and animal remains in convenient receptacles, but represent meaningful, structured activities; however, the specific purposes of this behaviour still remain a matter of debate.

At Danebury hillfort, 300 individual deposits of human remains were recovered during excavations (Cunliffe 1995a, 72). Variations in the mode of deposition were noted, ranging from complete corpse inhumations at the base of the storage pits, partial corpses and disarticulated material, to isolated elements or body parts (Cunliffe 1991; 1992; 1995a; Hill 1995; Whimster 1981).

The skeletal remains relating to whole corpse inhumations often indicate they had been tightly bound, or restrained, placed in a prone position or sprawled as if thrown carelessly into the open pit, sometimes with blocks of flint placed on top of the bodies (Cunliffe 1995a, 72-79). Frequently, the overall impression was not one of respectful treatment.

Although Cunliffe considers alternative explanations for this material, including ritual killings and dismemberment, display of bodies of enemies or even insult cannibalism, he states "the 'best fit' explanation is that we are seeing in these special depositions the final resting places of ancestors whose mortal remains were being used in a rare act of propitiation" (Cunliffe 1995a, 76). However, Craig *et al*. (2005, 166) state;

"It would seem that the time is ripe for a reinterpretation of the ancestor ... Human bodies placed in unusual or liminal places – perhaps separated from others or treated in a manner different from the norm – may represent social outcasts or those who died in unusual circumstances, rather than ancestors".

These activities were considered to be more closely related to endemic regional warfare and social negotiations between the living than specific deposition related to supplication or communications with deities and commemoration of ancestors. In consideration of the range exhibited by the human osteological profiles of the pit deposits, Craig *et al*. (2005, 167) state "no single explanation is likely to account for the appearance and distribution of the entire skeletal record".

Craig *et al*. (2005, 171) also note that the demographic profile of the Danebury death assemblage is more reflective of some socially controlled selection process, rather than a natural mortality profile; the greatest number of individuals occur in the adolescent age range, a sector that is normally underrepresented in a death assemblage. Women and children are also underrepresented in the demographic profile; far fewer children are present among the complete corpse inhumations than the partial corpse depositions (Cunliffe 1995a, 72-79; Cunliffe and Poole 1991, 457-461). Cunliffe (1995a, 78) also notes that while the numbers of males remained constant through time, there were significant fluctuations in the numbers of females deposited in pits throughout the time span of use.

Hill (1995) suggests it is misleading to separate the treatment of human remains from other deposits in these Iron Age contexts and considers the human material was deposited in a structured way in association with other material. He highlights specific combinations of deposited material, the resulting pit assemblage as a whole being the focus of activities rather than purely the manipulation of human remains. He considers that human remains were deposited in a structured way according to 'rules of deposition' relating to their position in the pit and specific associations with other classes of material (1995, 54). With regard to their interpretation, Hill stresses the contextual approach "… all the elements of this depositional practice were treated in similar ways and formed part of a web of associations" (1995, 100). However, regional variations were noted in how these codes or rules of deposition were expressed. For example at Winnall Down, groups of dog bones were commonly found with human remains, while at Danebury, there was a definite correlation between complete human corpse deposition and horse or cattle articulated remains (Hill 1995, 54).

Green (2001, 44) also notes the degree of associations between human and animal remains in Iron Age pit deposits and suggests the two categories were to some extent interchangeable. She suggests that certain human pit depositions were found associated with 'appropriate' animals, for example within a pit at Danebury, the body of a neonate infant was placed with that of a newborn calf (*ibid*.). She notes that there were recurring patterns in the archaeological record for repeated 'cultic activity' represented by associations of humans, horses and dogs: "The repeated association of human, horse and dog remains in Iron Age deposits may have significance, in terms of sacrifice" (2001, 45). Green (2001, 45) provides the example of the skeletons at Blewburton Hillfort, involving the deposition of the complete corpse of an adult male, a horse and a dog, suggesting such associations may be interpreted as retainer sacrifice. This highlights the dangers of how details, especially from older excavations, are repeated and become fixed in the literature.

Hill (1995, 105-6) highlights the similarity in the way humans and animals were treated with regard to their deposition in Iron Age pits and ditches (animals also occur as whole corpses, articulated bone groups or partial corpses, or isolated parts or skeletal elements) and suggests "we should recognise that from the Neolithic onwards archaeological deposits of human remains are never *simply* to do with the treatment of the dead". During this period in these contexts, the deposition of human remains, either as complete or partial corpses or isolated body parts, was something more and different from simple funerary behaviour. Hill also notes a temporal trend in the treatment of human remains. During the Middle Iron Age in the south of England, there was a peak in the deposition of partial corpses, skulls and articulated limbs; later on, evidence for the deposition of complete adult corpses became steadily more frequent, including a trend towards separating out those categories formerly mixed and an emphasis on distinct individuals (Hill 1995, 120).

Horses

Evidence for the deliberate deposition of animals is recognised as both complete burials and disarticulated remains, identified in a range of contexts in the first millennium BC (e.g. Grant 1984a; 1984b; 1991; Hill 1995; Wait 2004; Wilson 1999). Differences in skeletal parts present, taphonomic histories and the contexts of deposition show that post-mortem use of animal skeletons was a diverse and complex practice, and that part of this significance may have been transmitted through the manipulation of the skeleton and its deposition. Traditions of deposition, commonly identified in the Iron Age can be seen to be present in the Late Bronze Age (Brück 2001; Needham 1991) and can be seen to be incorporating and manipulating horse remains, for example the horse from pit F6 at Runnymede Bridge, Surrey (Done 1991) and that beneath a human skeleton at Cliffs End Farm, Kent (Stephanie Knight, pers. comm.). During the Iron Age complete, or near complete, horses were deposited in features associated with settlements (e.g. Grant 1984a; 1984b) as well as from cemetery contexts (e.g. Legge 1991; 1995)

Fruitful comparison of horses deposited with human remains may be drawn, in particular, between Blewburton Hill and the Iron Age and Romano-British enclosure site at Viables Farm, Hampshire (Millett and Russell 1982; 1984). At this site horse and other animal skeletons are associated with the burials of women. The double female human inhumation associated with a number of complete and partial animal skeletons, came from a pit dated to between the 3rd and 1st century BC (Millett and Russell 1982; 1984). Gibson (2004) suggests a later date for the pit, between the first century BC and the first century AD. Inhumation 1 was a female aged approximately 35-40 years and inhumation 2 was a female aged approximately 25-30 years (Millett and Russell 1982, 71-2). Animal remains from pit 5 include: two complete sheep burials; the majority of one, and another partial, horse skeleton and two partial cattle skeletons (Maltby 1982, 75).

Millett and Russell (1982, 88) recognise the considerable value of the meat placed in the Viables Farm pit, and infer that considerable importance was attached to the two individuals. The location of the burial pit at Viables Farm close to the entrance of the enclosure could indicate that the burials symbolically protected the opening to the site (Gibson 2004, 26). A similar interpretation could be suggested for the Blewburton Hill burial deposit, located as it is in the defensive perimeter of the hillfort.

At Blewburton Hill, the deliberate choice of a relatively healthy horse at the age of six, in its prime as a riding or driving animal, for deposition would represent significant loss to an individual or community. This could suggest a high status for the elderly woman. For example, Aldhouse-Green (1997, 4) suggests that the inclusion of a horse team with the chariot and its owner in the 'King's Barrow' in East Yorkshire was not only a rare event (as usually the horse harness only was buried to represent the animal), but that the 'dead warrior' must have been of high status to include the sacrifice of two such valuable beasts. Alternatively, if the Blewburton Hill horse was in fact suffering from septicaemia or a serious soft tissue infection, then it may well have been deemed expendable by its owners. In this context it is notable that the Viables Farm horse skeleton exhibits pathological bone (proliferative periosteal lesions) on a number of vertebrae from the atlas to sacrum and on several ribs (Maltby 1982; see also Bendrey 2008). This suggests a systemic infection in this animal that would have been evident to the human owners, and perhaps meant that it was no longer fit for work.

A martial association between horses and men is a frequent feature of archaeological discussion (see, for example, Aldhouse-Green 1997, 3 and Creighton 2000, 14-21). The association of horse skeletons with female burials at Blewburton Hill, Oxfordshire and Viables Farm, Hampshire, however, argue against the exclusive association between male humans and horses. Whilst the importance of horse in warfare cannot, and is not, denied, these sites act as a reminder that the roles and significances of the horse spread throughout human society.

The presence of a number of other horse skeletons from the site could indicate an important place for this animal at Blewburton Hill. Harding (1967, 85) claims that at least 10 horse skeletons, of probable Iron Age date, have been found at Blewburton Hill and describes the following: two found in the entrance of the hillfort in 1948-49; two found in the entrance passage in 1967; one found buried in a pit further towards the interior in 1967. In addition to these, there is the skeleton described in this paper, and another partial skeleton was also found in Cutting F (Collins 1952, 27-8). Harding (1976, 143) has suggested that the horses were in pairs, presumably reflecting their use as two-horse teams for drawing wheeled vehicles. There are two pairs of horse skeletons from the site (illustrated in Harding 1976, plates VIII and IX) and although these may have been driving-pairs, without analysis of the bones this is speculation. However, the presence of these four skeletons in the area of the western entrance could indicate an important role for the horse at Blewburton Hill, perhaps similar to the Iron Age hillfort at Bury Hill, Hampshire, where an unusually high proportion of horse bones was identified (Hamilton 2000).

Dogs

The healed traumata to the head and spine of the Blewburton Hill dog, some of which is longstanding, indicate a history of accident, abuse, or 'occupational' injury. Although the fracture to the left radius has united, it is nevertheless the site of persistent and probably debilitating infection. At the time of death, the most significant pathological conditions for this animal were the unhealed and infected fractures of the left fore and right hind feet. Because these injuries are on opposing sides the dog could not have stood without considerable pain, and is unlikely to have been able to move any distance on its feet, if at all. As a dog, therefore, it may well have been considered 'unfit for purpose'.

The deliberate despatch of dogs, and subsequent burial in special deposits, has been argued for in a number of Iron Age sites in southern Britain, and the presence of articulated dog remains in pits has been extensively catalogued by Wait (1985) and discussed by other workers. For example, Grant has postulated the deliberate killing of dogs in the Late Iron Age special deposits at Danebury (Grant 1984a), and Armour-Chelu (1987) has presented a similar argument for the placement of dogs at significant positions at Late Iron Age Poundbury. Clutton-Brock (1982) considers that three dogs from Late Iron Age pits at Bramdean were deliberately buried and that dogs from this site held a particular significance reflected in the perforated dog metapodials, or 'dogfoot pendants', recovered during excavation.

On the matter of specific burial in the Iron Age of dogs with humans, with or without the presence of other species, there has been less discussion although some do provide an insight into the relationship between human and dog. At Broadstairs, the head of a human skeleton rested on a stone which in turn rested on the skeleton of a dog whose body lay beneath the skull and upper chest of the human. The dog's head itself had been placed over a stone (Champion, pers. comm.), and at Gussage All Saints (Harcourt 1979) articulated horse and dog bones accompanied the skeleton of an adult male.

Evidence from the Early to Mid Iron Age burial at Dibbles Farm, Christon (Everton 1988) perhaps provides a more detailed comparison with the Blewburton remains. The articulated skeletons of two dogs, at least one of which was male, overlay each other and were placed at the feet of an adult male human. The dogs were adult, but not elderly, and both were around 50cms high at the shoulder. The bones of the extremities had become mixed, but it was clear that at least one dog had suffered injuries to the right forefoot which had given rise to osteoarthritis in the right radio-humeral joint. Periostitis and fusion of two of the right metacarpals, and osteitis in another, together with eburnation in yet another metacarpal, point to chronic and persistent lameness in at least one dog.

Detailed pathological examination of dog remains has only become routine in more recent years, and so it is not yet possible to argue that dogs interred in Iron Age 'ritual' deposits were expendable animals. However, the possibility should be borne in mind that these dogs may not necessarily be significant as individuals, or have a particular association with the humans with which they

Levels of analysis: understanding the deposit

To understand such deposits as the example discussed from Blewburton Hill, analysis needs to be undertaken at different levels, including: the individuals, the combined deposit in the feature, and the position in the site and the landscape. In consideration of the overall interpretation, many factors need to be addressed with regard to the sample being evaluated, including: excavation history and completeness, post-excavation curation of finds, differential preservation and internal site topography. Although it may not be possible to identify or comprehend the intent or purpose of the noted human behaviour witnessed by this skeletal assemblage, it is possible to better define the evidence for past behaviour.

The Blewburton Hill skeletons appear to have been deliberately interred together. The presence of the smaller bones of the skeletons suggest that they were not redeposited here from elsewhere after any significant post-mortem delay, and the absence of weathering and carnivore gnawing also suggests relatively quick deposition.

That the skeletons and other finds recovered represent a single act of deposition is indicated by the fact that conjoining pieces of the same pot were found at the top and the bottom of the excavated material containing the skeletons (Collins 1952, 30-31). Disturbance of the skeletal parts may have occurred during the process of decomposition of the bodies, and settling of the fill of the feature. This could explain the movement of the human skull into the chest cavity of the horse (perhaps pushed in by soil as the pleura decomposed).

The disposition of the skeletons may reflect the process by which the human and horse entered the ditch. If an inert human body was tied astride the horse, as Collins (1952, 31) suggests, and the pair were tipped from the top of the rampart and rolled down the slope into the ditch (a total height of some 20ft), then this rolling could drag the human body to the underside of the animal. In this scenario, whether the bodies went in from the top of the rampart (c.20ft) or from the western edge of the ditch (c.8ft), the horse is likely to have rolled, whether dead or dying, forcing the human to the belly side.

An alternative explanation is that the bodies were deliberately placed in these positions, although this does seem less likely considering the evident difficulty that would be involved in such a procedure. Aldhouse-Green (1997) suggests that the horse's vigorous sexuality was an important part of its symbolism of fertility and prosperity, but the identification of both the human and horse skeletons as female would seem to annul any sexual interpretation behind the positioning of the burials. The presence of over 100 Bunter quartzite pebbles may also be part of the structured deposition. Bunter pebbles derive from Triassic sandstones, which occur in many parts of the country. They can occur elsewhere as glacial erratics in Pleistocene deposits, that is rocks and pebbles transported by glaciers and meltwater from the areas where they formed (Angela Houghton, pers. comm.). They even occur on the tops of the downs, as glacial outwash deposits formerly covered much of the area; however, most tend to be found in the valley gravels. This number in a relatively small feature is likely to represent a deliberate collection of the stones from around the area (Lesley Dunlop, pers. comm.).

Location is also an important factor of such acts of deposition (Brück 2001, 150; Hill 1995, chapter 11), and should be taken into account when interpreting finds. It must be remembered that these locations were not simply repositories for burials. Their uses and interrelationships with other features in the landscape were complex and significant. The placement of the skeletons in the defensive perimeter of the hillfort at Blewburton Hill is no doubt of significance.

Conclusions

Our understanding of the past is based upon identifying patterns in the archaeological evidence. Where hypotheses are based on a small number of archaeological finds, and especially discoveries from older excavations, without returning to source data misleading patterns can ensue. It is essential that we reanalyse key material from older excavations, and apply new methods and approaches to this analysis. Haselgrove et al. (2001, 9) in their paper identifying strategic areas central to future Iron Age research state "Vast banks of uninterrogated data lie in museum archives, which need to be continually researched and reassessed in the light of developing theory and new methodologies".

This paper underlines this approach, and demonstrates the importance of reanalysis. It is only through revisiting collections and publishing data based on up-to-date methods and approaches that it will be possible to successfully rethink former hypotheses. As well as collecting fresh data from the osteological remains, it is also important to reconsider the combined assemblage, in terms of the relationship of the constituent parts to each other and the wider site and environment. In applying this approach, this reanalysis of the Blewburton Hill skeletons has contributed new information, and suggests a more complex meaning and set of associations than previously assigned to this deposit.

Acknowledgements

Thanks are due to Jill Greenaway (Reading Museum Service) for her kind assistance and allowing access to the Blewburton Hill archive, and to Angela Houghton (Reading Museum Service) and Lesley Dunlop (Berkshire Regionally Important Geological Sites Group) for advice on Bunter quartzite pebbles.

Bibliography

Aldhouse-Green, M. (1997) The symbolic horse in pagan Celtic Europe: an archaeological perspective. In. S. Davies and N. A. Jones (eds.) *The Horse in Celtic Culture: Medieval Welsh Perspectives*, 1-22. Cardiff, University of Wales Press.

Armour-Chelu, M. (1987) The animal bone. In. S.M. Davies and D. Grieve, The Poundbury pipeline: archaeological observations and excavations'. *Dorchester Natural History and Archaeological Society Proceedings* 106, 86-87.

Baker, J. and Brothwell, D. R. (1980) *Animal Diseases in Archaeology*. London, Academic Press.

Baxter, G. M. and Turner, A. S. (2002) Diseases of bones and related structures. In, T. S. Stashak, (ed.) *Adams' Lameness in Horses*, Fifth edition, 401-457. Philadelphia, Lippincott Williams & Williams.

Bendrey, R. (2007a) New methods for the identification of evidence for bitting on horse remains from archaeological sites. *Journal of Archaeological Science* 34, 1036-1050.

Bendrey, R. (2007b) Ossification of the interosseous ligaments between the metapodials in horses: a new recording methodology and preliminary study. *International Journal of Osteoarchaeology* 17, 207-213.

Bendrey, R. (2008) A possible case of tuberculosis or brucellosis in an Iron Age horse skeleton from Viables Farm, Basingstoke, England'. In, Z. Miklikova and R. Thomas, (eds.) *Current Research in Animal Palaeopathology. Proceedings of the Second ICAZ Animal Palaeopathology Working Group Conference*, 19-26. Oxford, British Archaeological Report International Series 1844.

Bertone, A. L. (2002) The metacarpus and metatarsus. In. T. S. Stashak, (ed.) *Adams' Lameness in Horses*, Fifth edition, 800-830. Philadelphia, Lippincott Williams and Williams.

Brück, J. (2001) Body metaphors and technologies of transformation in the English middle and late Bronze Age'. In. J. Brück, (ed.) *Bronze Age Landscapes: Tradition and Transformation*, 149-160. Oxford, Oxbow.

Buikstra, J. E. and Ubelaker, D. H., (1994) *Standards for Data Collection from Human Skeletal Remains. Proceedings of a seminar at The Field Museum of Natural History*. Fayetteville, Arkansas, Arkansas Archaeological Survey Research Series 44.

Chamberlain, A. T. (1994) *Human Remains*. London, British Museum Press.

Clutton-Brock, J. (1982) The animal bone. In, B. T. Perry, Excavations at Bramdean, Hampshire, 1973 to 1977. *Proceedings of the Hampshire Field Club and Archaeological Society* 38, Fiche 44-54.

Collins, A. E. P. (1947) Excavations on Blewburton Hill, 1947. *Berkshire Archaeological Journal* 50, 4-29.

Collins, A. E. P. (1952) Excavations on Blewburton Hill, 1948 and 1949. *Berkshire Archaeological Journal* 53, 21-64.

Collins, A. E. P. and Collins, F. J. (1959) Excavations on Blewburton Hill, 1953. *Berkshire Archaeological Journal* 57, 52-73.

Cornevin, C. and Lesbre, X. (1894) *Traité de l'Age des Animaux Domestiques: d'après les Dents et les Productions Épidermiques*. Paris, Librairie J-B Baillière et Fils.

Craig, C. R., Knüsel, C. J. and Carr, G. C. (2005) Fragmentation, mutilation and dismemberment: an interpretation of human remains on Iron Age sites. In. M. Parker Pearson, and I. J. N. Thorpe (eds.) *Warfare, Violence and Slavery in Prehistory. Proceedings of a Prehistoric Society Conference at Sheffield University*, 165-180. Oxford, British Archaeology Report International Series 1374.

Creighton, J. (2000) *Coins and Power in Late Iron Age Britain*. Cambridge, Cambridge University Press.

Cunliffe, B. (1991) *Iron Age Communities in Britain*, Third edition. London, Routledge.

Cunliffe, B. (1992) Pits, preconceptions, and propitiation in the British Iron Age. *Oxford Journal of Archaeology* 11, 69-83.

Cunliffe, B. (1995a) *Danebury: an Iron Age Hillfort in Hampshire. Volume 6: a Hillfort Community in Perspective*. London, Council for British Archaeology Research Report 102.

Cunliffe, B. (1995b) *Iron Age Britain*. London, Batsford/English Heritage.

Cunliffe, B. and Poole, C. (1991) *Danebury: an Iron Age Hillfort in Hampshire. Volume 5. The Excavations, 1979-88: the Finds*. London, Council for British Archaeology Research Report 73.

Done, G. (1991) The animal bone. In. S. Needham (ed.) *Excavation and Salvage at Runnymede Bridge, 1978: the Late Bronze Age Waterfront Site*, 327-342. London, British Museum Press.

Everton, R. E. (1988) The dog skeletons from pit XLIV. In, E. Morris (ed.) The Iron Age occupation at Dibbles Farm, Christon. *Somerset Archaeology and Natural History* 132, 54-55.

Gibson, C. (2004) The Iron Age and Roman site of Viables Two (Jays Close), Basingstoke. *Proceedings of the Hampshire Field Club and Archaeological Society* 59, 1-30.

Grant, A. (1984a) Animal husbandry. In. B. Cunliffe (ed.) *Danebury: an Iron Age Hillfort in Hampshire. Volume 2. The Excavations 1969-1978: the Finds*, 496-548. London, Council for British Archaeology Research Report 52.

Grant, A. (1984b) Survival or sacrifice? A critical appraisal of animal bones in Britain in the Iron Age. In. C. Grigson and J. Clutton-Brock (eds.) *Animals and Archaeology 4: Husbandry in Europe*, 221-227. Oxford, British Archaeological Report International Series 227.

Grant, A. (1991) Economic or symbolic? Animals and ritual behaviour. In. P. Garwood, D. Jennings, R. Skeates and J. Toms (eds.) *Sacred and Profane: Proceedings of a Conference on Archaeology, Ritual and Religion, Oxford, 1989*, 109-114. Oxford, Oxford University Committee for Archaeology.

Green, M. A. (2001) *Dying for the Gods: Human Sacrifice in Iron Age and Roman Europe*. Stroud, Tempus.

Hamilton, J. (2000) Animal bones. In. B. Cunliffe and C. Poole, (eds.) *The Danebury Environs Programme. The Prehistory of a Wessex Landscape. Volume 2, Part 2. Bury Hill, Upper Clatford, Hants, 1990*, 67-73. Oxford, English Heritage and Oxford University Committee for Archaeology Monograph 49.

Harcourt, R. A. (1974) The dog in prehistoric and early historic Britain. *Journal of Archaeological Science* 1, 151-175.

Harcourt, R. A. (1979) The animal bones. In. G. Wainwright (ed.) *Gussage All Saints: an Iron Age Settlement in Dorset*, 150-160. London, H.M.S.O.

Harding, D. W. (1967) Blewburton. *Current Archaeology* 4, 83-87.

Harding, D. W. (1976) Blewburton Hill, Berkshire: re-excavation and reappraisal. In. D. W. Harding (ed.) *Hillforts: Later Prehistoric Earthworks in Britain and Ireland*, 133-146. London, Academic Press.

Haselgrove, C. (1999) The Iron Age. In. J. R. Hunter and I. B. M. Ralston (eds.) *The Archaeology of Britain: an Introduction from the Upper Palaeolithic to the Industrial Revolution*, 113-134. London, Routledge.

Haselgrove, C., Armit, I., Champion, T., Creighton, J., Gwilt, A., Hill, J. D., Hunter, F. and Woodward, A. (2001) *Understanding the British Iron Age: an Agenda for Action*. Salisbury, Trust for Wessex Archaeology.

Hawkey, D. E. and Merbs, C. F. (1995) Activity-induced musculoskeletal stress markers (MSM) and subsistence strategy changes among ancient Hudson Bay Eskimos. *International Journal of Osteoarchaeology* 5, 324-338.

Hill, J. D. (1995) *Ritual and Rubbish in the Iron Age of Wessex*. Oxford, British Archaeological Report British Series 242.

Katz, D. and Suchey, J. M. (1986) Age determination of the male os pubis. *American Journal of Physical Anthropology* 69, 427-436.

Kieswalter, L. (1888) *Skelettmessungen an Pferden als Beitrag zur Theoretischen Grundlage der Beurteilungslehre des Pferdes*. Dissertation, Leipzig.

Legge, A. J. (1991) The animal bones. In, I. M. Stead (ed.) *Iron Age Cemeteries in East Yorkshire*, 140-147. London, English Heritage Archaeological Report 22.

Legge, A. J. (1995) A horse burial and other grave offerings. In, K. Parfitt (ed.) *Iron Age Burials from Mill Hill, Deal*, 146-152. London, British Museum Press.

Loth, S. R. and Iscan, M. Y. (1989) Morphological assessment of age in the adult: the thoracic region. In, M. Y. Iscan (ed.) *Age Markers in the Human Skeleton*, 105-136. Springfield, Illinois, Charles C Thomas.

Lovejoy, C. O., Meindl, R. S., Pryzbeck, T. R. and Mensforth, R. P. (1985) Chronological metamorphosis of the auricular surface of the ilium: a new method for the determination of age at death. *American Journal Physical Anthropology*, 68, 15-28

Maltby, M. (1981) Iron Age, Romano-British and Anglo-Saxon animal husbandry – a review of the faunal evidence. In. M. Jones and G. W. Dimbleby (eds.) *The Environment of Man: the Iron Age to the Anglo-Saxon Period*, 155-203. Oxford, British Archaeological Report British Series 87.

Maltby, M. (1982) The animal bones. In. M. Millett and D. Russell, An Iron Age burial from Viables Farm, Basingstoke. *Archaeological Journal*, 139, 75-81.

Millett, M. and Russell, D. (1982) An Iron Age burial from Viables Farm, Basingstoke. *Archaeological Journal*, 139, 69-90.

Millett, M. and Russell, D. (1984) An Iron Age and Romano-British site at Viables Farm, Basingstoke. *Proceedings of the Hampshire Field Club and Archaeological Society*, 40, 49-60.

Needham, S. (1991) *Excavation and Salvage at Runnymede Bridge, 1978: the Late Bronze Age Waterfront Site*. London, British Museum Press.

Roberts, C. A. and Cox, M. (2003) *Health and Disease in Britain from Prehistory to the Present Day*. Stroud, Sutton.

Silver, I. (1969) The ageing of domestic animals. In, D. Brothwell and E. S. Higgs (eds.) *Science and Archaeology, Second edition*, 250-268. London, Thames and Hudson.

Sisson, S. and Grossman, J. D. (1966) *The Anatomy of Domestic Animals*, Fourth edition. London, W.B. Saunders Company.

Stecher, R. M. and Goss, L. J. (1961) Ankylosing lesions of the spine. *Journal of the American Veterinary Medical Association*, 138, 248-255.

Trotter, M. (1970) Estimation of stature from intact long bones. In, T. D. Stewart (ed.) *Personal Identification in Mass Disasters*, 71-83. Washington, National Museum of Natural History, Smithsonian Institution.

Wait, G. A. (1985) *Ritual and Religion in Iron Age Britain*. Oxford, British Archaeological Report British Series 149.

Wait, G. A. (2004) Human and animal burials. In. G. Lambrick and T. Allen (ed.) *Gravelly Guy, Stanton Harcourt: the Development of a Prehistoric and Romano-British Community*, 221-257. Oxford, Oxford University School of Archaeology, Thames Valley Landscapes Monograph No. 21.

Whimster, R. (1981) *Burial Practices in Iron Age Britain. A Discussion and Gazetteer of the Evidence c700 BC – AD 43*. Oxford, British Archaeological Report British Series 90.

Wilson, B. (1999) Displayed or concealed? Cross cultural evidence for symbolic and ritual activity depositing Iron Age animal bones. *Oxford Journal of Archaeology*, 18, 297-305.

Authors' Affiliations

Robin Bendrey,
Department of Archaeology,
University of Winchester,
West Hill,
Winchester,
Hampshire,
SO22 4NR,
UK.

Stephany Leach,
Archaeology Department,
University of Reading,
Whiteknights,
Reading,
Berkshire,
RG6 6AH,
UK.

Kate Clark,
Moonrakers,
Lockerley Green,
Lockerley,
Nr Romsey,
Hampshire,
SO51 0JN,
UK.

6. Structured deposition or casual disposal of human remains? A case study of four Iron Age sites from southern England.

Anna Russell

Abstract

Most human remains from the Iron Age consist of isolated, disarticulated bones discovered in pits and ditches. These deposits are often found in conjunction with faunal deposits, but research into the presence of disarticulated faunal remains, and the possible concurrence of structured deposition, has been somewhat limited. By comparing the composition of faunal remains in features with and without human remains present, it was hoped it would be possible to establish whether there are any trends that may suggest structured deposition where human bones are present, perhaps as part of funerary practices. The faunal remains from four Iron Age sites in Wessex were assessed in terms of species proportions, body part representation and taphonomy, also features with human bones were compared to those without. This study shows that there are indeed signs of a more structured deposition in features with human bone on the sites studied. The difficulties of studies of this nature are discussed and recommendations for further work are put forward.

Introduction

Bone remains are often amongst the most plentiful of all the classes of archaeological evidence recovered during an excavation (Grant 1991). In general, animal bones have been studied simply to assess the contents of the meat diet, and to determine trends in the basic subsistence patterns of the settlement under consideration (Maltby 1985). Human remains, on the other hand, are usually analysed to gain information about past populations, mortality profiles and palaeopathology. It is with this information that we try to gain an insight into the economy, society and culture of past populations. Very rarely are animal and human bones considered together. Faunal analyses are habitually published in excavation reports as separate entities, often with apparently little connection to other aspects of the excavation, and they are hardly ever incorporated into general discussions about the settlements and societies involved (Maltby 1985). In addition, archaeological reports are often not conducive to combining analyses of different classes of finds together and it is not easy to cross-reference finds of human bone together with animal bone.

The aim of this research, undertaken as a Masters dissertation, was to try to use the composition of faunal remains as a way to analyse funerary practices in a period of time when complete human burials are so rare in Britain.

Previous Studies

Human remains have always been recognised during the excavation of Iron Age sites in southern England, but until recently, disarticulated remains were considered to be deposited as rubbish, their apparent casual disposal and domestic context drawing little attention (Hill 1995, 14). Despite the recognition of a range of different types of deposits of human remains, emphasis is often placed on complete bodies and their common occurrence in pits (*ibid*).

Although some archaeological reports allude to associations between human and animal bone and the structuring of faunal deposits (for example see Grant 1984a; Hamilton 2000), these reports seldom do more than skim the surface of this phenomenon. Hill's work, 'Ritual and Rubbish in the Iron Age of Wessex' (Hill 1995), was one of the first to take a more in-depth look at the presence of disarticulated human remains on Iron Age sites, and the associated faunal remains. He concluded that there were spatial patterns and thus structured deposition evident in features of later prehistoric sites. There are, however, many gaps in our understanding of structured deposition, in particular the possible links between disarticulated human remains, and the deposits in which they are found. Obviously there is a need to look more closely at the disarticulated human remains on Iron Age sites, particularly in conjunction with the faunal remains. It is hoped that this study will shed some light on this subject and provide a foundation on which to built future studies into an area that has so far been overlooked by zooarchaeologists and human osteologists alike.

Structured Deposition

When considering the burial rituals of the Iron Age, the evidence available for study is highly variable in quantity and quality. One of the only ways we can assess this aspect of the Iron Age is by calling upon the direct archaeological data available, in the form of structures and deposits (Cunliffe 2005, 543). It has been shown that only a tiny fraction of all material discarded on an Iron Age site enters archaeologically recoverable contexts and this is not a random sample (Hill 1995, 130). Certain types of finds were commonly deposited together, in a certain order and in certain places, while others were in general, excluded. What is important is that this patterning is not entirely a result of natural processes, rather it is produced by the way people deposited material in pits, ditches, post holes etc. These deposits can be considered 'structured'. These structured deposits are often interpreted as being ritual in nature, but 'structured deposition' and 'ritual' are not one and the same. The archaeological identification of ritual is a contentious issue, which is not easily tackled in a domestic context. Compounding this problem is the lack of rigorous definitions as to what a special or ritual deposit is (Hill 1995, 16).

Religious rites and ceremonies do, however, usually follow strict rules and as such, ritual offerings can be thought of as deposits produced by standardised, repetitive and stereotyped actions. If such structured patterns are traceable in bone assemblages, it may be possible to use this material to interpret the nature of activities and, more importantly, consider the intention behind these activities (Galik 2002).

The possibility that certain accumulations of bones may be the result of some kind of ritual deposition must be considered (Maltby 1996), but more secular processes may also produce a 'structured' deposit. In many instances the Associated Bone Groups (ABGs) (see Morris, Chapter 3), assumed to be a result of ritual deposition may in fact be interpreted as the carcasses or parts of animals not required for consumption for some reason, or 'non-typical' butchery waste (*ibid*). These deposits are no less structured but are not ritual in nature.

Daily carcass processing and refuse maintenance strategies could produce the archaeological patterns seen in zooarchaeological deposits; just because a deposit is 'special', in that it is distinct from other assemblages, does not make it ritual, but instead, a product of differently structured daily refuse maintenance strategies or taphonomic accidents (Wilson 1992). Different parts of any carcass may be valued for a variety of uses and it is logical to assume that activities, such as those involved in butchery, should produce distinct patterns in the faunal record (Maltby 1985). It is also important to consider that deposits often thought not to be 'special', such as deposits of butchery waste, may have been part of a ritual activity such as feasting (Galik 2002).

Three major problems hinder the interpretation of faunal assemblages: insufficient knowledge of the expected nature of the assemblages created by postulated activities, admixing of bones from different activities, and biases created by other sources of sample variation. Several authors have pointed out that it can be very misleading to rely on purely functional explanations for animal bone distributions. Animals are important in the belief systems of many societies and the possibility that the symbolic roles of animals were reflected in the treatment of their carcasses should not be ignored (Maltby 1985).

Archaeological patterns are as much produced by differential post-depositional preservation, and the varying processes by which assemblages enter different types of features, as they are related to the activities or refuse maintenance strategies that created that material (Hill 1995, 17). ABGs and other so called 'special' deposits may only be special because of their chance incorporation into deep sub-soil features where they could escape subsequent attrition, erosion, gnawing and scattering that destroyed the vast majority of Iron Age rubbish (Wilson 1992).

An important question to ask is why does votive deposition matter? It matters because it is an integral part of a complex relationship between people and objects, which can be both socially and economically significant (Osborne 2004). There is always the possibility that some bones were deliberately deposited with ceremonial or ritual significance, and the existence of such 'special' deposits has been recorded by zooarchaeologists such as Grant in her interpretation of Danebury (Grant 1984a; 1984b). The presence of 'special' deposits such as ABGs, particularly when their presence coincides with human bones, is often interpreted as having special significance (e.g. Bullock and Allen 1997). What must be taken into consideration is what archaeologists deem to be special deposits in the present, may not have been special in the past (Hill 1995, 17). People in the past were different in many ways and we cannot assume what we deem to be special today, human remains for example, had the same significance for our ancestors. We must recognise that human remains could have been treated in much the same way as refuse.

Iron Age Funerary Processes

The British Iron Age is in many areas characterised by an invisible method of disposal of the dead (Whimster, 1977), a trend that is also seen in parts of mainland Europe such as the Netherlands. This not only presents a problem for archaeologists trying to determine any formal burial practices, but also requires us to consider the radically different ways the human body was perceived and treated after death (Carr and Knüsel 1997).

Most human remains from Iron Age Wessex consist of isolated bones or disarticulated joints discovered in pits and ditches, hillfort ramparts and enclosure boundaries (*ibid*). Although efforts have been made to explain the absence of more complete human remains, in terms of hypothetical practices that would leave no archaeologically recognisable traces, there have been few attempts to consider in detail the scattered human remains found on many Iron Ages sites.

Archaeologists cannot excavate funerals, only the deposits resulting from such practices. For the largest part of prehistoric populations, we have no physical remains or traces of funerals of the dead at all. In many cultures the funerary practices actively contribute to the removal of any traces of the dead. Disposal in, or on, rivers; cremation and scattering the ashes; or excarnation are all possibilities (Cunliffe 2000). Funerary practices such as excarnation, the exposure of bodies in trees, on platforms, or on the ground surface, may lead to the complete destruction of any remaining bones.

The presence of disarticulated remains could be explained by the practice of secondary burial, which is described by Metcalf and Huntington (1991, 97) as:

'the regular and socially sanctioned removed of relics of some or all deceased persons from a place of temporary storage to a permanent resting place.'

The first phase of secondary burial is usually excarnation, leaving the body somewhere while the flesh decays (Carr and Knüsel 1997). Frequently the practice of excarnation, which until recently was quite widespread in the world, was accompanied by a belief that a liminal period existed between the physical death and the time when the spirit finally left the body (Cunliffe 2000).

Secondary burial seems a likely explanation for the presence of disarticulated human remains found on most Iron Age settlement sites. Isolated articulated limbs could be derived from recently deceased individuals where some soft tissue still remains to hold the limbs together. Alternatively the body could have been processed in some way i.e. dismembered and defleshed before decay (Carr and Knüsel 1997).

Excarnation and secondary burial may have involved bringing only a token representative of the body back on site, which would explain the small proportion of human remains recovered compared to the number of people who must have died during that period (*ibid*). The presence of isolated human bones could be explained in terms of ancestors' bones being brought back to the settlement from the excarnation platforms, perhaps as part of the final act that completed a liminal phase of disposal (Cunliffe 1992).

Archaeological evidence for excarnation comes from the analysis of the condition of the bones, i.e. they may be expected to show a certain degree of weathering (Carr and Knüsel 1997). Exposed bodies would also be extremely vulnerable to attack by animal scavengers; dogs, foxes, rats and mice are able to dismember a body, spreading parts of it over a wide area, especially if decomposition is well under way (Smith 2006). This would certainly explain why some human remains on Iron Age sites tend to have animal gnawing marks present. The composition of the skeletal assemblage can also provide some evidence. Very small bones are vulnerable to consumption and loss, which may explain the general loss of such elements from the archaeological record. It is important however to bear in mind that preservation potential is primarily a function of a bone's size, shape, density and other physical characteristics.

The human remains found on settlements in southern England often show clear patterns of deposition, both spatially and temporally, and between hillforts and smaller settlements. It has been shown that certain parts of the body and certain deposits were favoured at certain places and times; for example, parts of bodies are found regularly in enclosure ditches on earlier Iron Age sites, with the frequency declining through the Iron Age. During the Middle Iron Age we see a predilection to placing the skulls of adult males and long bones, often from the right side, within hillforts. Interestingly, there is a similarity between the patterns of deposition of human remains and so-called 'associated bone groups' or 'ABGs' of animal deposits (Fitzpatrick 1997).

Methods

The Iron Age sites of Battlesbury Bowl (Hambleton and Maltby unpublished; McKinley unpublished), Suddern Farm (Cunliffe and Poole 2000a), Houghton Down (Cunliffe and Poole 2000b) and Nettlebank Copse (Cunliffe and Poole 2000c) were selected from the Wessex area for inclusion in this study. The selection process mostly involved picking sites from which the relevant detailed information was available which included: general information about the site; information on the excavation techniques; complete access to the faunal remains data including: NISP (number of identified specimens per taxon), body part representation, information down to feature and where possible, context level, information on the taphonomy of the assemblages including information on the presence of weathering, erosion, butchery and gnawing and information on the presence of any possible ABGs or 'special' deposits. Also required was complete access to the human remains data, including information on both complete burials and disarticulated, scattered material and information on the body parts represented, information on the taphonomy of the deposits, including information on the presence of weathering, erosion, butchery and gnawing and, most importantly, the ability to correlate the data concerning human and faunal remains.

All features containing human bones were selected and at least the same number of features, which did not contain human bone were also recorded. Where possible the selection of these features took into consideration the site phase and the location of the feature. Taking these factors into consideration hopefully allowed for the selection of control features of similar phasing and positioning as features containing human bone. Apart from this, the selection of these pits was as random as possible.

For each feature the following information was recorded

- Date/phase
- Number of human deposits, type of deposit
- Total NISP of faunal deposits
- Species NISP
- Information on body area for main domesticates
- Presence of ABGs noted and recorded
- Taphonomic information and butchery evidence recorded

These data were entered into an especially created database. From these data the composition of the animal bone assemblage by site, feature type and phase could be determined.

The data recorded from these sites were used to answer two main questions:

1. Are there any trends which may suggest structured deposition in features with human bone present?
2. Could differences in animal bone deposition be the result of structured deposition sometimes associated with funerary practice?

Results

Comparison of Features Containing Human Bone with those in which Human Bone is absent and those with ABGs present.

The proportions of the main species recorded for each site were calculated per feature, per phase, per feature category (i.e. with human bone present, without human bone present and with ABGs present) and finally grouped into:

- 'Human Features' – features with human bone present (without animal ABGs).
- 'Non-Human Features' – features with no human bone nor ABGs present
- 'ABG Features' – features with associated animal bone groups present but no human bone

All species proportions were calculated using NISP values excluding ABGs. It was felt important to exclude ABGs as these can seriously affect NISP counts and therefore species proportions.

Estimations of species abundance are heavily dependent upon what parts of the settlement are excavated (Maltby 1996). The features excavated are only a small sample of the features present on the sites, and the features analysed in this study are a small sample of the excavated features.

Battlesbury Bowl

Battlesbury Bowl is an Iron Age site situated in Warminster in the vicinity of the Salisbury Plain and Wylye Valley. Excavations at Battlesbury Bowl comprised a c. 418m long strip located immediately to the north of the Iron Age hillfort of Battlesbury Camp (Ellis *et al* 2008). An extensive spread of Late Bronze Age/Early Iron Age activity was identified with the majority of features dated to the 8th-7th centuries BC with a small number of features of 10th-9th and 6th-4th century BC date also recorded (*ibid*).

Figure 6.1 shows there are clear differences between features with human bone present and those where human bone was absent. In features with human bone there are higher proportions of cattle and pig, and lower proportions of sheep/goat. These differences are statistically significant when chi square tests are applied (Appendix 1.1). Features with human bone present are also unlike features with ABGs present, once again they contain relatively more cattle and pig and fewer sheep/goat.

This is also a statistically significant difference (Appendix 1.2). (ABG features more closely resemble the control features without human bone).

Despite the similarities between ABG features and the features without human bone, they are significantly different statistically (Appendix 1.3). Although chi squared tests do not measure actual differences, the subtotals indicate that it is the differences in the observed and expected frequencies of horse and dog that contribute most to the variation between these categories of feature. Horse remains are commonly found as ABGs in the archaeological record, often in association with dog remains (Grant 1991). An example of this type of deposit can be found at Danebury where a dog and horse were buried together in a single pit (Grant 1984a, 534). This trend could explain the higher than expected proportions of horse in the ABG features on this site, even though these deposits themselves were not identified in the site report as ABGs.

There is also a higher than expected proportion of corvids in the ABG features; the proportion of corvids in these features is far higher than that in the features with human bone present and the features without human bone. Raven, or other corvid, ABGs are relatively common on Iron Age Sites; over a dozen ABGs were discovered at Danebury (Grant 1984b). There were indeed raven ABGs identified in the features analysed from Battlesbury (excluded from NISP counts) as well as a number of disarticulated corvid remains not identified as ABGs, which may have become disarticulated through post-depositional movement. Ravens and other corvids are closely associated with Celtic religious beliefs and deities; this has often led to these remains being classed as ritual deposits (Cunliffe 1992). If this is indeed the case then it is interesting that these types of deposits are not seen in association with the human remains on this site. On the other hand, ravens and other corvids are known to frequent rubbish dumps and may pick at carcasses (Coy 1984), in which case the lack of corvid remains in features with human bone may suggest that these scavengers did not have access to these features.

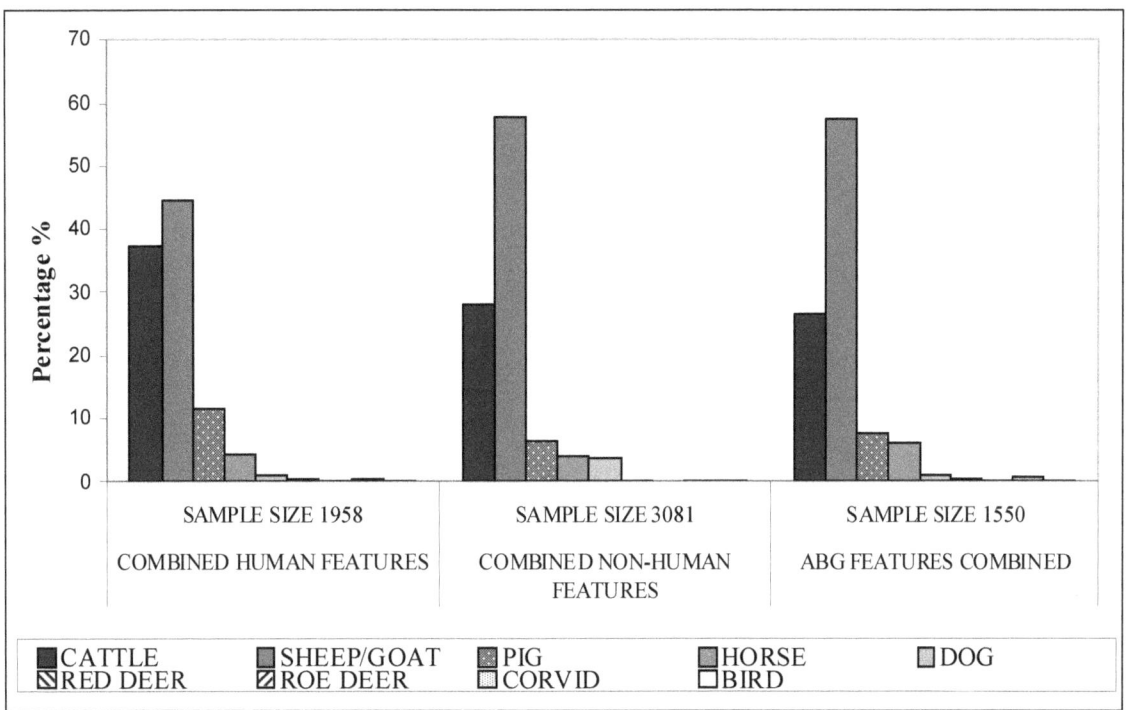

Figure 6.1 Proportions of species in features with human remains, without human remains and with ABGs (ABGs excluded from NISP) at Battlesbury Bowl.

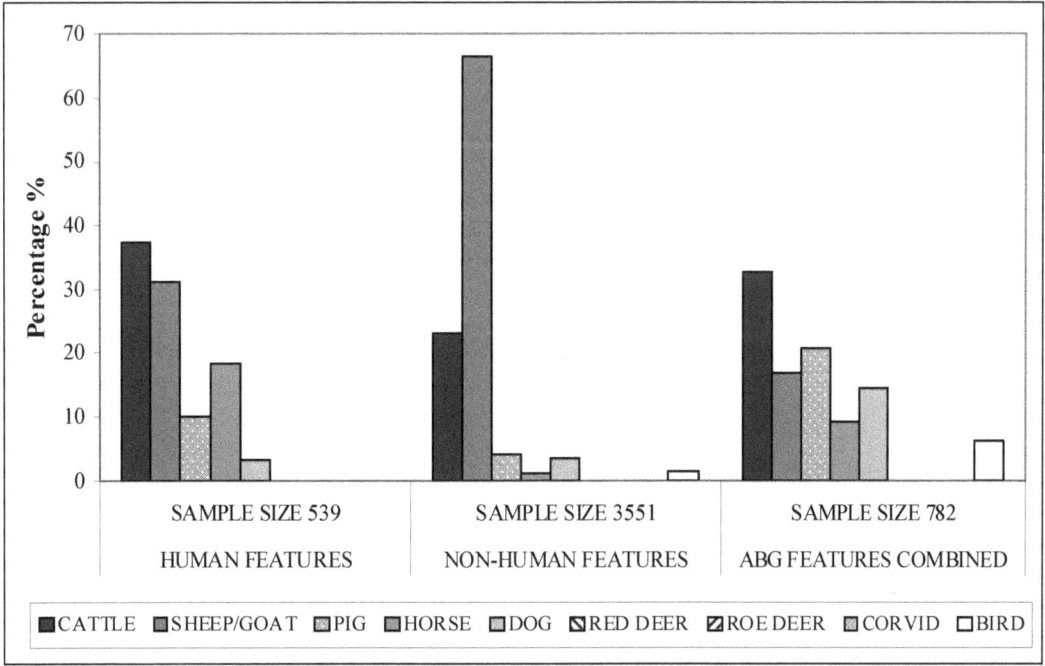

Figure 6.2 Proportions of species in features with human remains, without human remains and with ABGs (ABGs excluded from NISP) at Suddern Farm.

Suddern Farm

The site of Suddern Farm, Hampshire (Cunliffe and Poole 2000a) consists of a ditched enclosure with evidence of occupation from the Early Iron Age to the Romano-British period. Evidence for settlement comes from the presence of a number of post-hole and pits. The settlement was enclosed throughout the Iron Age with a number of ditches being constructed and re-cut throughout this period. The excavation revealed 78 pit structures on the site. Human remains were found in seven features (Poole 2000a) (the early and middle Iron Age cemetery found on the site was not included in this study). These consisted of two cases of partial skeletons

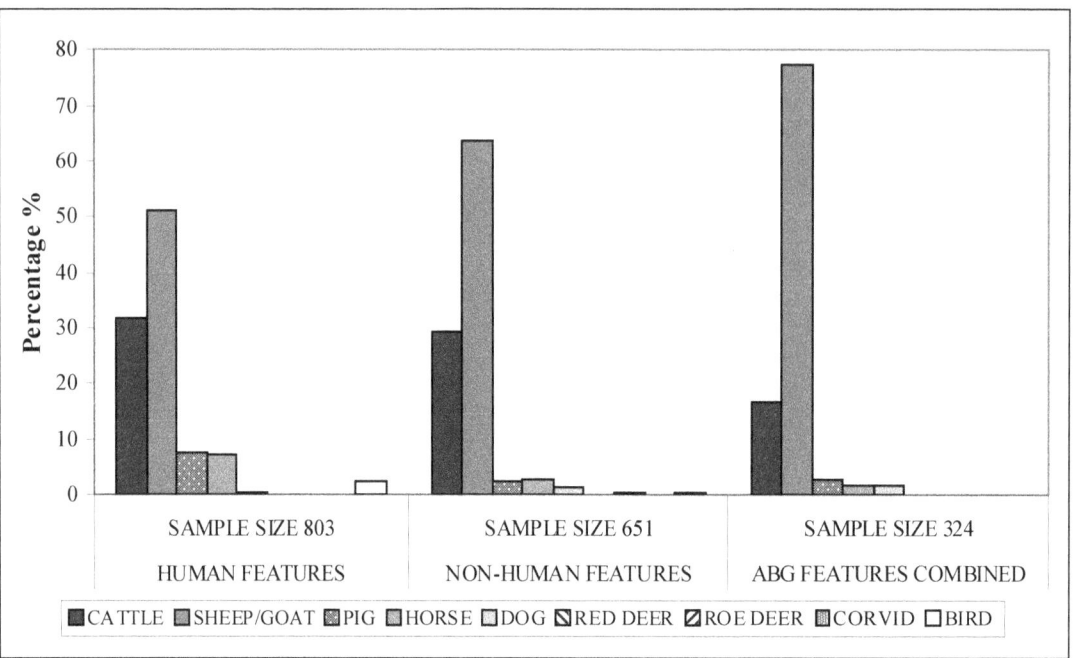

Figure 6.3 Proportions of species in features with human remains, without human remains and with ABGs (ABGs excluded from NISP) at Houghton Down.

and five cases of isolated bones. Twelve ABGs were present in six pits.

At Suddern Farm, the differences in the proportions of species seen in features with human bone, without human bone, and with ABGs, are substantial and highly significant statistically (Figure 6.2 and Appendix 1.4-1.6). On this site there are significantly more disarticulated cattle, pig and horse elements in features with human bone compared with features without human bone. A chi square test of these results showed a highly significant difference between the species proportions in these categories of feature (Appendix 1.4). The features with human bone are more similar in species proportions to features with ABGs present, but these two categories of feature are still significantly different (Appendix 1.5). In this case differences in the observed and expected frequencies of pig, horse, dog and bird contributed most of the variation. The non-human features have a very high percentage of sheep/goat unlike Battlesbury Bowl, the features with human bones included higher than expected numbers of horse bones. Iron Age assemblages from southern England are comprised mainly of sheep and cattle with a low incidence of pig (Hambleton 1999). As such, the high proportion of pig seen in human and ABG features is significant.

This site showed the most statistically significant differences between features with human bone and those without. This is particularly interesting as this site produced an unusually rich array of 'special deposits' of both bones and artefacts (Poole 2000a).

Houghton Down.

The site of Houghton Down, Hampshire (Cunliffe and Poole 2000b) like Suddern Farm consists of an enclosed settlement with evidence of occupation from the Early Iron Age. There is a break in occupation in the beginning of the third century which appears to last two or three centuries. Evidence of occupation comes from a number of roundhouse structures, post-holes and pits. Twenty-eight pits were excavated, of which three contained disarticulated human bone fragments (Poole 2000b). In total, 20 ABGs were present in six of the pits.

Looking at the comparison of species proportions in the different categories of feature on this site (Figure 6.3), it can be seen that the differences between the features with human bone present and features without human bone are nowhere near as marked as on the sites of Suddern Farm (Figure 6.2) and Battlesbury Bowl (Figure 6.1). There are however still differences; the features with human bone have higher proportions of pig, horse and bird and lower proportions of sheep/goat. These differences are statistically significant (Appendix 1.7-1.9). In contrast with the other samples, the features with ABGs had the highest proportion of sheep/goat and the lowest of cattle.

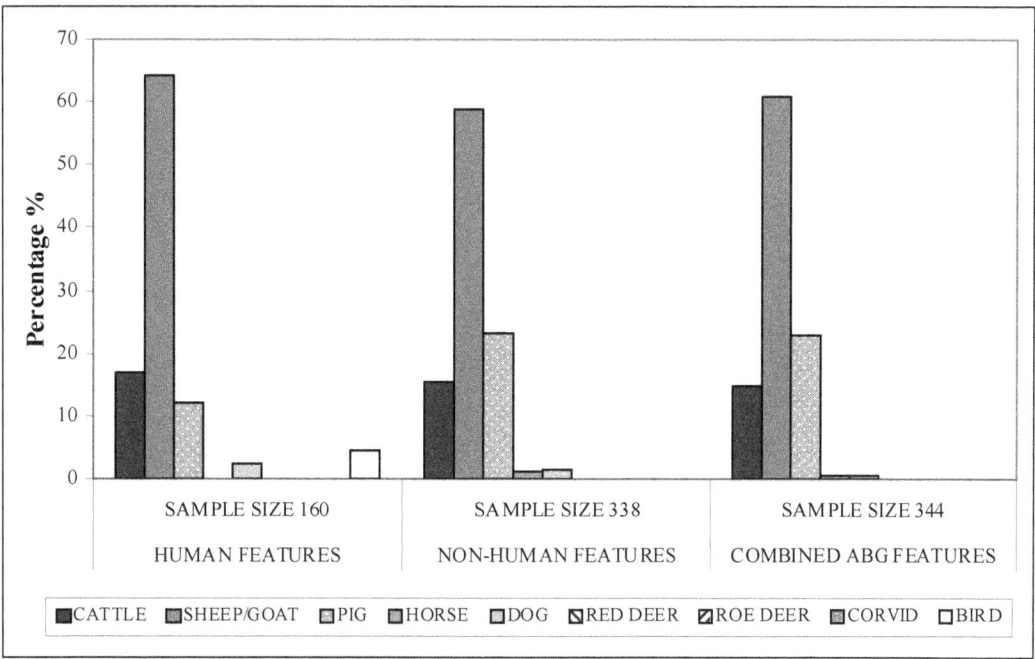

Figure 6.4 Proportions of species in features with human remains, without human remains and with ABGs (ABGs excluded from NISP) at Nettlebank Copse.

Nettlebank Copse

Nettlebank Copse, Hampshire (Cunliffe and Poole 2000c) consists of an Early Iron Age unenclosed small farmstead abandoned around 300BC, at which time a banjo enclosure was constructed around the site. The excavated pits belong to the early Iron Age settlement, with 28 pits being investigated. Human remains consisting of isolated bone fragments were found in one pit and two quarry features. In total six ABGs were discovered in three pits.

All categories of features on this site have similar proportions of species (Figure 6.4). There are no significant differences between features containing human bone, features without human bone and features with ABGs (Appendix 1.10-1.12). The features without human bone have almost identical species proportions to the features with ABGs present. On this site the features without human bone actually have higher proportions of pig than the features with human bone present. The site does not follow the trends seen on the other sites analysed.

Inter-Site Comparisons

Despite inter-site differences in the species proportions seen in features with human bone present (Figure 6.5), there does appear to be a general trend across the sites, for features with human bone present to have more cattle and pig than features without human bone. On the sites of Battlesbury Bowl, Suddern Farm and Houghton Down these differences are statistically significant. Battlesbury Bowl, Suddern Farm and Houghton Down show high proportions of cattle and at Suddern Farm cattle is in fact the best represented species in features with human bone.

This is noteworthy because Iron Age sites on chalkland sites on southern England in general, including these sites, tend on the whole to be dominated by sheep/goat. The majority of Iron Age assemblages consist mainly of sheep and cattle, with the majority of samples having more sheep than cattle, and with a low incidence of pig (Hambleton 1999). The majority of Wessex assemblages have high percentages of sheep ranging from c. 40-70%, slightly lower percentages of cattle (c. 20-50%), and low percentages of pig (c. 0-20%) (Hambleton 1999, 46). Sheep/goat is the dominant species on all the sites analysed in this study (Figure 6.6). As such, it is interesting that the features with human bone show higher percentages of cattle than the site average (Figure 6.5). Pig bones usually rank well behind sheep and cattle on most British sites, and where proportions of pig are high this is usually a reflection of local ecological conditions (Maltby 1996). Pig proportions on these sites followed the general trend for Wessex and were low, but importantly, they were fairly prominent in features with human bone present on all sites in this study, being found in higher than expected proportions in features with human bone in Battlesbury Bowl, Suddern Farm and Houghton Down. These results suggest the purposeful deposition of cattle and pig bones in features with human bone.

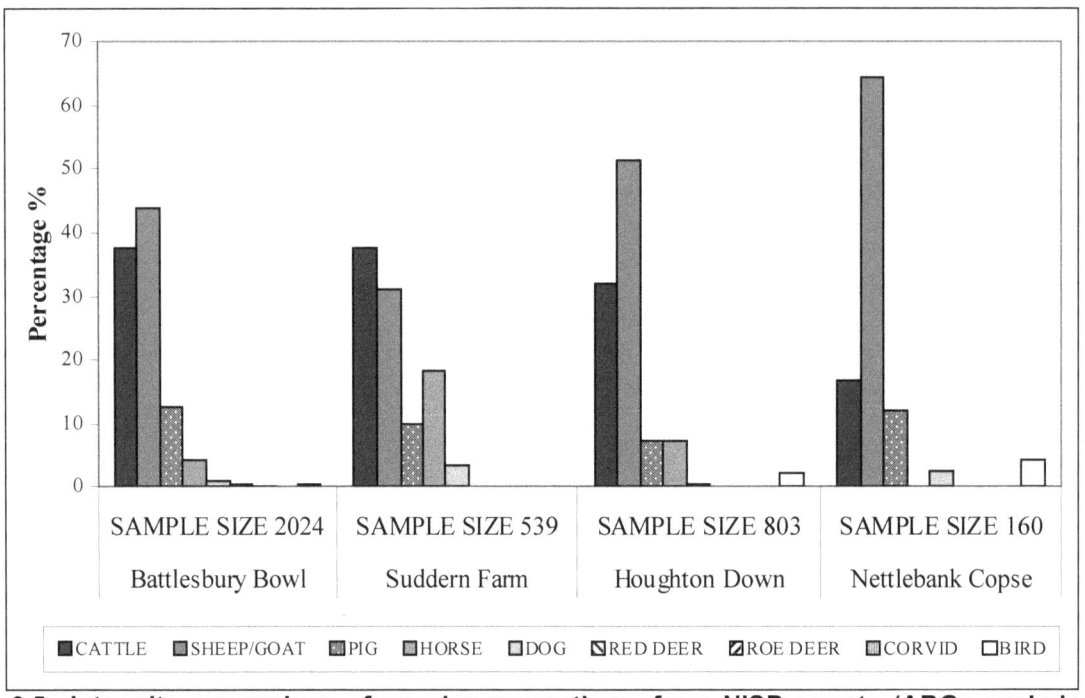

Figure 6.5 Inter-site comparison of species proportions, from NISP counts (ABGs excluded from NISP), in features with human bone present.

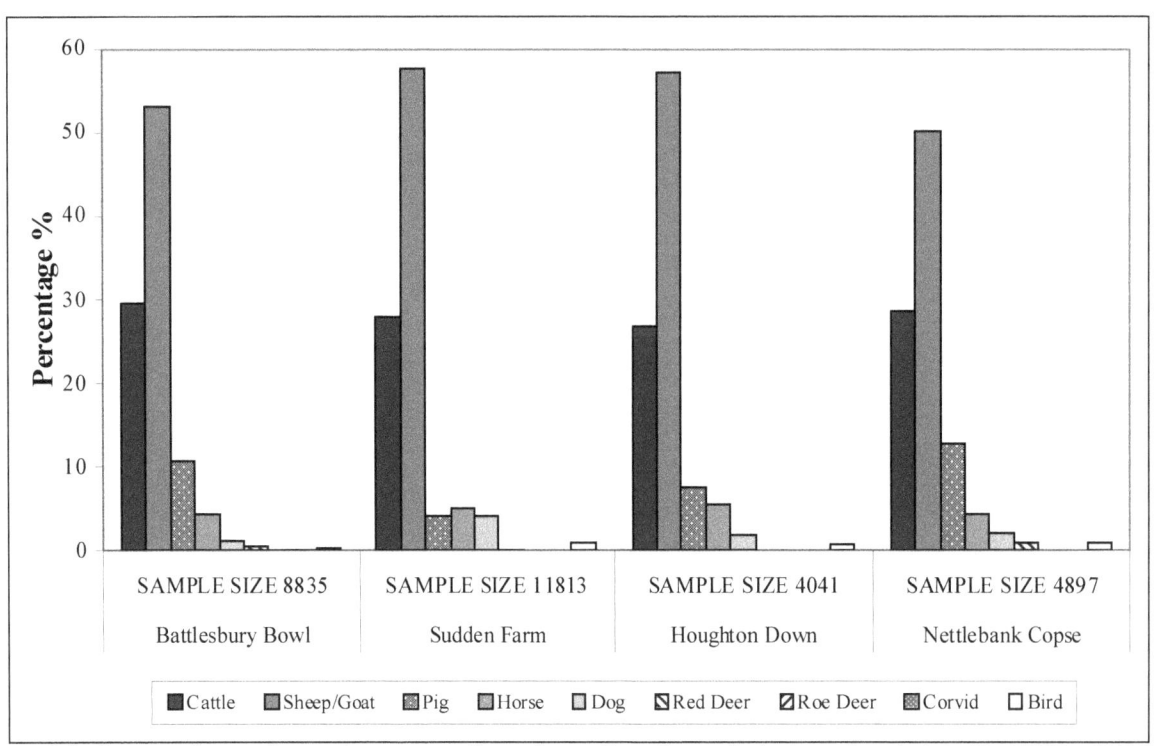

Figure 6.6 Comparison of species proportions from the sites of study using total site NISPs (ABGs excluded from NISP).

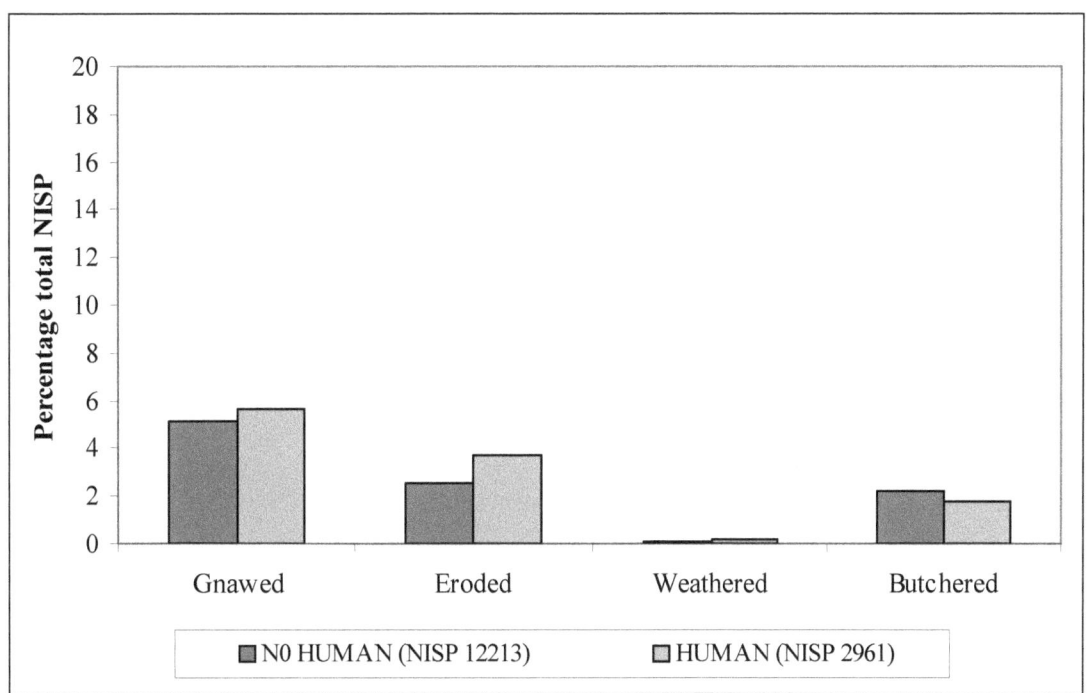

Figure 6.7 Percentage of bones with taphonomic and butchery evidence at Battlesbury Bowl in features with and without human bone.

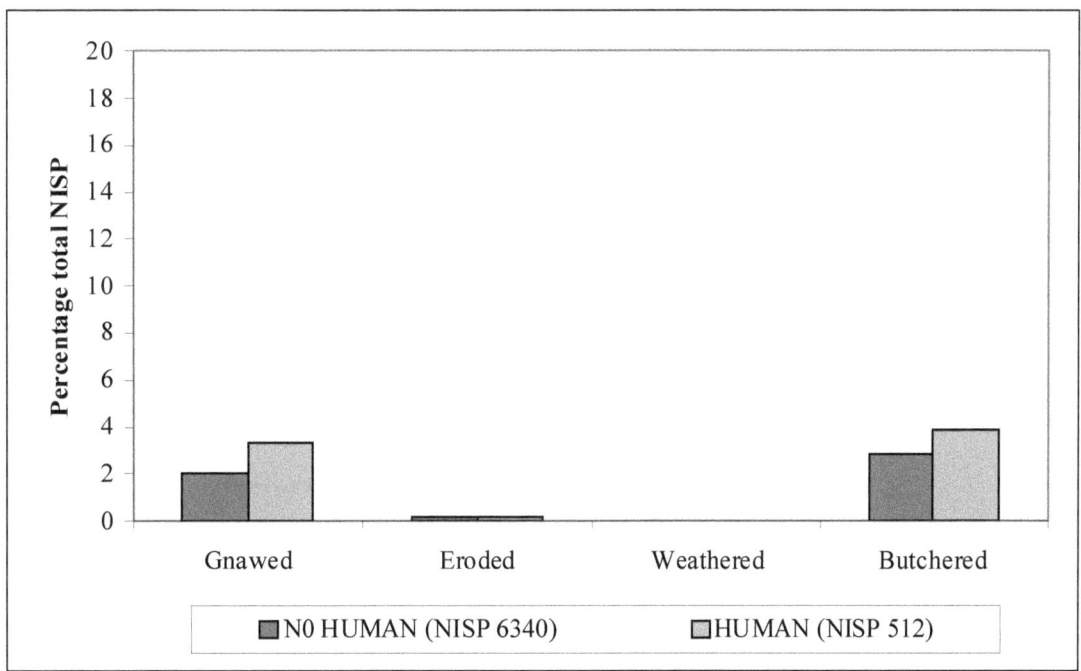

Figure 6.8 Percentage of bones with taphonomic and butchery evidence at Suddern Farm in features with and without human bone.

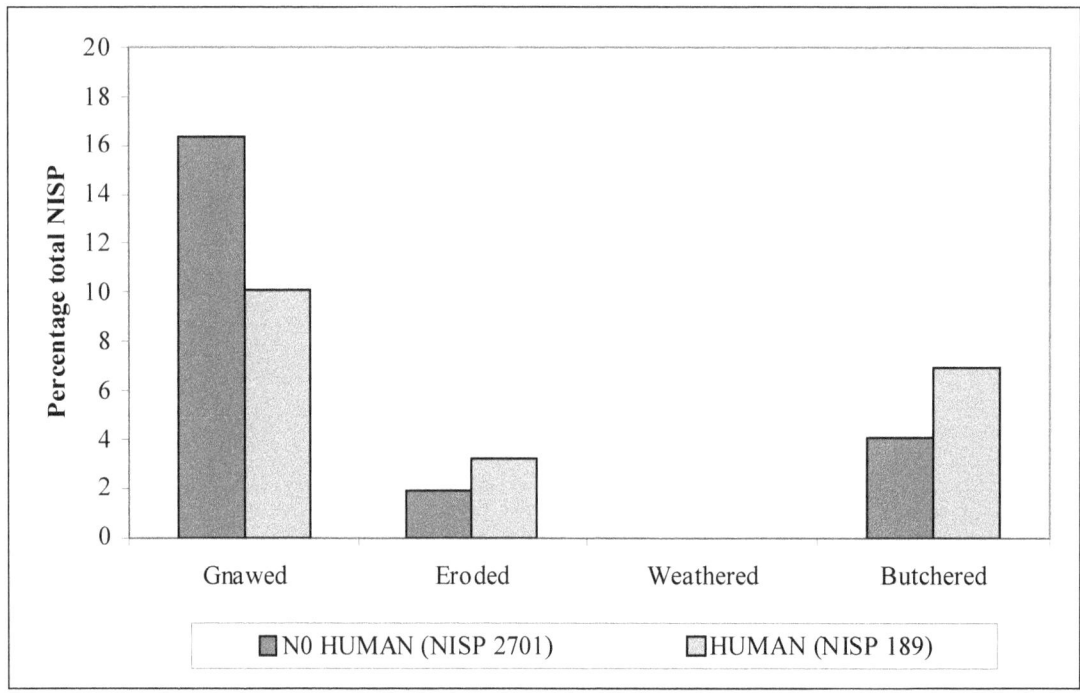

Figure 6.9 Percentage of bones with taphonomic and butchery evidence at Houghton Down in features with and without human bone.

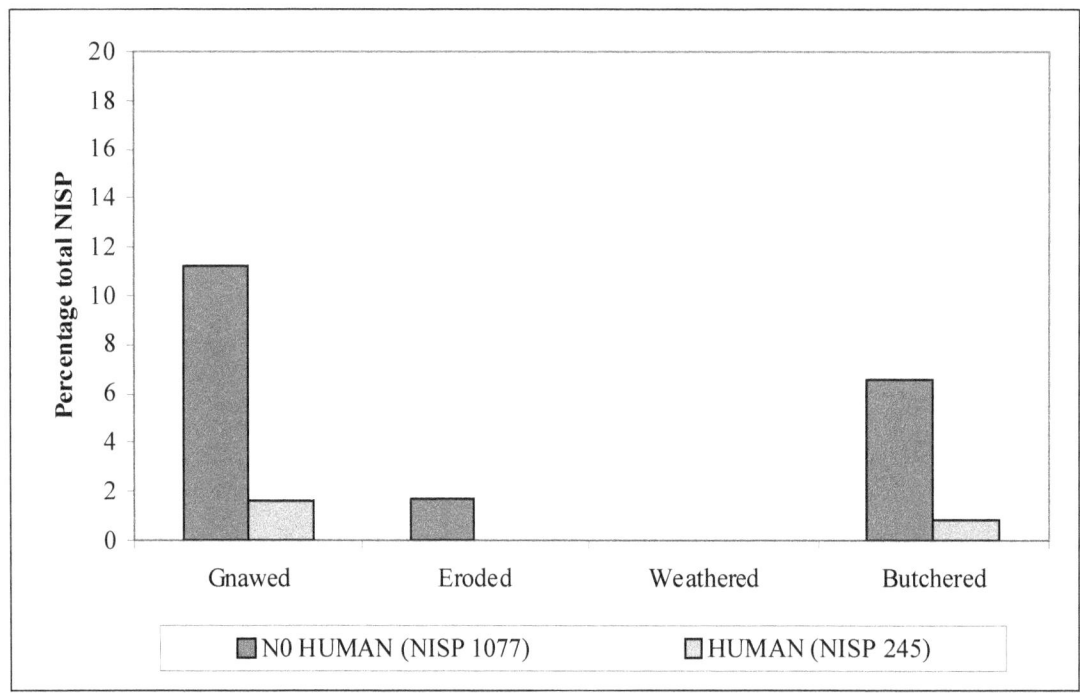

Figure 6.10 Percentage of bones with taphonomic and butchery evidence at Nettlebank Copse in features with and without human bone.

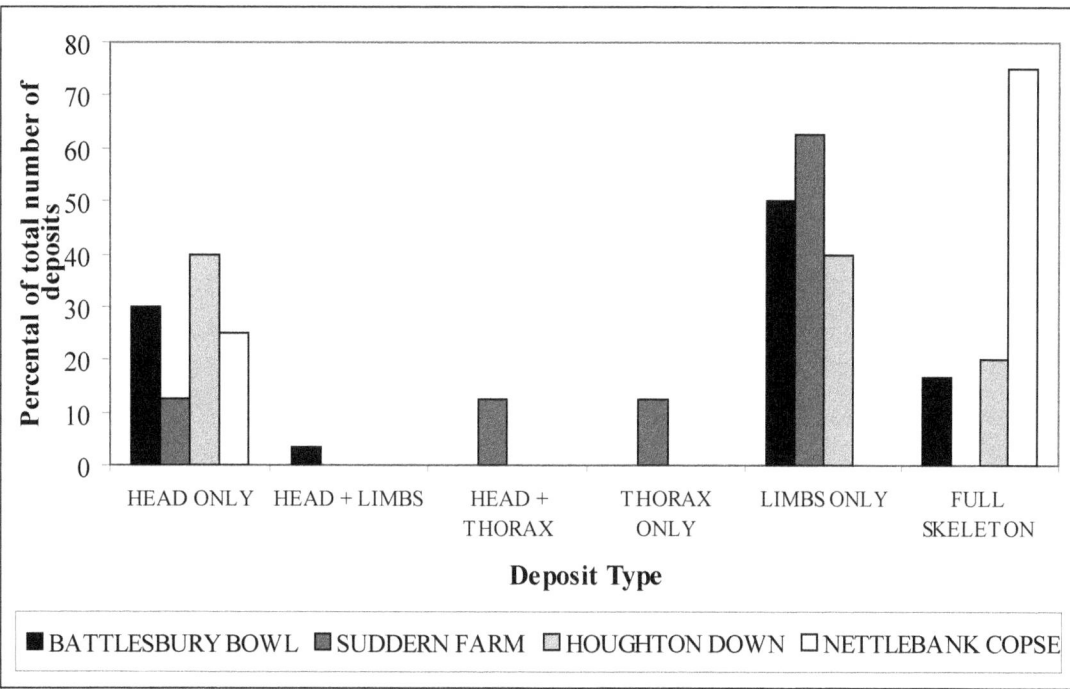

Figure 6.11 Types of human deposits as a percentage of the total number per site (NB. The category 'Full Skeleton' refers to deposits with all body areas present and not necessarily to complete skeletons).

Most Iron Age faunal samples from southern England produce evidence for horse with fragment counts usually contributing 10-20% of the total number of cattle and horse fragments (Maltby 1996). Suddern Farm and Houghton Down have higher than expected frequencies of horse in features with human bone present. At Suddern Farm, horse makes up 32.7% of the cattle/horse fragments in compared to 4.9% in features absent of human bone. At Houghton Down 18.3% of the cattle/horse fragments are from horse in features with human bone present compared to 8.6% in features without human bone. These differences are quite large and may indicate a tendency to deposit horse remains in features with human bone present. This is not seen at Battlesbury Bowl or Nettlebank Copse. Bones from deer and other wild animals form only a tiny part of the samples from these sites. This is the norm for most Iron Age sites and hunting appears to have been of little economic importance in the majority of cases (Maltby 1996). There does not appear to be any differences between features with and without human bone present in the proportions of these species, although it would be difficult to see any trends with the small sample sizes of these species.

Nettlebank Copse shows the least evidence for structured deposition (in terms of species proportions) in features with human bone. Assemblages from these features on this site closely resemble features without human bone. The other sites studied do however show signs of differential deposition between features with human bone and features without human bone and there are definitely some inter-site similarities.

There is also interesting inter-site variation in terms of taphonomy and butchery percentages with all sites showing different patterns (Figures 6.7-6.10). On the sites displaying higher percentages of gnawing, Houghton Down (Figure 6.9) and Nettlebank Copse (Figure 6.10), there is far less gnawing in features with human bone. This suggests that most of the contents of these deposits were inaccessible to dogs at any stage and were perhaps covered soon after deposition. On the sites showing lower percentages of butchery and other taphonomic observations, Battlesbury Bowl (Figure 6.7) and Suddern Farm (Figure 6.8), there is little difference between the features with and without human bone. The only significant difference is seen in the amount of erosion seen in features from Battlesbury Bowl where there are relatively more eroded bones in features with human bone.

Human Deposits

Deposits of human bone comprising all areas of the body were found on all sites especially Suddern Farm, and were particularly common at Nettlebank Copse. The majority of deposits were of heads and limbs while areas of the thorax were infrequently represented (Figure 6.11). This trend was also recorded at the sites of Danebury and Gussage All Saints (Walker 1984). This could be the result of recovery bias, as skull fragments and long bones are more easily recognised which may enhance their retrieval during excavation (*ibid*). It is also possible that this trend is a result of structured deposition.

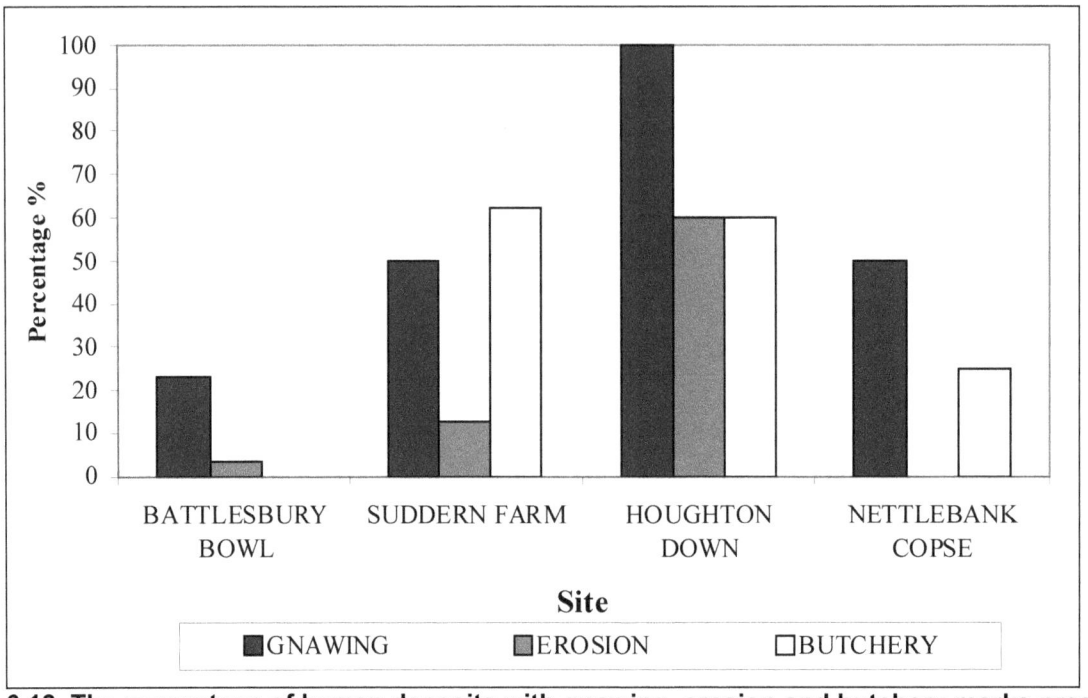

Figure 6.12 **The percentage of human deposits with gnawing, erosion and butchery marks present.**

The skull was an important symbol to the Celts who considered it as the source of life and it is possible that this was also the case for Iron Age people (Walker 1984). The removal of a skull from a body could be associated with victory over an enemy and trophy collection, or alternatively it could be an act of veneration of ancestors (*ibid*). If either of these theories is correct, then what is the meaning of depositing these skulls in pits? Is it as part of a ritual or propitiatory act, or does it merely represent the casual disposal of old skulls? The presence of so many isolated long bones on these sites could be a result of taphonomy or it could imply a preference to deposit certain parts of the anatomy for purposes other than simple burial. Most of the human bones from the sites studied here were very fragmentary and many of the human bones from Battlesbury Bowl were recorded as being trampled. Several of the human bones from the Danebury Environs sites were recorded as showing signs of burning which would alter the survival of the bone assemblage and may suggest that some of these bones were cremated or at least in contact with fire before secondary deposition.

A high percentage of human bones showed evidence of gnawing (Figure 6.12). Gnawing generally only occurs when bones are relatively fresh, and as such, suggests that many of the human bones were available to scavengers soon after death. This may also explain the lack of areas of the torso in these deposits; it is quite feasible that carnivores might entirely consume smaller flesh-carrying bones such as ribs (Walker 1984). However, ribs and vertebrae survive in the animal bone assemblage, which was also subjected to scavenging. Sixty percent of human bones from Houghton Down showed signs of erosion and erosion was also present, in smaller percentages, on human bones from Battlesbury Bowl and Suddern Farm. Human bones from the Danebury Environs sites show high levels of butchery. This suggests that bodies were dismembered before their deposition in pits. It does not tell us, however, whether this process occurred while the bodies were fresh or partially decayed. The archaeological indicators for exposure of bodies include: animal gnawing on bones; scattered, isolated, fragmentary, weathered bones; disarticulated skeletons; and incomplete skeletons (Carr 1997). The human bones from the sites studies in this work show nearly all these signs and as such, it is likely that these remains were excarnated before disposal in pits, postholes, ditches and quarries.

Conclusions

This study has shown that there are indeed signs of more structured depositions in features where human bone was present on Iron Age sites in southern England. Faunal deposits in features with human bone present often display significantly different species proportions, taphonomy and butchery patterns to features with no human bone present. These results lead to the question of why? Why are pig and cattle bones seemingly preferentially deposited in features with human bone deposits? As cattle and pigs are found in far lower frequencies than sheep, they may have been seen as having greater value, perhaps having a higher status, leading to their inclusion in the secondary burials of human remains.

A wider range of samples and analyses, which take into account contextual variability within features, is required before any definitive statements can be made about the possibility for structured deposition in features with human bone (Maltby 1996). The analyses undertaken in this study have yet to fully take into account the problems of intra-site variability and this study is only the beginning of a much larger task. Much more detailed comparisons of features with and without human bone on Iron Age sites are required to clarify the situation and determine if any conclusions drawn from this study are truly correct.

The past few decades have witnessed an encouraging increase in the amount of data available to archaeologists from faunal studies (Maltby 1996) and this data should be used to add to the research performed here. Many factors can create variability in faunal assemblages. Previous intra-site studies of Iron Age sites have shown how factors of differential preservation or variations in the butchery and disposal of carcasses of different ages can significantly affect zooarchaeological samples (Maltby 1996). Samples from different sites can vary greatly in their contents and there is a need for further analyses to see if any of these differences are due to structured deposition related to the presence of human remains, in particular the disarticulated remains so common on Iron Age sites. Given samples of good quality and of a decent size a more detailed picture of these deposition practices may be obtained. Several analyses have already indicated the presence of structured deposition in terms of ABGs (Grant 1984b; Hill 1995) and to some extent human burials, but there still remains a big gap in the analyses undertaken on features with disarticulated human bones present.

More accessibility to complete faunal and human bone reports is required to enable the development of this area of research. One of the biggest difficulties in this study was getting the relevant data from both the faunal and human bone reports to an adequate level and with good compatibility.

For other sites it was the case of one or the other. In some cases only the faunal data were available at the required standard; in other cases, only the human data were available. The main problem appears to arise from the segregation of faunal and human bone data so early on in the post-excavation programmes. Often, disarticulated remains are glossed over in favour of the analysis of more complete human remains. It is still not uncommon for some disarticulated human remains to be included in the animal bones, sent to the faunal specialists and therefore not examined by the human osteologists at the same time as the other human material, or even overlooked completely. Ultimately it boils down to the question of who is responsible for the analysis of the occurrence of human bone in faunal deposits – zooarchaeologists or human osteologists? This task may ultimately fall to zooarchaeologists but more integration and communication with human osteologists is required.

Due to time restraints many aspects of the faunal and human remains could not be explored. One of the main areas omitted in this study concerns the age profiles of the faunal assemblage. There may be differences in the proportion of animals of different ages represented in features with and without human bone, which would be interesting to explore. In addition further work could be done on the relative abundance of different elements of animals as well as humans.

This study has shown that there is a lot of potential in the study of faunal deposits in features with human bone. There is much we do not know about the mortuary rites of Iron Age people and their attitudes to animals and much to be gleaned from further examination of the faunal remains in these deposits. Continued research of this nature can only add to our knowledge of Iron Age Societies.

Acknowledgments

I am indebted to the following for their contributions to this research: my supervisors, Ellie Hambleton and Mark Maltby for their continued advice, guidance and support, and for allowing me to use the faunal data from Battlesbury Bowl; Wessex Archaeology for allowing me to use the unpublished faunal data from Battlesbury Bowl; Julie Hamilton for providing me with the faunal databases for Suddern Farm, Houghton Down and Nettlebank Copse; and James Morris for all his help.

Bibliography

Bullock, A. E. and Allen, M. J. (1997) Animal bones. In. R. J. C. Smith, F. Healy, M. J. Allen, E. L. Morris, I. Barnes and P. J. Woodward (eds.), *Excavations along the Route of the Dorchester By-pass, Dorset, 1986-1988*, 194-195. Dorchester, Wessex Archaeological Report 1.

Carr, G. and Knüsel, C. (1997) The ritual framework of excarnation by exposure as the mortuary practice of the early and middle Iron Ages of central southern Britain. In. A. Gwilt and C. Haselgrove (eds.) *Reconstructing Iron Age Societies*, 167-173. Oxford, Oxbow Monograph 71.

Coy, J. (1984) The bird bones. In. B. Cunliffe (ed.), *Danebury: an Iron Age Hillfort in Hampshire. Volume 2. The Excavations 1969-1978: the Finds*, 527-531. London, Council for British Archaeology Research Report 52.

Cunliffe, B. (1992) Pits, preconceptions and propitiation in the British Iron Age. *Oxford Journal of Archaeology* 11, 69-83.

Cunliffe, B. (2000). *The Danebury Environs Programme. The Prehistory of a Wessex Landscape. Vol 1. Introduction.* Oxford, English Heritage and

Oxford University Committee for Archaeology Monograph 49.

Cunliffe, B. (2005) *Iron Age Communities in Britain: an account of England, Scotland and Wales from the 7th Century BC until the Roman Conquest*, 4th Edition. London, Routledge.

Cunliffe, B. and Poole, C. (2000a) *The Danebury Environs Programme. The Prehistory of a Wessex Landscape. Vol 2. Part 3. Suddern Farm, Middle Wallop, Hants, 1991 and 1996*. Oxford, English Heritage and Oxford University Committee for Archaeology Monograph 49.

Cunliffe, B. and Poole, C. (2000b) *The Danebury Environs Programme. The Prehistory of a Wessex Landscape. Vol 2. Part 6. Houghton Down, Stockbridge, Hants, 1994.* Oxford, English Heritage and Oxford University Committee for Archaeology Monograph 49.

Cunliffe, B. and Poole, C. (2000c) *The Danebury Environs Programme. The Prehistory of a Wessex Landscape. Vol 2. Part 5. Nettlebank Copse, Wherwell, Hants, 1993.* Oxford, English Heritage and Oxford University Committee for Archaeology Monograph 49

Ellis, C and Powell, A.B. with Hawkes, J. (2008) *An Iron Age Settlement outside Battlesbury Hillfort, Warminster and Sites along the southern Range Road*, 84-93. Salisbury, Wessex Archaeological Report 122.

Fitzpatrick, A. P. (1997) Everyday Life in Iron Age Wessex. In A. Gwilt and C. Haselgrove (eds.) *Reconstructing Iron Age Societies*, 73-86. Oxford, Oxbow Monograph 71.

Galik, A. (2002) An Iron Age bone assemblage from Durezza Cave, Carinthia, Austria: detecting ritual behaviour through archaeozoological and taphonomical analyses. In. S. J. O'Day, W. Van Neer, A. Ervynck, (eds.) *Behaviour behind Bones. The Zooarchaeology of Ritual, Religion, Status and Identity. 9th ICAZ Conference*, 54-61, Oxford, Oxbow.

Grant, A (1984a) The animal husbandry. In. B. Cunliffe, *Danebury: an Iron Age Hillfort in Hampshire. Volume 2,* 496-548. London, Council for British Archaeology Research Report 52.

Grant, A. (1984b) Survival or sacrifice? A critical appraisal of animal burials in the Iron Age. In. C. Grigson and J. Clutton-Brock (eds.) *Animals in Archaeology 4: Husbandry in Europe*, 221-228. Oxford, British Archaeological Report British Series 227.

Grant, A. (1991). Economic or symbolic? In. P. Garwood (ed.) *Sacred and Profane, Proceedings of a Conference of Archaeology, Ritual and Religion, Oxford, 1989*, 109-114. Oxford, Oxford Committee for Archaeology Monograph 32.

Hambleton, E. (1999). *Animal Husbandry Regimes in Iron Age Britain. A Comparative Study of Faunal Assemblages from British Iron Age Sites.* Oxford, British Archaeological Report British Series 282.

Hambleton E and Maltby M. (unpublished). Animal Bones from Excavations at Battlesbury Bowl, Wiltshire. Bournemouth University Animal Bone Archive Report for Wessex Archaeology.

Hamilton, J. (2000) The animal bones. In. B. Cunliffe and C. Poole, *The Danebury Environs Programme. The Prehistory of a Wessex Landscape. Vol 2. Part 3. Suddern Farm, Middle Wallop, Hants, 1991 and 1996*, 175-192. Oxford, English Heritage and Oxford University Committee for Archaeology Monograph 49.

Hill, J. D. (1995) *Ritual and Rubbish in the Iron Age of Wessex*. Oxford, British Archaeological Report British Series 242.

Maltby, M. (1985) Patterns in faunal assemblage variability. In. G. Barker and C. Gamble (eds.) *Beyond Domestication in Europe*, 33-67. London, Academic Press.

Maltby, M. (1996) The exploitation of animals in the Iron Age: the archaeozoological evidence. In. T. C. Champion and J. R. Collis (eds.) *The Iron Age in Britain and Ireland: Recent Trends*, 17-27. Sheffield, University of Sheffield J. R. Collis Publications.

McKinley, J. I. (unpublished). Battlesbury Bowl, Warminster (44896) Human Bone Archive Report. Wessex Archaeology.

Metcalf, P. and Huntington, R. (1991) *Celebrations of Death. The Anthropology of Mortuary Ritual*, 2nd Edition. Cambridge, Cambridge University Press.

Osborne, R. (2004) Hoards, votives, offerings: the archaeology of the dedicated object. *World Archaeology* 36, 1-10

Poole, C. (2000a) Special deposits. In. B. Cunliffe and C. Poole, *The Danebury Environs Programme. The Prehistory of a Wessex Landscape. Vol 2. Part 3. Suddern Farm, Middle Wallop, Hants, 1991 and 1996*, 143-151. Oxford, English Heritage and Oxford University Committee for Archaeology Monograph 49

Poole, C. (2000b) Special Deposits. In B. Cunliffe and C. Poole, *The Danebury Environs Programme. The Prehistory of a Wessex Landscape. Vol 2. Part 6. Houghton Down, Stockbridge, Hants, 1994*, 123-126. Oxford. English Heritage and Oxford University Committee for Archaeology Monograph 49.

Poole C. (2000c) Special Deposits. In B. Cunliffe and C. Poole. *The Danebury Environs Programme. The Prehistory of a Wessex Landscape. Vol 2. Part 5. Nettlebank Copse, Wherwell, Hants, 1993*, 93-98. Oxford. English Heritage and Oxford University Committee for Archaeology Monograph 49.

Smith, M. (2006) Bones chewed by canids as evidence for human excarnation: a British case study. *Antiquity* 80, 671-685.

Walker, L. (1984) The deposition of human remains. In. B. Cunliffe, *Danebury: an Iron Age Hillfort in Hampshire. Volume 2,* 496-548. London,

Council for British Archaeology Research Report 52.

Whimster, R. (1977) Iron Age burial in Southern Britain. *Proceedings of the Prehistoric Society* 43, 317 – 327.

Wilson, B. (1992) Considerations for the identification of ritual deposits of animal bones in Iron Age pits. *International Journal of Osteoarchaeology* 2, 341-349.

Author's Affiliation

Anna Russell
Universiteit Leiden
Faculty of Archaeology
P.O. Box 9515
2300 RA Leiden,
The Netherlands

Appendix

Battlesbury Bowl Species Proportions

Statistical Test 1.1

- Null Hypothesis: there is no difference in the relative frequencies of cattle, sheep/goat, pig, horse, and dog between features with human bone present and features absent of human bone at the site of Battlesbury Bowl.

OBSERVED

	Cattle	S/G	Pig	Horse	Dog	TOTAL
HUMAN	731	874	224	86	21	1936
NO HUMAN	862	1779	195	121	112	3069
TOTAL	1593	2653	419	207	133	5005

EXPECTED

	Cattle	S/G	Pig	Horse	Dog	TOTAL
HUMAN	616.2	1026.2	162.1	80.1	51.4	1936
NO HUMAN	976.8	1626.8	256.9	126.9	81.6	3069
TOTAL	1593	2653	419	207	133	5005

$$X^2 = \sum \frac{(O-E)^2}{E}$$

$X^2 = 140.2 (1.d.p.)$

At 4df and $\alpha = 0.01$ $X^2_{Crit} = 15.09$. Therefore the null hypothesis can be rejected and there is a highly significant difference between features with human bone present and features absent of human bone at the site of Battlesbury Bowl.

Statistical Test 1.2

- Null Hypothesis: there is no difference in the relative frequencies of cattle, sheep/goat, pig, horse, and dog between features with human bone present and features with ABGs present at the site of Battlesbury Bowl.

OBSERVED

	Cattle	S/G	Pig	Horse	Dog	TOTAL
HUMAN	731	874	224	86	21	1936
ABG	412	890	119	94	15	1530
TOTAL	1143	1764	343	180	36	3466

EXPECTED

	Cattle	S/G	Pig	Horse	Dog	TOTAL
HUMAN	638.4	985.3	191.6	100.5	20.1	1935.9
ABG	504.6	778.7	151.4	79.5	15.9	1530.1
TOTAL	1143	1764	343	180	36	3466

$$X^2 = \sum \frac{(O-E)^2}{E}$$

$X^2 = 76.1 (1.d.p.)$

At 4df and $\alpha = 0.01$ $X^2_{Crit} = 15.09$. Therefore the null hypothesis can be rejected and there is a highly significant difference between features with human bone present and features with ABGs present at the site of Battlesbury Bowl.

Statistical Test 1.3

- Null Hypothesis: there is no difference in the relative frequencies of cattle, sheep/goat, pig, horse, and dog between features absent of human bone and features with ABGs present at the site of Battlesbury Bowl.

OBSERVED	Cattle	S/G	Pig	Horse	Dog	TOTAL
NO HUMAN	862	1779	195	121	112	3069
ABG	412	890	119	94	15	1530
TOTAL	1274	2669	314	215	127	4599

EXPECTED	Cattle	S/G	Pig	Horse	Dog	TOTAL
NO HUMAN	850.2	1781.1	209.5	143.5	84.7	3069
ABG	423.8	887.9	104.5	71.5	42.3	1530
TOTAL	1274	2669	314	215	127	4599

$$X^2 = \sum \frac{(O-E)^2}{E}$$

$X^2 = 40.5$ (1.d.p.)

At 4df and $\alpha = 0.01$ $X^2_{Crit} = 15.09$. Therefore the null hypothesis can be rejected and there is a highly significant difference between features absent of human bone and features with ABGs present at the site of Battlesbury Bowl.

Suddern Farm Species Proportions

Statistical Test 1.4

- Null Hypothesis: there is no difference in the relative frequencies of cattle, sheep/goat, pig, horse, and dog between features with human bone present and features absent of human bone at the site of Suddern Farm.

OBSERVED	Cattle	S/G	Pig	Horse	Dog	TOTAL
HUMAN	202	167	54	98	18	539
NO HUMAN	816	2366	150	42	126	3500
TOTAL	1018	2533	204	140	144	4039

EXPECTED	Cattle	S/G	Pig	Horse	Dog	TOTAL
HUMAN	135.9	338	27.2	18.7	19.2	539
NO HUMAN	882.1	2195	176.8	121.3	124.8	3500
TOTAL	1018	2533	204	140	144	4039

$$X^2 = \sum \frac{(O-E)^2}{E}$$

$X^2 = 555.7$ (1.d.p.)

At 4df and $\alpha = 0.01$ $X^2_{Crit} = 15.09$. Therefore the null hypothesis can be rejected and there is a highly significant difference between features with human bone present and features absent of human bone at the site of Suddern Farm.

Statistical Test 1.5

- Null Hypothesis: there is no difference in the relative frequencies of cattle, sheep/goat, pig, horse, and dog between features with human bone present and features with ABGs present at the site of Suddern Farm.

OBSERVED	Cattle	S/G	Pig	Horse	Dog	TOTAL
HUMAN	202	167	54	98	18	**539**
ABG	256	131	163	72	112	**734**
TOTAL	**458**	**298**	**217**	**170**	**130**	**1273**

EXPECTED	Cattle	S/G	Pig	Horse	Dog	TOTAL
HUMAN	193.9	126.2	91.9	72	55	**539**
ABG	264.1	171.8	125.1	98	75	**734**
TOTAL	**458**	**298**	**217**	**170**	**130**	**1273**

$$X^2 = \sum \frac{(O-E)^2}{E}$$

$X^2 = 110.0 (1.d.p.)$

At 4df and $\alpha = 0.01$ $X^2_{Crit} = 15.09$. Therefore the null hypothesis can be rejected and there is a highly significant difference between features with human bone present and features with ABGs present at the site of Suddern Farm.

Statistical Test 1.6

- Null Hypothesis: there is no difference in the relative frequencies of cattle, sheep/goat, pig, horse, and dog between features absent of human bone and features with ABGs present at the site of Suddern Farm.

OBSERVED	Cattle	S/G	Pig	Horse	Dog	TOTAL
NO HUMAN	816	2366	150	42	126	**3500**
ABG	256	131	163	72	112	**734**
TOTAL	**1072**	**2497**	**313**	**114**	**238**	**4234**

EXPECTED	Cattle	S/G	Pig	Horse	Dog	TOTAL
NO HUMAN	886.2	2064.1	258.7	94.2	196.7	**3499.9**
ABG	185.8	432.9	54.3	19.8	41.3	**734.1**
TOTAL	**1072**	**2497**	**313**	**114**	**238**	**4234**

$$X^2 = \sum \frac{(O-E)^2}{E}$$

$X^2 = 856.7 (1.d.p.)$

At 4df and $\alpha = 0.01$ $X^2_{Crit} = 15.09$. Therefore the null hypothesis can be rejected and there is a highly significant difference between features absent of human bone present and features with ABG's present at the site of Suddern Farm.

Houghton Down Species Proportions

Statistical Test 1.7

- Null Hypothesis: there is no difference in the relative frequencies of cattle, sheep/goat, pig, horse, and dog between features with human bone present and features absent of human bone at the site of Houghton Down.

OBSERVED	Cattle	S/G	Pig	Horse	Dog	TOTAL
HUMAN	255	410	59	57	4	785
NO HUMAN	191	415	16	18	9	649
TOTAL	446	825	75	75	13	1434

EXPECTED	Cattle	S/G	Pig	Horse	Dog	TOTAL
HUMAN	244.1	451.6	41.1	41.1	7.1	785
NO HUMAN	201.9	373.4	33.9	33.9	5.9	649
TOTAL	446	825	75	75	13	1434

$$X^2 = \sum \frac{(O-E)^2}{E}$$

$\underline{X^2 = \mathbf{43.5(1.d.p.)}}$

At 4df and $\alpha = 0.01$ $X^2_{Crit} = 15.09$. Therefore the null hypothesis can be rejected and there is a highly significant difference between features with human bone present and features absent of human bone at the site of Houghton Down.

Statistical Test 1.8

- Null Hypothesis: there is no difference in the relative frequencies of cattle, sheep/goat, pig, horse, and dog between features with human bone present and features with ABGs present at the site of Houghton Down.

OBSERVED	Cattle	S/G	Pig	Horse	TOTAL
HUMAN	255	410	59	57	781
ABG	54	251	9	5	319
TOTAL	309	661	68	62	1100

EXPECTED	Cattle	S/G	Pig	Horse	TOTAL
HUMAN	219.4	469.3	48.3	44.0	781
ABG	89.6	191.7	19.7	18.0	319
TOTAL	309	661	68	62	1100

$$X^2 = \sum \frac{(O-E)^2}{E}$$

$\underline{X^2 = \mathbf{67.2(1.d.p.)}}$

At 3df and $\alpha = 0.01$ $X^2_{Crit} = 13.28$. Therefore the null hypothesis can be rejected and there is a highly significant difference between features with human bone present and features absent of human bone at the site of Houghton Down.

Statistical Test 1.9

- Null Hypothesis: there is no difference in the relative frequencies of cattle, sheep/goat, pig, horse, and dog between features absent of human bone and features with ABGs present at the site of Houghton Down.

OBSERVED	Cattle	S/G	Pig	Horse	Dog	TOTAL
NO HUMAN	191	415	16	18	9	649
ABG	54	251	9	5	5	324
TOTAL	245	666	25	23	14	973

EXPECTED	Cattle	S/G	Pig	Horse	Dog	TOTAL
NO HUMAN	163.4	444.2	16.7	15.3	9.3	648.9
ABG	81.6	221.8	8.3	7.7	4.7	324.1
TOTAL	245	666	25	23	14	973

$$X^2 = \sum \frac{(O-E)^2}{E}$$

$\underline{X^2 = \mathbf{22.0(1.d.p.)}}$

At 4df and $\alpha = 0.01$ $X^2_{Crit} = 15.09$. Therefore the null hypothesis can be rejected and there is a significant difference between features with human bone present and features absent of human bone at the site of Houghton Down.

Nettlebank Copse Species Proportions

Statistical Test 1.10

- Null Hypothesis: there is no difference in the relative frequencies of cattle, sheep/goat, pig, horse, and dog between features with human bone present and features absent of human bone at the site of Nettlebank Copse.

OBSERVED	Cattle	S/G	Pig	TOTAL
HUMAN	27	103	19	149
NO HUMAN	52	199	78	329
TOTAL	79	302	97	478

EXPECTED	Cattle	S/G	Pig	TOTAL
HUMAN	24.6	94.1	30.2	149
NO HUMAN	54.4	207.9	66.8	329
TOTAL	79	302	97	478

$$X^2 = \sum \frac{(O-E)^2}{E}$$

$\underline{X^2 = \mathbf{7.6(1.d.p.)}}$

At 2df and $\alpha = 0.01$ $X^2_{Crit} = 9.21$. Therefore the null hypothesis cannot be rejected and there is no significant difference between features with human bone present and features absent of human bone at the site of Nettlebank Copse.

Statistical Test 1.11

- Null Hypothesis: there is no difference in the relative frequencies of cattle, sheep/goat, pig, horse, and dog between features with human bone present and with ABGs present at the site of Nettlebank Copse.

OBSERVED	Cattle	S/G	Pig	TOTAL
HUMAN	27	103	19	149
ABG	51	210	79	340
TOTAL	78	313	98	489

EXPECTED	Cattle	S/G	Pig	TOTAL
HUMAN	23.8	95.4	29.9	149
ABG	54.2	217.6	68.1	340
TOTAL	78	313	98	489

$$X^2 = \sum \frac{(O-E)^2}{E}$$

$X^2 = 7.2$ (1.d.p.)

At 2df and $\alpha = 0.01$ $X^2_{Crit} = 9.21$. Therefore the null hypothesis cannot be rejected and there is no significant difference between features with human bone present and features with ABGs present at the site of Nettlebank Copse.

Statistical Test 1.12

- Null Hypothesis: there is no difference in the relative frequencies of cattle, sheep/goat, pig, horse, and dog between features absent of human bone and features with ABGs present at the site of Nettlebank Copse.

OBSERVED	Cattle	S/G	Pig	TOTAL
NO HUMAN	52	199	78	329
ABG	51	210	79	340
TOTAL	103	409	157	669

EXPECTED	Cattle	S/G	Pig	TOTAL
NO HUMAN	50.7	201.1	77.2	329
ABG	52.3	207.9	79.8	340
TOTAL	103	409	157	669

$$X^2 = \sum \frac{(O-E)^2}{E}$$

$X^2 = 0.1$ (1.d.p.)

At 2df and $\alpha = 0.01$ $X^2_{Crit} = 9.21$. Therefore the null hypothesis cannot be rejected and there no significant difference between features absent of human bone and features with ABGs present at the site of Nettlebank Copse.

7. Bone modification and the conceptual relationship between humans and animals in Iron Age Wessex

Richard Madgwick

Abstract

Bone modification has generally been marginalised as a tool for the interpretation of osseous material in complex archaeological records. As a result of the manner in which human and animal remains are traditionally studied and reported on, the analysis of taphonomic processes which affect the character of specimens between death and incorporation into forming deposits is often confined to butchery, burning and fragmentation. This paper argues that current methods of osteoarchaeological analysis fail to recognise the potential of a substantial and easily accessible source of information in paying little attention to the processes of weathering, gnawing, trampling, abrasion and longitudinal/spiral fracturing. More detailed taphonomic assessments have tended to focus on one specific process to answer a particular research question rather than taking a holistic approach to pre-depositional affects (e.g. Outram 2001). Consequently biographies of skeletal material are only partially complete, as the period in the material existence of bone prior to subterranean deposition is not fully investigated. The aforementioned taphonomic processes can provide substantial evidence for human decision making regarding the treatment of different classes of remains.

This research explores the potential of holistic taphonomic analysis in a sample of c.9500 human and faunal specimens from the Iron Age sites of Winnall Down and Danebury. These sites were selected as they are located in the heart of Wessex, an area about which there has been considerable discourse and disagreement regarding the nature of human and animal bone treatment in the Iron Age. Through comprehensive taphonomic analysis, highly regulated, socially circumscribed behaviours surrounding bone handling were revealed. These results are suggestive of separate practices relating to the treatment of human and faunal remains with the latter exhibiting significantly greater evidence of exposure. The analysis of bone modification in features containing both human and faunal remains reveals a blurring of the boundary between human and animal identities, as the treatment of the two classes of material differs to a significantly lesser degree than when analysing the entire assemblage. Therefore each class of material is subjected to a more closely related mode of treatment. This might be seen as indicative of a conceptual proximity of human and faunal remains.

Iron Age Deposits in Wessex

This paper demonstrates the potential of commonly marginalised taphonomic processes in the understanding of complex archaeological records. It opens with a brief background on human and faunal remains in the Iron Age archaeological record of Wessex and is followed by a summary of the processes of weathering, abrasion, trampling, gnawing and fracturing with data analysis and interpretations concluding the paper.

The treatment of human and animal remains prior to and during deposition in Iron Age Wessex is notable. Human remains are recovered in a range of distinctive configurations, including isolated bones and skulls, disarticulated limbs, partial inhumations or complete inhumations from ditches, enclosure boundaries, ramparts and most commonly, pits (Hill 1995, 13). In addition, in central/southern England, finds of human remains account for only a small proportion of settlements' inhabitants, with Wait (1985, 90) suggesting that those recovered account for only approximately 6% of the population in the early/middle Iron Age. Faunal material is regularly recovered in a manner uncharacteristic of domestic refuse. Deposits do not only contain disarticulated material of the main domesticates, but also fully articulated skeletons, articulated limbs and skulls. Also bones of dogs and horses, as well as right sided elements are over-represented compared to their number in the 'normal' assemblage on site (Cunliffe 1995; Cunliffe and Poole 1995; Grant 1984a; 1984b, Green 1992; Morris 2008; Woodward 1993). Human and faunal remains are frequently recovered in association with each other (Figure 7.1), and with a range of other cultural debris, most commonly pottery, but also quernstone fragments, metalwork, worked bone, plant remains, spindle whorls and loomweight fragments (Hill 1995, 20-22; Walker 1984). These deposits are predominantly found in the Wessex region of southern England, particularly Dorset, Wiltshire, Oxfordshire and Hampshire (Wait 1985, 88) and are being noted in increasing numbers elsewhere in England. It is important to emphasise the diversity and complexity of depositional practice, as all manner of configurations of associations, remains categories and feature types have been found on both non-hillfort settlements and hillfort sites.

In the past, deposits containing human remains and/or articulated faunal material have often been classified as 'ritual' (Grant 1984b; Grant 1991; Hambleton 1999, 11; Wilson 1999) or 'special' (Grant 1984a; Hill 1996). However the validity of using unusual configurations of skeletal material in the identification of ritual is unproven and consequently this approach provides little more than a convenient way of dividing Iron Age deposits into 'atypical' and 'typical' at initial analysis. This division is based on deposit content and articulation level and fails to

Figure 7.1 Pit 923, from Danebury showing the mass of material in various states of articulation (reproduced with the kind permission of the Danebury Trust).

consider taphonomic modification. Therefore this demarcation may oversimplify these heterogeneous groups of material, as it is possible that all deposits exhibit structure in their treatment and provide evidence of human decision making far beyond a mere concern for optimal disposal. Consequently this research involves the analysis of material from a range of deposits, both those defined as ritually significant and domestic. A holistic analysis of taphonomic modification has the potential to reveal the choices made in the pre-depositional treatment of different classes of remains and the way in which these are a reflection of the relationship between humans and animals.

Taphonomic Modifications

This section discusses issues surrounding preservation in order to demonstrate the potential contribution of taphonomic analysis and to highlight possible problems and solutions in data collection, analysis and interpretation. A complete discussion of taphonomy cannot be presented within the confines of this paper and therefore only a shortened summary of each process is offered.

Gnawing

Gnawing is often the most common and earliest occurring of taphonomic processes (Fernández-Jalvo et al. 2002; 355). This modification is generally indicative of ground extract bones from subterranean contexts. Canids habitually gnaw all bones, including skulls, mandibles and horn cores. Other agents of gnawing include humans (Binford 1981, 147), pigs (Greenfield 1988) and, to a lesser extent, deer (Kahlke 1990; Kierdorf 1994; Sutcliffe 1977) and other non-carnivorous ungulates (Brain 1967; Fernández-Jalvo et al. 2002, 356; Sutcliffe 1973). Depending on scavenger and tooth class, a range of marks can be produced including striations, furrows, pits, punctures, square-based grooves and ragged edges (Buikstra and Ubelaker 1994, 98; Fisher 1995; Smith 2006). In spite of the variation in marks, gnawing is easily distinguished from other taphonomic processes when using low powered magnification (Fisher 1995). Studies have demonstrated that scavengers gnaw bones in patterned ways (Bonnischen 1973; Haynes 1980; Hill

1976; Miller 1969; 1975; Sutcliffe 1973, 1977) by targeting areas rich in cancellous bone such as epiphyses, vertebral bodies and iliac crests (Bochenski and Tornberg 2003; Brain 1980; 1981, 21; Gifford-Gonzales 1989; Haynes 1980; Johnson 1989; Laudet and Fosse 2001; Maguire *et al.* 1980). However contrary to this, in studying fossil bones from Spain, Andrews and Fernández-Jalvo (1997, 199) found that although articular ends were favoured by scavengers, there was no relationship between the robusticity of elements and gnawing prevalence.

Poorly preserved bone tends to exhibit less evidence of gnawing and experiments by Haynes (1980) demonstrated that severe weathering obscures gnawing through the removal of the outer layer of lamellar bone. However Potts (1986) counters this, as his studies indicated both cut and gnaw-marks to be evident on severely weathered bone. Ground level exposure can take place for extended periods without gnawing occurring, as demonstrated in an experiment by Andrews and Cook (1985, 679), where no gnawing evidence was present on a well preserved cow skeleton exposed for 7½ years in Britain. Therefore the nature of the environment and its fauna has a substantial affect on the degree of gnawing within an assemblage.

Weathering

Weathering is defined as the process whereby microscopic organic and inorganic bone components are separated and destroyed by physical and chemical agents operating *in situ*, once flesh and connecting tissue have degraded (Behrensmeyer 1978). This modification is strongly indicative of sub-aerial exposure, as most analysts agree that the impact of weathering in subterranean contexts is negligible (e.g. Behrensmeyer 1978; Maat 1993). The process is characterised by the cracking, exfoliation, splitting and disintegration of bone (Fisher 1995; Steele and Carson 1989; White 2000, 411) and split-line cracks on antlers and horns (Dunbar *et al.* 1989). Cracking is generally organised longitudinally, and is most abundant on long bone shafts, eventually leading to split-line fractures (Andrews and Fernández-Jalvo 1997; Tappen 1969; 1971; 1976). Experiments indicate that weathering is a progressive and irreversible process that follows a linear pattern regardless of environment (Andrews 1995; Behrensmeyer 1978; Brain 1967; Isaac 1967; Sokal and Rohlf 1969, 12; Tappen and Peske 1970; Voorhies 1969).

Exposure of bone does not always cause weathering cracks, as experiments have demonstrated that skeletal material can be rapidly buried through disturbance (Andrews 1995; Behrensmeyer 1978) and short term exposure in mild environments leaves no evidence of weathering (Lyman 1994, 364). A range of studies has highlighted causes of variation in preservation in different environments (Hill 1989). Sunlight, freezing, vegetation, temperature and texture of the sediment; microbial activity and repeated wetting and drying all impact upon weathering rates (Brain 1981; Brothwell 1981, 7; Child 1995; Guadelli and Ozouf 1994; Hedges 2002; Janaway 1990; Lam 1992; Littleton 2000; Lyman 1994, 358; Micozzi 1986; Nicholson 1996; Ortner *et al.* 1972; Tappen 1994; Von Endt and Ortner 1984). Bone degrades more quickly in open habitats due to wide temperature and moisture fluctuations whereas consistently very moist or dry environments decelerate the process (Behrensmeyer 1978; Hedges 2002) as does shelter (Janaway 1987).

Experiments have also demonstrated that boiling increases the porosity of bone and consequently increases the weathering rate, although conventional boiling times of 1-9 hours have very little effect (Roberts *et al.* 2002). The shape of elements or parts of elements is another contributing factor (Henderson 1987). Tubular elements like long bones are more susceptible to weathering with compact elements (such as carpals) being less frequently affected (Giffford-Gonzales 1989; Lambert *et al.* 1985; Potts 1986; Von Endt and Ortner 1984). Weathering evidence is consequently usually most common on long bones and elements such as the pelvis, mandible, scapula and calcaneus and when all elements are assessed, Potts (1986) has demonstrated that results tend to be biased towards a lack of weathering. In spite of the range of factors affecting the rate of weathering, experiments by Miller (1975) have shown a statistically significant correlation between exposure duration and weathering stage.

Trampling

Trampling results from the disturbance of skeletal material on the ground surface by human and animal agents. This causes shallow, sub-parallel striations on bones, due to the etching of material by soil particles (Andrews 1995, 148; Andrews and Fernández-Jalvo 1997; Behrensmeyer *et al.* 1986; Courtin and Villa 1982; Fiorillo 1989; Olsen and Shipman 1988). As striations are not created by hooves, which are softer than bone, but rather by particles in the soil, certain sediments induce greater evidence of trampling. Effects tend to be more severe in sandy, coarse sediments (Behrensmeyer *et al.* 1989; Denys 2002; Fiorillo 1989). Evidence of trampling is strongly indicative of (at least) short term exposure of bone at ground surface level.

The effects of trampling have often been marginalised in archaeological research (Behrensmeyer *et al.* 1989). However some researchers have cited the process as being a major cause of fragmentation (e.g. David 1990; Haynes 1980; Lyman 1994, 377; Stiner *et al.* 1995; Walters 1988). Spiral fractures, suggestive of fresh bone breakage and longitudinal fractures, indicative of dry bone breakage have been proposed as evidence for trampling (Agenbroad 1989; Saunders 1977). However, experiments by Fiorillo (1989), Johnson (1989) and Outram (2001) have demonstrated that such fractures and patterns of recovery have a range of causes, including butchery for marrow extraction (spiral fractures) and cryoturbation (longitudinal fractures).

It has commonly been stated that striations caused by trampling can at times be confused with cut-marks (e.g. Behrensmeyer *et al.* 1986; Bunn 1981; Fiorillo 1984, 1989; Lyman 1994, 377; Oliver 1989; Olsen and Shipman 1988; Potts and Shipman 1981). However, research has demonstrated that trampling evidence can be distinguished from butchery marks and sedimentary abrasion, as trampling tends to cause large numbers of closely spaced, shallow striations on affected fragments, exhibiting considerable variation in depth, width and direction (Andrews 1995; Andrews and Cook 1985; Olsen and Shipman 1988). Research also indicates that smaller skeletal elements, such as carpals and tarsals generally exhibit less trampling evidence, probably as they easily become covered by sediment (Olsen and Shipman 1988; Potts 1986). Following this, exposure of bones need not always induce trampling marks, as skeletal material can be rapidly buried in soft soils (Fiorillo 1989; Olsen and Shipman 1988), areas with dense vegetation protect bones (Fiorillo 1989) and some zones within sites are less commonly accessed.

Abrasion

Abrasion is defined as the gradual erosion of a bone's surface by any agent through physical force (Bromage 1984) and is characterised by smoothness, progressing to a glossy polish through the removal of external lamellar bone (Behrensmeyer 1982). In addition, broken edges become smooth and rounded (Behrensmeyer 1988) and a loss of surface detail occurs (Behrensmeyer 1990). Abrasion has a diverse aetiology and although most causes are strongly indicative of ground surface exposure, as noted below, some processes occur in subterranean contexts. Causes include contact with flowing water (Bromage 1984; Denys 2002; Nicholson 1992), human and animal movement (Andrews and Fernández-Jalvo 1997; Argast *et al.* 1987; Brain 1981, 15; Haynes 1980; Lyman 1994, 381), carnivore licking (Haynes and Stanford 1984), using bone as a tool (Fisher 1995), exposure to acidic conditions (Gordon and Buikstra 1981), earthworm activity (Armour-Chelu and Andrews 1994) and the churning of material in shallow subterranean contexts (Haynes 1980). In general it is very difficult to differentiate between causes of abrasion (Olsen and Shipman 1988), although Bromage (1984) attempted to characterise the micromorphology of different sources. Research has demonstrated that weathered material is more susceptible to abrasion (Andrews 1995, Behrensmeyer 1990; Cook 1995) due to loss of elasticity, once the organic component of bone has degraded (Martill 1990).

Fracturing

Longitudinal and spiral fractures were also recorded. Longitudinal fractures can arise through the weakening of bone by weathering or erosion combined with trampling or disturbance (Andrews and Fernández-Jalvo 1997; Tappen 1969, 1971, 1976). Spiral fractures can be caused by the trampling of fresh bones (Agenbroad 1989; Saunders 1977). However these distinctive fractures may also result from long bones being intentionally smashed when fresh for the extraction of marrow (Outram 2001). Consequently interpretation of these fracture patterns is complex, as both can occur independently of agents of trampling and are not always indicative of sub-aerial exposure.

Summary

Consideration of taphonomy now plays an important role in the analysis and interpretation of human and faunal material. However, in spite of this, most taphonomic processes remain far from fully understood. Standardised stages and vocabulary are required for all aforementioned processes to enable reliable comparisons, although the diversity of marks made by processes such as trampling and abrasion have complicated such attempts in the past (Fisher 1995). The complexity of patterns of preservation in similar contexts has long been recognised (e.g. Rietti and Ruffer 1912), and the diversity and unpredictability of taphonomic processes must not be underestimated. The tendency to look for comprehensive laws in bone preservation is erroneous (Hill 1989), as every microenvironment has a unique suite of factors influencing preservation. Patterns in preservation must be seen as resulting from a multifarious interaction between wide-ranging variables (Henderson 1987). Consequently all factors affecting the rate and nature of processes must be carefully considered in interpretation, as reconstructing taphonomic histories is a complex task. However, except in certain exceptional circumstances, the taphonomic modifications described above are indicative of sub-aerial exposure and in analysing a range of taphonomic processes on a substantial sample, the patterns revealed reflect intentional treatment by human agents.

Methodology

This research presents a focused taphonomic analysis of remains from the sites of Winnall Down and Danebury, in order to shed light on the conceptual relationship between human and animal bones, as reflected in their pre-depositional treatment. Data collection was undertaken using a 10x magnification hand lens under the light of a 60 watt lamp. Although taphonomic overprinting undoubtedly caused some modifications to be overlooked (Shipman 1989), every effort was made to study the entire surface of each fragment systematically.

Table 7.1 Stages for the identification of different levels of gnawing severity.

Stage 1, Slight gnawing, with intermittent pits, punctures, furrows or square-edged grooves evident on the bone.
Stage 2, Moderate gnawing, with around half of the affected edge of a fragment covered with gnaw-marks. Ragged edges begin to appear in worst affected areas.
Stage 3, Severe gnawing, with at least 80% of the affected edge covered with gnaw-marks. This causes the removal of epiphyses on long bones and will leave a ragged edge at the affected end of the diaphysis.

Feature type, depth, element, species, age class, burning and butchery were also recorded for each fragment, as these affect the prevalence of other processes and may have a role in dictating modes of treatment. As no accepted standards exist for the recording of gnawing, the author's own stages were applied (Table 7.1).

Data collection for weathering used Behrensmeyer's (1978) stages for medium/large mammals, with the most advanced stage covering more than 1cm² of weathering damage recorded. Although these stages impose arbitrary divisions on a continuous process, they remain the most appropriate way of quantifying weathering, as although the temporal meaning of weathering data has been questioned (Potts 1986), for the purposes of this research it is not necessary to put a timescale to exposure, but rather to note variation in different classes of remains. Due to the complexity of interpreting trampling, a presence/absence analysis was employed rather than grading severity. This was deemed appropriate as severity of trampling does not reflect exposure duration. When striations were evident, particular care was taken in distinguishing them from other modifications following the guidance of Andrews and Cook (1985). Biases relating to soil type were not considered to have had a substantial effect on the degree of trampling evidence, as both Danebury and Winnall Down are located on the Hampshire chalkland.

Abrasion was also scored as either present or absent. This was deemed appropriate as the process need not occur in a linear pathway and the rounding of fragmented ends of bones cannot be compared to the polished appearance of a section of diaphysis in terms of severity. As most causes of abrasion indicate exposure, it was not critical to differentiate processes for the purposes of this research. Fiorillo's (1988) abrasion indices were not employed in this research, as stages were produced using Nebraskan material and cannot be confidently applied to British material, as they are not experimentally determined (Cook 1995). For the purposes of this paper, longitudinal fractures and spiral breaks were not distinguished, as both may provide evidence for trampling. Fractures were recorded for mandibles and all post-cranial elements except for carpals and tarsals, which are generally too small for fracturing to occur through trampling. Bones of the cranium were also not included, as fragments were generally too small to be sure of the direction of the fracture.

The Sample

9,493 bone fragments were analysed of which 5,183 (967 human, 4,216 animal) were from Winnall Down and 4,310 from Danebury (1,934 human, 2,376 animal). These sites were selected as they are both in the heartland of the central/southern region that has been the focus of so much research on the deposition of skeletal material (and little on bone modification) in the past. The prehistoric settlement of Winnall Down, Hampshire is situated less than 2km north-east of Winchester and was fully excavated in 1976-9 as part of the M3 construction project. The main occupation of the site occurred throughout the Iron Age and early Roman period (Fasham 1985). Excavations yielded in excess of 14,000 animal bone fragments (Maltby 1985). Human skeletons from the site represent 31 individuals with a further 78 instances of scattered bone being recovered (Bayley *et al.* 1985). The hillfort of Danebury is situated near Andover in the chalkland of Hampshire. The site was settled throughout the Iron Age with occupation peaking in the early and middle phases (Cunliffe 2003, 161-2). In excess of 240,000 animal bone fragments were recovered from the site (Grant 1991). Three hundred depositions of human remains representing a minimum of 91 individuals were recovered, although in reality, due to the large amount of disarticulated material, the figure is likely to be far higher (Cunliffe 1991b).

A selection of features containing only humans, only animals and both humans and animals were sampled from Winnall Down. Human remains from features without faunal material were all in an articulated state. The sample of mixed features and features containing only faunal material included both articulated and disarticulated remains, although in various instances features comprised only disarticulated material. Features included quarry pits, scoops and postholes, although the vast majority of sampled remains came from storage pits. This was the case, as the majority of remains from the site derived from these features (Maltby 1985) and they also provided most examples of features containing both human and faunal remains, a crucial feature type for the purposes of this study. Due to incomplete archived material, insufficient human bone was sampled from Winnall Down for statistical testing to be carried out. Therefore two charnel pits that were rich in human bone were sampled from Danebury. Overall 1593 fragments were analysed from features containing only faunal remains, 7405 from mixed features and 495 from features containing only human material.

Analysis

Statistical tests (either Chi² or Mann-Whitney) were systematically applied to the data to reveal patterns in treatment of different classes of remains. Chi² tests of difference were applied for nominal datasets and Mann-Whitney for ordinal datasets. For weathering and gnawing tests, where samples were of sufficient size, all stages were included in the statistical analysis. However, when expected values were prohibitively low, data was pooled to conduct presence/absence analyses. As highlighted in the taphonomy section, research has demonstrated that long bones are more susceptible to weathering and analysis tends to be biased towards a lack of weathering when all elements are included (Giffford-Gonzales 1989, Lambert *et al.* 1985; Potts 1986; Von Endt and Ortner 1984). Consequently, when samples were of a sufficient size, tests concerned with weathering were also conducted on long bones only. Graphs summarising gnawing and weathering do not show stage 0 modification (unmodified material), as the omission of this category increases the clarity of patterns in other stages. However, all unmodified material was included in testing. Details of each statistical test are presented in the appendix.

Initially tests were carried out to assess differences in the prevalence of each modification between humans and animals. Results demonstrate significant differences for weathering (T1, $p = 0.000$), gnawing (T2, $p = 0.000$), abrasion (T3, $p = 0.000$), trampling (T4, $p = 0.000$) and longitudinal/spiral fracturing (T5, $p = 0.000$), with faunal remains being more commonly affected in every instance. This indicates that animal remains were exposed to a greater degree than human skeletal material. A series of tests was undertaken to ascertain whether other factors could account for the apparent differences. The level of articulation is one such factor, as significantly more disarticulated faunal material was sampled than disarticulated human bone (T6, $p = 0.000$). Unsurprisingly the difference in the degree of weathering of articulated and disarticulated fragments is significant (T7, $p = 0.000$), with the former exhibiting less modification. Similar significant differences are evident in gnawing (T8, $p = 0.000$), abrasion (T9, $p = 0.000$), trampling (T10, $p = 0.000$) and longitudinal/spiral fracturing (T11, $p = 0.000$). Therefore articulation levels have a significant effect on bone modification, with disarticulated material exhibiting greater evidence of exposure. This is to be expected, as for bones to remain in articulation, they must be joined by connecting tissue, and would therefore be, to some extent, protected from modification.

To be sure of the effect of articulation levels on modification the difference in weathering of articulated animal and human remains was tested. Results reveal no significant difference (T12, $p = 0.511$). However, testing the difference in weathering in disarticulated remains demonstrates animals to be significantly more modified (T13, $p = 0.000$) and thus exposed to a greater degree. This is also the case when only long bones are analysed (T14, $p = 0.000$). Small numbers of gnawed human bones prevented analysis of gnawing in articulated remains. However, analysis shows a significant difference in disarticulated material (T15, $p = 0.000$), again with faunal remains exhibiting greater evidence of exposure. Differences in the treatment of human and faunal remains are evident in disarticulated material only and consequently the further inclusion of articulated bone groups would only serve to distort results. Therefore further analysis was conducted on disarticulated remains only. The clear difference in modification between disarticulated human and faunal material is summarised in Figures 7.2-7.4.

The clear difference in human and animal modification suggests that no conceptual relationship exists between human and faunal remains in Iron Age Wessex, as it seems that each class of remains was subjected to entirely separate pre-depositional practices. However, in order to take a more thorough, holistic approach to revealing any symbolic connection, analysis is extended to taphonomic variation in material from features which contain both human and faunal remains (referred to as mixed features) and those which contain only faunal material (referred to as uniform features). This analysis has the potential to elucidate how the association of human material affects the way in which faunal material is treated. No testing could be carried out on features containing only humans, as all those sampled contained only articulated or partially articulated material.

As expected weathering (T16, $p = 0.000$), gnawing (T17, $p = 0.000$), abrasion (T18, $p = 0.008$), trampling (T19, $p = 0.000$) and longitudinal/spiral fracturing (T20, $p = 0.000$) are significantly more prevalent in animal rather than human fragments from mixed features. However, distinct differences are also evident in the treatment of faunal remains from mixed features and those from uniform features, with both weathering (T21, $p = 0.000$) and gnawing (T22, $p = 0.003$) being significantly more prevalent in material from uniform features (Figures 7.5 and 7.6). Weathering differences remain significant when only long bones are analysed (T23, $p = 0.000$).

As presented in Figures 7.7 and 7.8, abrasion (T24, $p = 0.008$), trampling (T25, $p = 0.000$) and longitudinal/spiral fracturing (T26, $p = 0.000$) are also all more common on animal bone from uniform features. As all modifications are significantly more frequent on faunal material from uniform features rather than mixed features, the association of human bone appears to impact upon the way that animal remains are treated, with those in association exhibiting significantly less evidence of exposure.

It is not possible to discuss all the research findings within the confines of this paper. However, the results

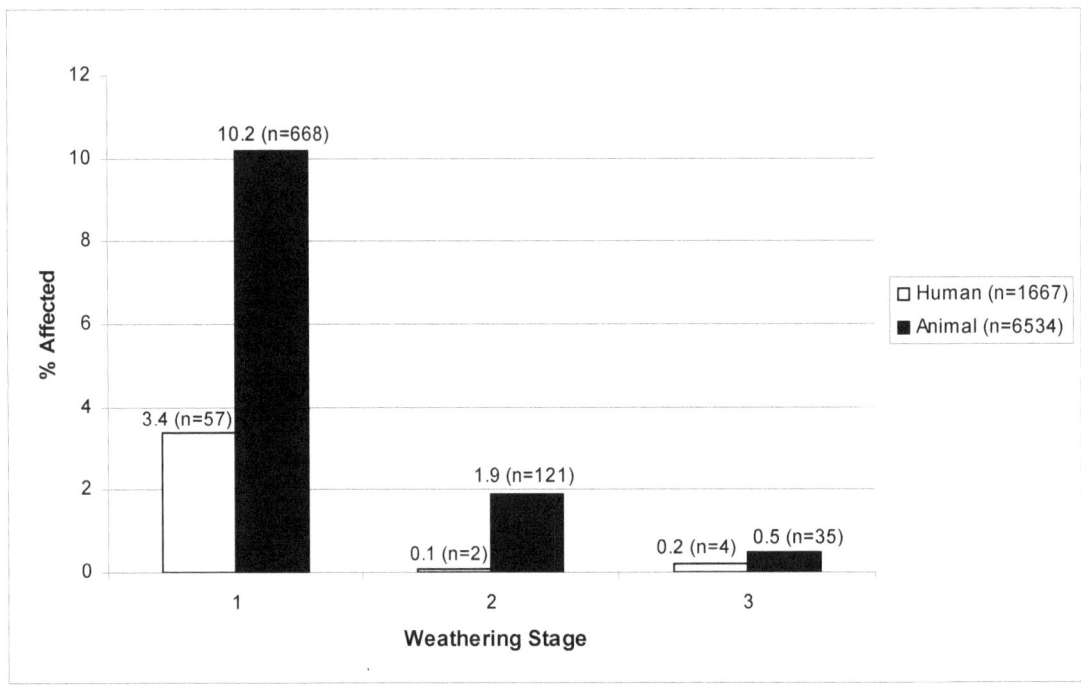

Figure 7.2 The percentage of disarticulated human and faunal remains in different weathering stages (stage 0 not included in order to emphasise patterns in the prevalence of other stages, 87.4% of faunal fragments show no weathering, as do 96.2% of human specimens).

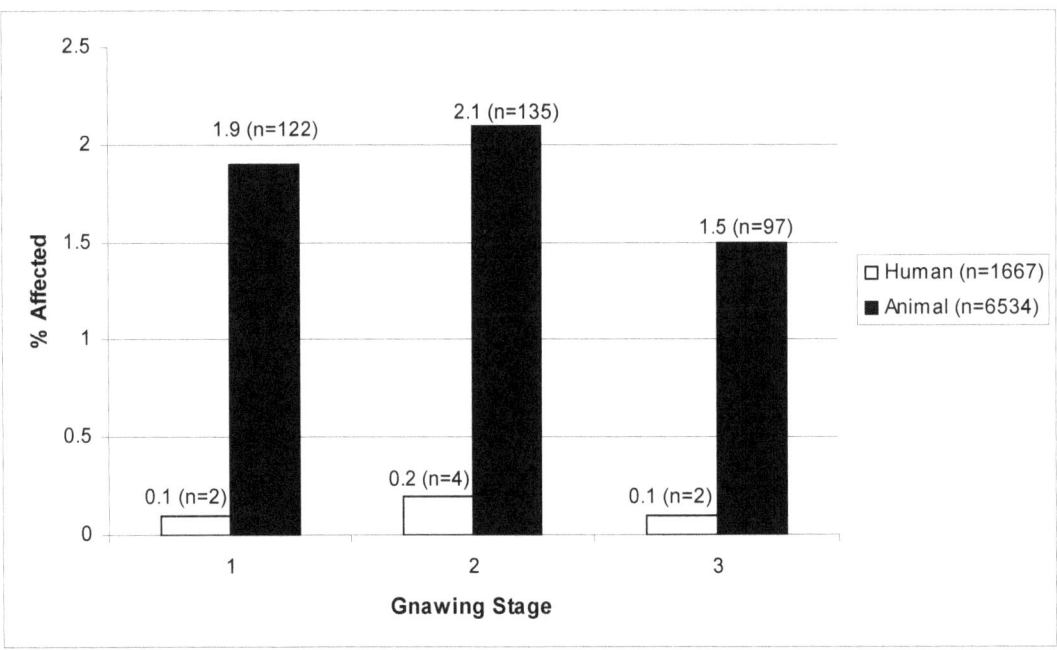

Figure 7.3 The percentage of disarticulated human and faunal remains in different gnawing stages (stage 0 not included in order to emphasise patterns in the prevalence of other stages, 94.6% of faunal fragments exhibit no evidence of gnawing, as do 99.5% of human specimens).

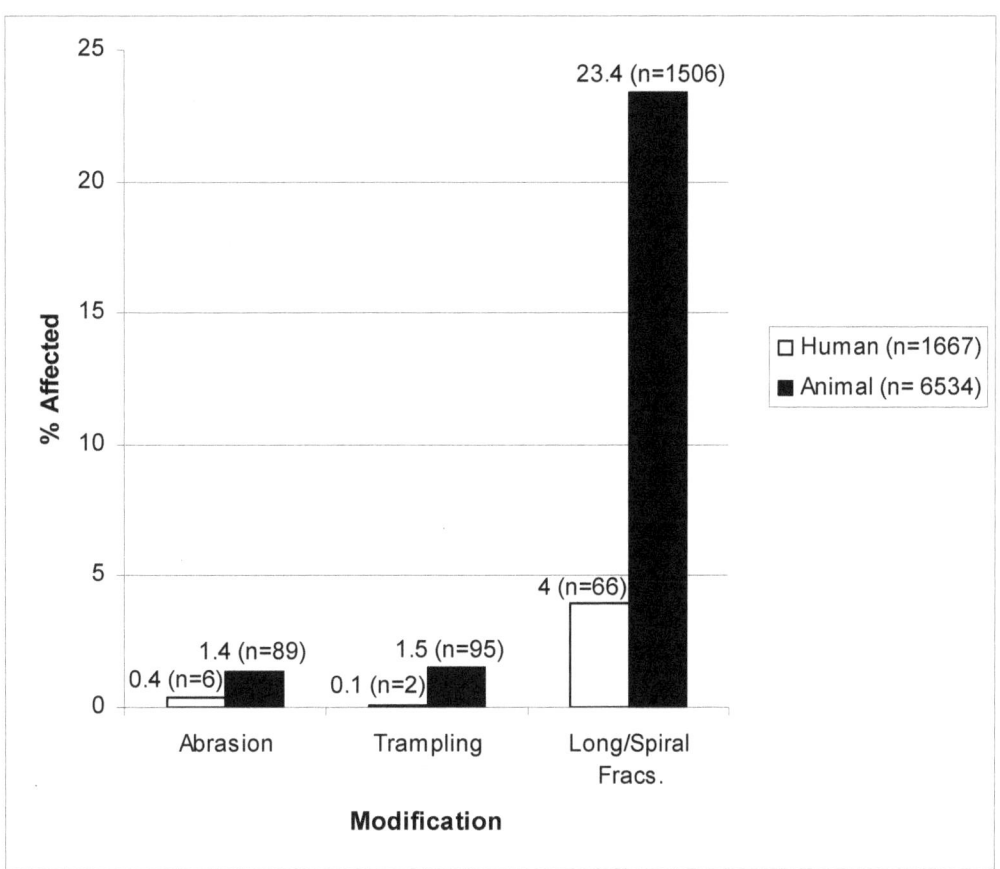

Figure 7.4 The percentage of disarticulated human and faunal remains affected by abrasion, trampling and longitudinal/spiral fracturing.

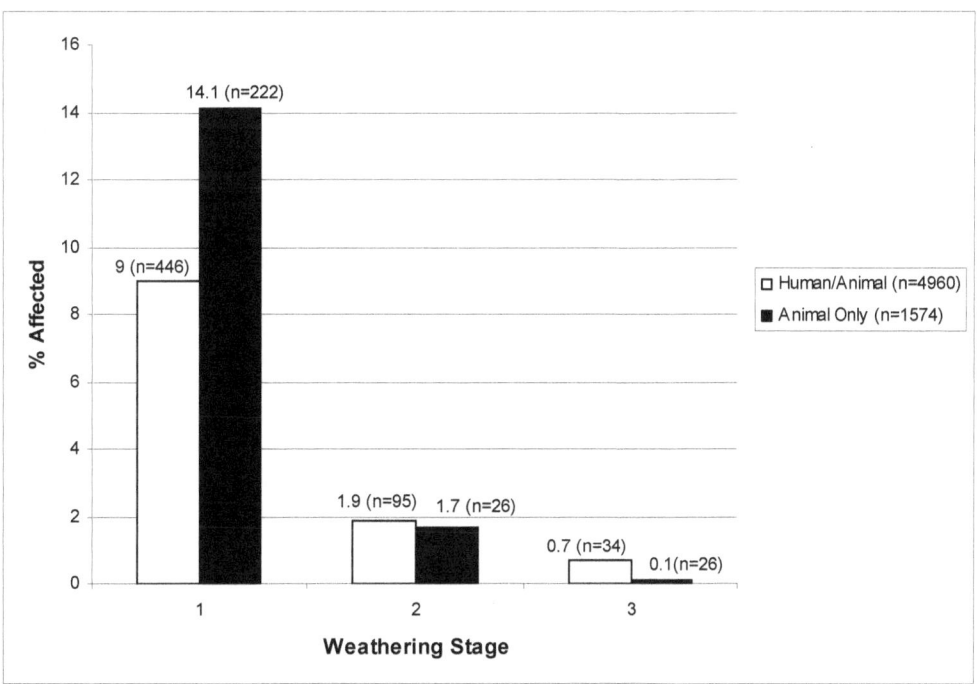

Figure 7.5 The percentage of animal bones in uniform features (those that contain only faunal remains) and mixed features (those that contain both human and faunal remains) in different weathering stages (stage 0 not included in order to emphasise patterns in the prevalence of other stages, 88.4% of remains from mixed features exhibit no weathering evidence, as do 84.1% of fragments from uniform features).

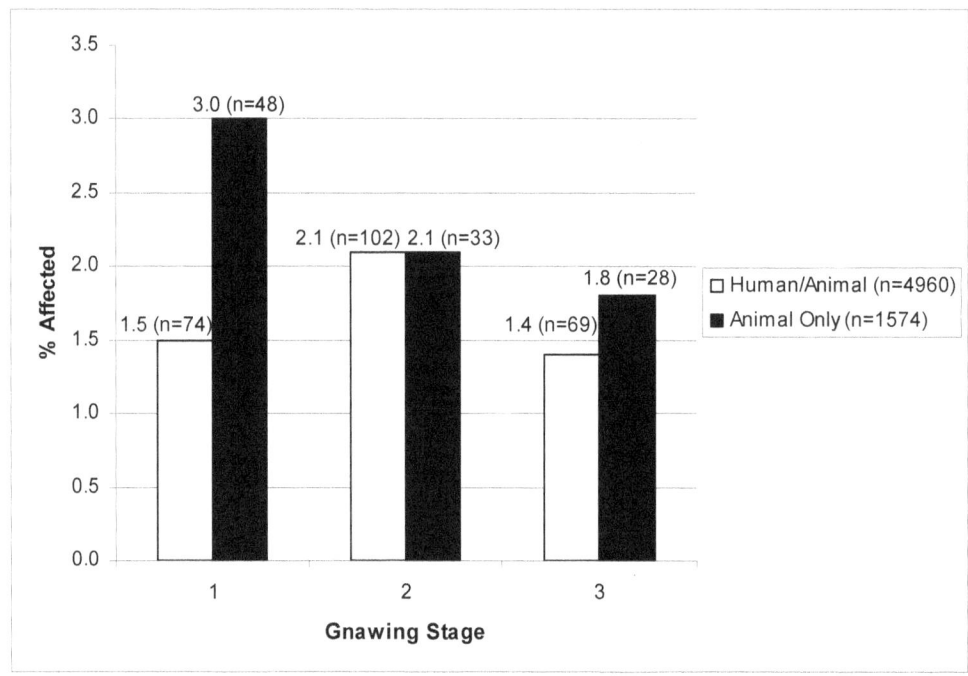

Figure 7.6 The percentage of animal bones from uniform features (those that contain only faunal remains) and mixed features (those that contain both human and faunal remains) in each gnawing stage (stage 0 not included in order to emphasise patterns in the prevalence of other stages, 95% of remains from mixed features exhibit no evidence of gnawing, as do 93.1% of fragments from uniform features).

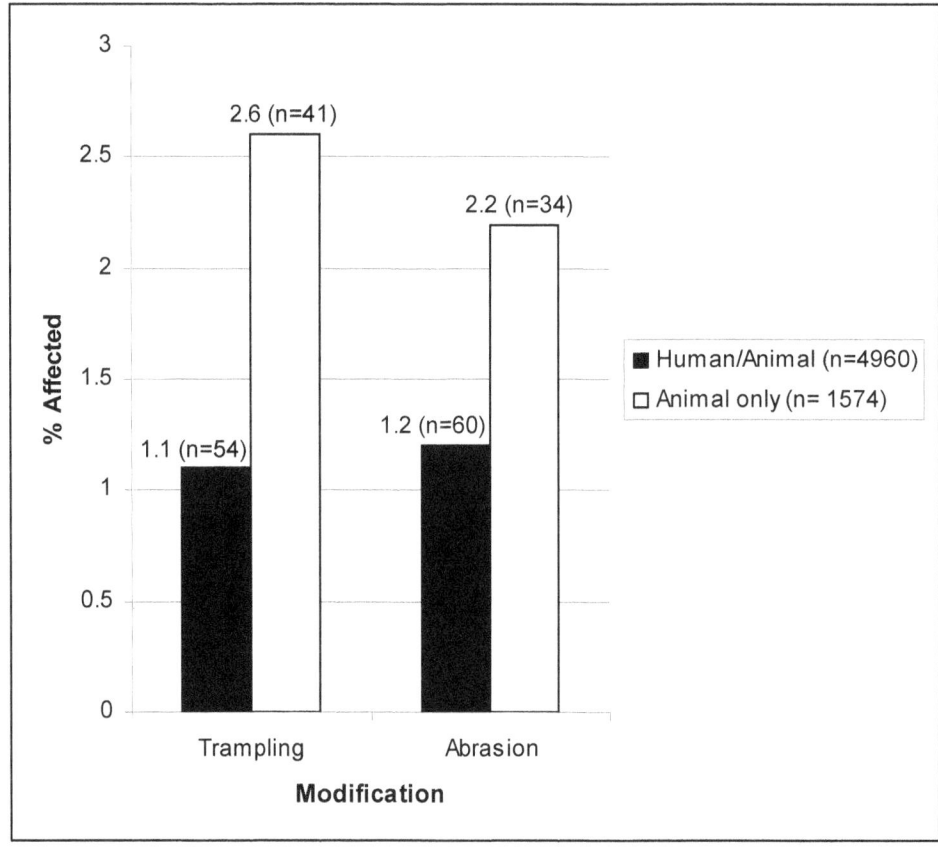

Figure 7.7 The percentage of animal bones from uniform features (those that contain only faunal remains) and mixed features (those that contain both human and faunal remains) that are affected by trampling and abrasion.

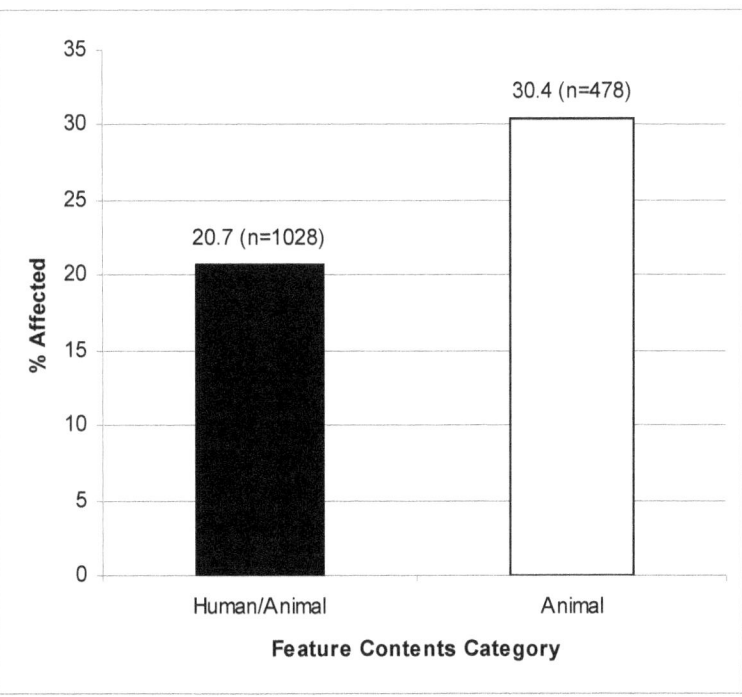

Figure 7.8 The percentage of animal bones from uniform features (those that contain only faunal remains) and mixed features (those that contain both human and faunal remains) that are affected by longitudinal and spiral fracturing. The sample of faunal fragments from mixed features comprised 4960 fragments with uniform features comprising 1574 fragments).

also revealed that dog and horse remains were treated significantly differently from other animals (Madgwick 2008).

Consequently a concentration of one species category (e.g. other animals) in mixed or uniform features could be responsible for the apparent difference in treatment. However, statistical testing revealed that the differences in bone modification in mixed and uniform features transcend species categories. Bones from uniform features exhibit greater evidence of weathering for dog/horse remains (T27, p = 0.000) and other animals (T28, p = 0.000). This remains the case when only including long bones in testing (T29, p = 0.002 for dog/horse, T30, p = 0.007 for other animals). Other modifications are also more prevalent in uniform features for each of the species categories. Gnawing (T31, p = 0.000 for dog/horse, T32, p = 0.038 for other animals), abrasion (T33, p = 0.004 for dog/horse, T34, p = 0.035 for other animals) and trampling (T35, p = 0.001 for dog/horse, T36, p = 0.001 for other animals) are all significantly more common in uniform features. Longitudinal/spiral fracturing reveals the same difference in dog/horse (T37, p = 0.000), although no difference was apparent for other animals (T38, p = 0.591). Therefore the contents of features has a clear effect on the modification of bones (at least for animals), with those from uniform features (those that contain only animal bone) exhibiting greater modification and therefore having been exposed to a significantly greater extent.

Discussion

Data analysis has revealed clear patterns in the taphonomic pathways of different classes of remains. The highly statistically significant results are indicative of prescribed practices in the pre-depositional treatment of skeletal material in Iron Age Wessex. The most striking finding is the differential treatment of disarticulated human and animal remains, with faunal material exhibiting significantly greater evidence of exposure in every instance. All possible sampling and taphonomic biases were systematically discounted from responsibility for this difference. Therefore it is clear that faunal remains were sub-aerially exposed to a significantly greater degree than human skeletal material. These findings emphatically refute the suggestion that human remains were indiscriminately disposed of in the Iron Age (e.g. Bersu 1940; Cunliffe 1991a, 505; Cunnington 1933) and demonstrate that specific considerations were given to the treatment of different classes of remains.

Initially these findings may be considered to suggest entirely unconnected practices in the treatment of the two classes of material, with only the feature in which they were deposited linking them. However, further analysis reveals more complex, inter-related modes of treatment. Results demonstrate that modification of animal bones is significantly more frequent when human remains are not found in association with them. As other factors that could be responsible for this difference have been discounted, evidence suggests a distinct practice whereby faunal remains deposited in features that contain humans, are exposed to a lesser degree. As statistical testing has demonstrated that humans display far less evidence of exposure, this can be viewed as faunal material being subjected to a mode of handling akin to that of the humans with which they are deposited and asserts that the two classes of remains are in fact inherently linked in their pre-depositional treatment.

The nature of the relationship of human and faunal remains may be bi-directional, with the association of animals affecting the way that humans are treated, just as the association of humans affects the way in which animals are treated. However, no analysis could be undertaken on features containing only human remains, as all those sampled comprised only articulated material. In spite of the quantity of bone fragments, Hill (1995, 54) has highlighted that it is, in fact, very rare for disarticulated human remains to be deposited without the association of faunal remains. This in itself provides interesting indications of how the association of faunal material affects the treatment of human remains. Bones from features containing only human remains exhibit the least evidence of exposure, as attested to by all remains being in at least a partially articulated state. The taphonomic analysis demonstrates that human material in mixed features provides greater evidence of exposure. Faunal remains from mixed features display even more modification and finally animal bones from features containing only animal material exhibit the greatest evidence of exposure.

The findings demonstrate that formalised modes of treatment relating to specific combinations of human and faunal material were employed in Iron Age Wessex. This indicates that neither class of remains was disposed of indiscriminately and that the bones of animals had far greater importance in society than mere waste material. These practices are suggestive of a society that prizes faunal species far beyond their value as domesticates, and whose relationship with animals runs far more deeply than that of consumer and consumed. This is demonstrated in the way that remains were not disposed of in the most effortless, convenient way, but rather time, consideration and energy was invested in the treatment of different classes of remains.

Analysis demonstrates that, in Iron Age Wessex, humans and animals were conceived of in fundamentally different ways, but not as entirely unconnected entities. Patterns in the treatment of remains suggest that symbolic relationships between humans and animals were deeply embedded in the fabric of society. Although there is a clear separation between humans and animals, for remains in mixed features, there is a degree of blurring of the boundary between human and animal identities, as indicated by the juxtaposition of modes of treatment. The conceptual proximity of humans and animals is demonstrated in the manner in which bones are treated in a similar way to the opposing class of remains when deposited in association. This might indicate recognition of a developed, almost human-like identity of animals. The symbolic importance of animals in Celtic life and ritual is well supported. Green (1992, 92) states that animals were of great importance as food, in hunting and in warfare and were of equal importance in death and religion in Iron Age society. The enhanced status of animals is alluded to in their prevalence in Celtic art (Green 1992). However, their social role in death is far more complex than previous suggestions of animal sacrifice (Grant 1984a; 1984b; Green 1992, 3; Holleyman 1937; Wait 1985, 153) or fertility rite relating to grain storage (Barrett 1989; Bradley 1981; 1984, 159; 1990, 183; Cunliffe 1983, 164; Cunliffe and Poole 1995), as specific modes of treatment are adhered to for all classes of remains from different features, not just those recovered from so-called 'special' deposits.

This research is concerned with the treatment of human and faunal remains between the death of individuals and incorporation into forming deposits and has demonstrated the close physical and conceptual relationship between humans and animals. It is highly plausible that this symbolic relationship would also be apparent in the treatment of animals during life. Production and consumption practices may also be permeated by rules and culturally prescribed behaviours that reflect the social value of domesticates that extends beyond meat, milk, wool, draught or hunting companion.

The aim of this paper is not to reveal the exact nature of social practices involving the pre-depositional treatment of different classes of remains. It is rather to reveal how a holistic taphonomic analysis of osseous material can contribute to our understanding of the perceptions of humans and animals within the communities of Iron Age Wessex. Human and faunal material was treated significantly differently within the sample and therefore remains were clearly distinguished and not subjected to homogeneous practices. However, the conceptual proximity of humans and animals is attested to by their closely related modes of treatment when deposited together. Without fine-grained taphonomic analysis, this relationship in pre-depositional treatment would remain unnoticed. Therefore in this age of a taphonomy-aware zooarchaeology, a greater focus on bone modification beyond the level of butchery and burning is required. Fleeting comments on the surface preservation of material have limited interpretative potential and consequently all modifications must be quantified in the same way as butchery and burning, as other taphonomic modifications are equally valid as interpretative tools. Processes such as weathering, abrasion, trampling and to a lesser extent gnawing have been marginalised in previous research, as they have often been regarded as incidental and not the product of human decision making. However just as cultural norms and values are reflected in production and consumption, so too are they in practices relating to deposition. Therefore these processes must become an integral part of the analysis and interpretation of faunal assemblages, in order to gain more complete biographies of skeletal material.

Acknowledgements

My thanks go to Jacqui Mulville, James Morris and Mark Maltby for their thoughtful comments on drafts of this paper and to Jo Sofaer for her guidance while conducting the research. In addition, I am indebted to David Allen and Kay Ainsworth for assistance with accessing the material and Siân Iles for providing much needed support throughout.

Bibliography

Agenbroad, L. D. (1989) Spiral fractured mammoth bone from non-human taphonomic processes at Hot Springs mammoth site. In. R. Bonnischen and M. H. Sorg (eds) *Bone Modification*, 139-148. Orono, Maine, Centre for the Study of the First Americans, Institute for Quaternary Studies, University of Maine.

Andrews, P. (1995) Experiments in taphonomy. *Journal of Archaeological Science* 22, 147-153.

Andrews, P. and Cook, J. (1985) Natural modifications to bone in a temperate setting. *Man* 20, 675-691.

Andrews, P. and Fernández-Jalvo, Y. (1997) Surface modifications of the Sima los Huesos fossil humans. *Journal of Human Evolution* 33, 191-217.

Argast, S. Farlow, J. D., Gabet, R. M., and Brinkman, D. L. (1987) Transport-induced abrasion of fossil reptilian teeth: implications for the existence of tertiary dinosaurs in the Hell Creek Formation, Montana. *Geology* 15, 927–930.

Armour-Chelu, M. and Andrews, P. 1994. Some effects of bioturbation by earthworms (oligochaeta) on archaeological sites. *Journal of Archaeological Science* 21, 433-443.

Barrett, J. C. (1989) Food, gender and metal: questions of social reproduction. In. M. L. S. Sorensen and R. Thomas (eds.) *The Bronze Age-Iron Age Transition in Europe,* 304-320. Oxford. British Archaeological Report International Series 484.

Bayley, J. Fasham, P. J. and Powell, F. V. H. (1985) The human skeletal remains. In. P. J. Fasham (ed) *The Prehistoric Settlement at Winnall Down, Winchester*, 119-122. Winchester, Hampshire Field Club Monograph 2.

Behrensmeyer, A. K. (1978) Taphonomic and ecological information from bone weathering. *Paleobiology* 4, 150-162.

Behrensmeyer, A. K. (1982) Time resolution in fluvial vertebrate assemblages. *Paleobiology* 8, 211-227.

Behrensmeyer, A. K. (1988) Vertebrate preservation in fluvial channels. *Palaeogeography, Palaeoclimatology, Palaeoecology* 63, 183-199.

Beherensmeyer, A. K. (1990) Bones. In. D. E. G. Briggs and P. R. Crowther (eds) *Palaeobiology: a Synthesis*, 232-235. Oxford, Blackwell.

Behrensmeyer, A. K., Gordon, K. D. and Yanagi, G. T. (1986) Trampling as a cause of bone surface damage and pseudo-cutmarks. *Nature* 319, 768-771.

Behrensmeyer, A. K., Gordon, K. D. and Yanagi, G. T. (1989) Non-human bone modification in Miocene fossils from Pakistan. In. R. Bonnischen and M. H. Sorg (eds) *Bone Modification*, 99-120. Orono, Maine, Centre for the Study of the First Americans, Institute for Quaternary Studies, University of Maine.

Bersu, G. (1940) Excavations at Little Woodbury, Wiltshire, part 1. *Proceedings of the Prehistoric Society* 6, 30-111.

Binford, L. R. (1981) *Bones: Ancient Men and Modern Myths*. New York, Academic Press.

Bochenski, Z. M. and Tornberg, R. (2003) Fragmentation and preservation of bird bones in uneaten food remains of the gyrfalcon *Falco rusticolus*. *Journal of Archaeological Science* 30, 1665-1671.

Bonnischen, R. (1973) Some operational aspects of human and animal bone alteration. In. B. M. Gilbert (ed) *Mammalian Osteoarchaeology*, 9-24. Columbia, Missouri, Missouri Archaeological Society.

Bradley, R. (1981) Economic growth and social change: two examples from prehistoric Europe. In. A. Sheridan and G. Bailey (eds) *Economic Archaeology*, 231-238. Oxford, British Archaeological Report International Series 96.

Bradley, R. (1984) *The Social Foundations of British Prehistory*. London, Longman.

Bradley, R. (1990) *The Passage of Arms: an Archaeological Analysis of Prehistoric Hoards and Votive Deposits*. Cambridge, Cambridge University Press.

Brain, C. K. (1967) Bone weathering and the problem of pseudotools. *South African Journal of Science* 63, 97-99.

Brain, C. K. (1980) Some criteria for the recognition of bone collecting agencies in African caves. In. A. K. Behrensmeyer and A. P. Hill (eds) *Fossils in the Making*, 107–130. Chicago, University of Chicago Press.

Brain, C. K. (1981) *The Hunters or the Hunted? An Introduction to African Cave Taphonomy*. Chicago, University of Chicago Press.

Bromage, T. G. (1984) Interpretation of scanning electron microscopic images of abraded forming bone surfaces. *American Journal of Physical Anthropology* 64, 161-178.

Brothwell, D. (1981) *Digging up Bones*. New York, Cornell University Press.

Buikstra, J. and Ubelaker, D. (1994) *Standards for Data Collection from Human Skeletal Remains*. Fayetteville, Arkansas Archaeological Survey.

Bunn, H. T. (1981) Archaeological evidence for meat-eating by Plio-Pleistocene hominids from Koobi Fora and Olduvai Gorge. *Nature* 291, 574–577.

Child, A. M. (1995) Towards an understanding of the decomposition of bone in the archaeological environment. *Journal of Archaeological Science* 22, 165–174.

Cook, E. (1995) Sedimentology and Taphonomy of Wealden (Lower Cretaceous) Bone Accumulations. University of Bristol, PhD Thesis.

Courtin, J. and Villa, P. (1982) Une expérience de piétinement. *Bulletin Société Préhistorique Française* 79, 117–23.

Cunliffe, B. (1983) *Danebury: Anatomy of an Iron Age Hillfort*. London, Batsford.

Cunliffe, B. (1991a) *Iron Age Communities in Britain*, Third edition. London, Routledge.

Cunliffe, B. (1991b) Population and behaviour. In. B. Cunliffe and C. Poole (eds.) *Danebury: an Iron Age Hillfort in Hampshire. Volume 5. 1979-1988: the Finds*, 418-425. London, Council for British Archaeology Research Report 73.

Cunliffe, B. (1995) Behaviour and belief. In. B. Cunliffe (ed.) *Danebury: an Iron Age Hillfort in Hampshire. Volume 6: a Hillfort Community in Perspective*, 72-79. London, Council for British Archaeology Research Report 102.

Cunliffe, B. (2003) *Danebury Hillfort*. Stroud, Tempus.

Cunliffe, B. and Poole, C. (1995) Pits and propitiation. In. B. Cunliffe (ed.) *Danebury: An Iron Age Hillfort in Hampshire. Volume 6: A Hillfort Community in Perspective*, 80-88. London, Council for British Archaeology Research Report 102.

Cunnington, M. 1933. Excavations in Yarnbury Castle Camp. *Wiltshire Archaeological Magazine* 46, 198-213.

David, B. (1990) How was this bone burnt? In. S. Solomon, I. Davidson and D. Watson (eds) *Problem Solving in Taphonomy: Archaeological and Palaeontological Studies from Europe, Africa and Oceania vol. 2*, 65–79. Brisbane, St. Lucia Press.

Denys, C. (2002) Taphonomy and experimentation. *Archaeometry* 44, 469-484.

Dunbar, J. S., Webb, D. S. and Cring, D. (1989) Culturally and naturally modified bones from a Paleo-Indian site in the Aucilla River, North Florida. In. R. Bonnischen and M. H. Sorg (eds) *Bone Modification*, 473-498. Orono, Maine, Centre for the Study of the First Americans, Institute for Quaternary Studies, University of Maine.

Fasham, P. J. (1985) The development of the site. In. P.J. Fasham (ed.) *The Prehistoric Settlement at Winnall Down, Winchester*, 9-45. Winchester, Hampshire Field Club Monograph 2.

Fernández-Jalvo, Y. (1992) Tafonomia de microvertebrados del complejo carstico de Atapuerca (Burgos). Universidad Complutense de Madrid, PhD Thesis.

Fernández-Jalvo, Y., Sanchez-Chillum, B., Andrews, P., Fernández-Lopez, P. and Alcala Martinez, L. (2002) Morphological taphonomic transformations of fossil bones in continental environments and repercussions on their chemical composition. *Archaeometry* 44, 353-361.

Fiorillo, A. R. (1984) An introduction to the identification of trample marks. *Current Research* 1, 47-48.

Fiorillo, A. R. (1989) An experimental study of trampling: implications for the fossil record. In. R. Bonnischen and M. H. Sorg (eds) *Bone Modification*, 61-72. Orono, Maine, Centre for the Study of the First Americans, Institute for Quaternary Studies, University of Maine.

Fisher, J. W. (1995) Bone surface modifications in zooarchaeology. *Journal of Archaeological Method and Theory* 2, 7-68.

Gifford-Gonzales, D. P. (1989) Ethnographic analogues for interpreting modified bones; some cases from East Africa. In. R. Bonnischen and M. H. Sorg (eds.) *Bone Modification*, 179-246. Orono, Maine, Centre for the Study of the First Americans, Institute for Quaternary Studies, University of Maine.

Gordon, C. C. and Buikstra, J. E. (1981) Soil pH, bone preservation and sampling bias at mortuary sites. *American Antiquity* 46, 566-571.

Guadelli, J. L. and Ozouf, J. C. (1994) Études expérimentales de l'action du gel sur les restes fauniques. Premiers resultants. *Artefacts* 9, 47–56.

Grant, A. (1984a) Animal husbandry. In. B. Cunliffe (ed.) *Danebury: an Iron Age Hillfort in Hampshire. Volume 2. The Excavations 1969-1978: the Finds*, 496-548. London, Council for British Archaeology Research Report 52.

Grant, A. (1984b) Survival or sacrifice? A critical appraisal of animal bones in Britain in the Iron Age. In. C. Grigson and J. Clutton-Brock (eds.) *Animals and Archaeology 4: Husbandry in Europe*, 221-227. Oxford, British Archaeological Report. International Series 227.

Grant, A. (1991) Animal husbandry. In. B. Cunliffe and C. Poole (eds.) *Danebury: an Iron Age hillfort in Hampshire, Volume 5, 1979-1988: the Finds*, 447-487. London, Council for British Archaeology Research Report 73.

Green, M. (1992) *Animals in Celtic Life and Myth*. London, Routledge.

Greenfield, H. J. (1988) Bone consumption by pigs in a contemporary Serbian village: implications for the interpretation of prehistoric faunal assemblages. *Journal of Field Archaeology* 15, 473-479.

Hambleton, E. (1999) *Animal Husbandry Regimes in Iron Age Britain: a Comparative Study of Faunal Assemblages from British Iron Age Sites*. Oxford, British Archaeological Report British Series 282.

Haynes, G. (1980) Evidence of carnivore gnawing on Pleistocene and recent mammalian bones. *Paleobiology* 6, 341-351.

Haynes, G. and Stanford, D. (1984) On the possible utilisation of *Camelops* by early man in North America. *Quaternary Research* 22, 216-230.

Hedges, R. E. M. (2002) Bone diagenesis: an overview of processes. *Archaeometry* 44, 319-328.

Henderson, J. (1987) Factors determining the state of preservation of human remains. In. A. Boddington, A. N. Garland and R. C. Janaway (eds) *Death, Decay and Reconstruction: Approaches to Archaeology and Forensic Science*, 43-54. Manchester, University of Manchester Press.

Hill, A. (1976) On carnivore weathering and damage to bones. *Current Anthropology* 17, 335-336.

Hill, A. (1989) Problems and prospects of interpreting modified bones from the archaeological record. In. R. Bonnischen and M. H. Sorg (eds) *Bone Modification*, 285-289. Orono, Maine, Centre for the Study of the First Americans, Institute for Quaternary Studies, University of Maine.

Hill, J. D. (1995) *Ritual and Rubbish in the Iron Age of Wessex*. Oxford, British Archaeological Report British Series 242.

Hill, J. D. (1996) The identification of ritual deposits of animals. A general perspective from a specific study of 'special animal deposits' from the southern English Iron Age. In. S. Anderson and K. Boyle (eds) *Ritual Treatment of Human and Animal Remains*, 17-32. Oxford, Oxbow.

Holleyman, G. (1937) Harrow Hill excavations 1936. *Sussex Archaeological Collections* 78, 230-252.

Isaac, G. I. (1967) Towards the interpretation of occupation debris: some experiments and observations. *The Kroeber Anthropological Society Papers* 37, 31-57.

Janaway, R. C. (1987) The preservation of organic materials in association with metal artefacts deposited in inhumation graves. In. A. Boddington, A. N. Garland and R. C. Janaway (eds.) *Decay and Reconstruction: Approaches to Archaeology and Forensic Science*, 127–148. Manchester, University of Manchester Press.

Janaway, R. C. (1990) Experimental investigations of the burial environment of inhumation graves. In. D. E. Robinson (ed) *Experimentation and Reconstruction in Environmental Archaeology*, 147–149. Oxford, Oxbow.

Johnson, E. (1989) Human modified bones from early southern plains sites. In. R. Bonnischen and M. H. Sorg (eds) *Bone Modification*, 432-472. Orono, Maine, Centre for the Study of the First Americans, Institute for Quaternary Studies, University of Maine.

Kahlke, R. D. (1990) Beispiel einer Cerviden-osteophagie aus thüringen. *Zoologische Abhandlungen Staatliches Museum für Tierkunde Dresden* 45, 179-185.

Kierdorf, U. (1994) A fuller example of long bone change due to chewing by deer. *International Journal of Osteoarchaeology* 4, 209-213.

Lam, Y. M. (1992) Variability in the behaviour of spotted hyenas as taphonomic agents. *Journal of Archaeological Science* 19, 389-406.

Lambert, J. B., Simpson, S. V., Weiner, J. G. and Buikstra, J. E. (1985) Induced metal-ion exchange in excavated human bone. *Journal of Archaeological Science* 12, 85-92.

Laudet, F. and Fosse, F. (2001) Un assemblage d'os grignoté par les rongeurs au paléogène (Oligocène supérieur, phosphorites du Quercy). *Comptes Rendus de l'Académie des Sciences de Paris, Sciences de la Terre et des Planètes* 333, 185–200.

Littleton, J. (2000) Taphonomic effects of erosion on deliberately buried bones. *Journal of Archaeological Science* 27, 5-18.

Lyman, R. L. (1994) *Vertebrate Taphonomy*. Cambridge, Cambridge University Press.

Maat, G. J. R. (1993) Bone preservation, decay and its related condition in ancient human bones from Kuwait. *International Journal of Osteoarchaeology* 3: 77-86.

Madgwick, R. (2008) Patterns in the modification of animal and human bones in Iron Age Wessex: revisiting the excarnation debate. In. O. P. Davis, N. Sharples and K, E. Waddington (eds) *Changing Perspectives on the First Millennium BC*, 99-118. Oxford, Oxbow Books.

Maguire, J. M., Pemberton, D. and Collett, M. H. (1980) The Makapansgat limeworks grey breccia: hominids, hyenas, hystricids or hillwash? *Paleontologia Africana* 23, 75–98.

Maltby, J.M. (1985) The animal bones. In. P. J. Fasham (ed) *The Prehistoric Settlement at Winnall Down, Winchester*, 97-112. Winchester, Hampshire Field Club Monograph. 2.

Martill, D. M. (1990) Bones as stones: the contribution of vertebrate remains to the lithologic record. In. S. K. Donovan (ed) *The Processes of Fossilisation*, 270-292. New York, Columbia University Press.

Micozzi, M. S. (1986) Experimental study of postmortem change under field conditions: effects of freezing, thawing and mechanical injury. *Journal of Forensic Research* 31, 953–961.

Miller, G. J. (1969) A study of cuts, grooves and other marks on recent and fossil bone I: animal tooth marks. *Tebiwa* 12, 20-6.

Miller, G. J. (1975) A study of cuts, grooves and other marks on recent and fossil bone II: weathering cracks, fractures, splinters and other similar natural phenomena. In. E. W. Swanson (ed) *Lithic Technology: Making and Using Stone Tools*, 129-136. Chicago, Aldine.

Morris, J. (2008) Associated bone groups; one archaeologists rubbish is another's ritual deposition. In. O. Davis, N. Sharples and K. Waddington, (eds) *Changing Perspectives on the First Millennium BC*, 83-98. Oxford, Oxbow Books.

Nicholson, R. (1992) Bone survival: the effects of sedimentary abrasion and trampling on fresh and cooked bone. *International Journal of Osteoarchaeology* 2, 79-90.

Nicholson, R. (1996) Bone degradation, burial medium and species representation: debunking the myths, an experiment based approach. *Journal of Archaeological Science* 23, 513-33.

Oliver, J. S. (1989) Analogues and site context: bone damages from Shield Trap Cave (24CB91), Carbon County, Montana, USA. In. R. Bonnischen and M. H. Sorg (eds) *Bone Modification*, 73-99. Orono, Maine, Centre for the Study of the First Americans, Institute for Quaternary Studies, University of Maine.

Olsen, S. L. and Shipman, P. (1988) Surface modification on bone: trampling versus butchery. *Journal of Archaeological Science* 15, 535-553.

Ortner, D., Von Endt, D. W. and Robinson, M. S. (1972) The effect of temperature on protein decay in bone: its significance in nitrogen dating of archaeological specimens. *American Antiquity* 37, 514-520.

Outram, A. K. (2001) A new approach to identifying bone marrow and grease exploitation: why the "indeterminate" fragments should not be ignored. *Journal of Archaeological Science* 28, 401-410.

Potts, R. (1986) Temporal span of bone accumulations at Olduvai Gorge and implications for early hominid foraging behaviour. *Palaeobiology* 12, 25-31.

Potts, R. and Shipman, P. (1981) Cut-marks made by stone tools on bones from Olduvai Gorge, Tanzania. *Nature* 291, 577-580.

Rietti, A. and Ruffer, M. A. (1912) On osseous lesions in ancient Egyptians. *Journal of Pathology and Bacteriology* 16, 439-465.

Roberts, S. J., Smith, C. I., Millard, A. and Collins, M. J. (2002) The taphonomy of cooked bone: characterising boiling and its physiochemical effects. *Archaeometry* 44, 485-494.

Saunders, J. J. (1977) Late Pleistocene vertebrates of the Western Ozark Highland, Missouri. *Illinois State Museum Reports of Investigations*, 33, 1-118.

Shipman, P. (1989) Altered bones from Olduvai Gorge, Tanzania: techniques, problems and implications of their recognition. In. R. Bonnischen and M. H. Sorg (eds.) *Bone Modification*, 317-334. Orono, Maine, Centre for the Study of the First Americans, Institute for Quaternary Studies, University of Maine.

Smith, M. (2006) Bones chewed by canids as evidence for human excarnation: a British case study. *Antiquity* 80, 671-685.

Sokal, R. R. and Rohlf, F. J. (1969) *Biometry*. San Francisco, Freeman.

Steele, D. G. and Carson, D. L (1989) Excavation and taphonomy of mammoth remains from the Duewall-Newberry site, Brazos County, Texas. In. R. Bonnischen and M. H. Sorg (eds) *Bone Modification*, 413-430. Orono, Maine, Centre for the Study of the First Americans, Institute for Quaternary Studies, University of Maine.

Stiner, M. C., Kuhn, S. L., Weiner, S. and Bar-Yosef, O. (1995) Differential burning, recrystallisation and fragmentation of archaeological bones. *Journal of Archaeological Science* 22, 223-37.

Sutcliffe, A. J. (1973) Similarities of bones and antlers gnawed by deer to human artefacts. *Nature* 246, 428-430.

Sutcliffe, A. J. (1977) Further notes on bones and antlers chewed by deer and other ungulates. *Deer* 4, 73-82.

Tappen, N. C. (1969) The relationship of weathering cracks and split-line orientation in bone. *American Journal of Physical Anthropology* 31, 191-197.

Tappen, N. C. (1971) Two orientational features of compact bone as predictors of split-line patterns. *American Journal of Physical Anthropology* 35, 129-140.

Tappen, N. C. (1976) Advanced weathering cracks as an improvement on split-line preparations for analysis of skeletal orientation in compact bone. *American Journal of Physical Anthropology* 44, 375-380.

Tappen, N. C. (1994) Bone weathering in the tropical rainforest. *Journal of Archaeological Science* 21, 667-673.

Tappen, N. C. and Peske, G. R. (1970) Weathering cracks and split line patterns in archaeological bone. *American Antiquity* 35, 383-386.

Von Endt, D. W. and Ortner, D. M. (1984) Experimental effects of bone size and temperature on bone diagenesis. *Journal of Archaeological Science* 11, 247–253.

Voorhies, M. (1969) Taphonomy and population dynamics of an early Pliocene vertebrate fauna, Knox County, Nebraska, 69. *Contributions to Geology, Special Papers No. 1*. Laramie, Wyoming, University of Wyoming Press.

Wait, G. A. (1985) *Ritual and Religion in Iron Age Britain*. Oxford, British Archaeological Report British Series 149.

Walker, L. (1984) The deposition of the human remains. In. B. Cunliffe (ed.) *Danebury: an Iron Age Hillfort in Hampshire. Volume 2. The Excavations 1969-1978: the Finds*, 496-548. London, Council for British Archaeology Research Report 52.

Walters, J. (1988) Fire and bones: pattern of discard. In. B. Meehan and R. Jones (eds) *Archaeology with Ethnography: an Australian Perspective*, 215–221. Canberra, Australian National University Press.

White, T. D. (2000) *Human Osteology*. San Diego, Academic Press.

Wilson, B. (1999) Symbolic and ritual activity in depositing Iron Age animal bones. *Oxford Journal of Archaeology* 18, 297-305.

Woodward, A. (1993) The cult of relics in prehistoric Britain. In. M. O. H. Carver (ed) *In Search of the Cult: Archaeological Investigations in Honour of P. Rahtz*, 1-7. Woodbridge, The Boydell Press.

Author's Affiliation

Richard Madgwick
School of History and Archaeology
Cardiff University
Humanities Building
Colum Drive
Cardiff
CF10 3EU
UK

Appendix

A key to the abbreviations used in the statistics table is presented below. The first entry in the description column in the table refers to the categories being tested for difference (e.g. H/A = humans and animals compared). Brackets denote the data selected for testing. For example (A) means only animals included in analysis and (A,LB) means only animal long bones included in the analysis. The final entry in the description refers to the variable being tested for difference (e.g. weathering, gnawing etc). In the direction of significance column, direction refers to which of the categories has a greater prevalence/severity of the variable in question, therefore H<A indicates that animal specimens have a greater prevalence (of e.g. weathering) than humans. All tests from T16 onwards were conducted on disarticulated material only.

* - continuity correction value used as values computed for a 2x2 table.
† - Fisher's exact test used, as more than 20% of boxes have expected values lower than 5.
A - Animal
ABR – Abrasion
ART – Articulation levels (compared)
ARTP – Articulation levels (proportions thereof)
CA – Features containing only animal specimens
CHA – Features containing human and animal specimens
CHI² - Chi² test
DF – Degrees of freedom
DH – Dog/Horse
DIS – Disarticulated
GNW – Gnawing stage (0-3)
H – Humans
LB – Long bones
LGCK- Longitudinal/Spiral fracturing

MWU – Mann Whitney test
OA – Animals other than dog or horse
TRMP - Trampling
WETH – Weathering stage (0-3)
WPA – Weathering (presence/absence)

Details of the statistical tests carried out (p<0.05). Refer to the key above for details of abbreviations and the use of the description column.

T	DESCRIPTION	TEST	N	CHI²/MWU VALUE	DF	EXACT SIGNIFICANCE	DIRECTION
1	H/A - WETH	MWU	9493	8723752.000	3	**0.000**	H<A
2	H/A - GNAW	MWU	9493	9071550.000	3	**0.000**	H<A
3	H/A - ABR	CHI²	9493	27.549*	1	**0.000**	H<A
4	H/A - TRMP	CHI²	9493	36.140*	1	**0.000**	H<A
5	H/A - LGCK	CHI²	9493	619.238*	1	**0.000**	H<A
6	H/A - ARTP	CHI²	9493	2970.309	3	**0.000**	A<H
7	ART - WETH	MWU	9493	8723752.000	3	**0.000**	ARTC<DIS
8	ART - GNW	MWU	9493	5067975.500	3	**0.000**	ARTC<DIS
9	ART - ABR	CHI²	9493	14.774*	1	**0.000**	ARTC<DIS
10	ART - TRMP	CHI²	9493	14.292*	1	**0.000**	ARTC<DIS
11	ART - LGCK	CHI²	9493	277.927*	1	**0.000**	ARTC<DIS
12	H/A (ARTC) - WETH	MWU	1292	35920.500	2	0.511	-
13	H/A (DIS) - WETH	MWU	8201	4962871.000	3	**0.000**	H<A
14	H/A (DIS, LB) - WETH	MWU	1215	80985.000	3	**0.000**	H<A
15	H/A (DIS) - GNW	MWU	8201	4962871.000	3	**0.000**	H<A
16	H/A (CHA) -WETH	MWU	6626	3806762.500	3	**0.000**	H<A
17	H/A (CHA) - GNW	MWU	6626	3947450.000	3	**0.000**	H<A
18	H/A (CHA) - ABR	CHI²	6626	8.286	1	**0.004**	H<A
19	H/A (CHA) - TRMP	CHI²	6626	253.044	1	**0.000**	H<A
20	H/A (CHA) - LGCK	CHI²	6626	12.832	1	**0.000**	H<A
21	CHA/CA (A) - WETH	MWU	6534	3747217.500	3	**0.000**	CHA<CA
22	CHA/CA (A) - GNW	MWU	6534	3827572.500	3	**0.003**	CHA<CA
23	CHA/CA (A, LB) - WETH	MWU	1024	80985.000	3	**0.000**	CHA<CA
24	CHA/CA (A) - ABR	CHI²	6534	6.956	1	**0.008**	CHA<CA
25	CHA/CA (A) - TRMP	CHI²	6534	62.096	1	**0.000**	CHA<CA
26	CHA/CA (A) - LGCK	CHI²	6534	18.125	1	**0.000**	CHA<CA
27	CHA/CA (DH) - WPA	CHI²	695	22.244*	1	**0.000**	CHA<CA
28	CHA/CA (OA) - WETH	MWU	2166	344248.500	3	**0.000**	CHA<CA
29	CHA/CA (DH, LB) - WPA	CHI²	139	9.284	1	**0.002**	CHA<CA
30	CHA/CA (OA, LB) - WETH	MWU	791	39806.500	3	**0.007**	CHA<CA
31	CHA/CA (DH) - GNW	MWU	695	25230.500	3	**0.000**	CHA<CA
32	CHA/CA (OA) - GNW	MWU	2166	361784.000	3	**0.038**	CHA<CA
33	CHA/A (DH) - ABR	CHI²	695	9.023* †	1	**0.004**	CHA<CA
34	CHA/A (OA) - ABR	CHI²	2166	4.450*	1	**0.035**	CHA<CA
35	CHA/A (DH) - TRMP	CHI²	695	11.404* †	1	**0.001**	CHA<CA
36	CHA/A (OA) - TRMP	CHI²	2166	10.100*	1	**0.001**	CHA<CA
37	CHA/A (DH) - LGCK	CHI²	695	15.664*	1	**0.000**	CHA<CA
38	CHA/A (OA) - LGCK	CHI²	2166	0.288*	1	0.591	-

8. More ritual rubbish? Exploring the taphonomic history, context formation processes and 'specialness' of deposits including human and animal bone in Iron Age pits.

Clare Randall

Abstract

Concentrations of animal bone, associated bone groups and human remains are common on British Iron Age sites, and in particular in pits. These have been shown in previous studies, especially by J. D. Hill, to occur in associated patterns, and have been interpreted as having ritual connotations. Sigwells, Charlton Horethorne, Somerset consists of an extensive pit scatter dating from the Middle Iron Age to the end of the Late Iron Age. The excavated area provided an animal bone assemblage of reasonable size, associated bone groups, human remains and a range of other objects and materials. In addition, the extensive wet sieving programme provided plant macrofossils and microartefacts and enabled an integrated approach to its study. The combination of zooarchaeological and taphonomic information with other artefactual and ecofactual data provides far richer interpretive possibilities. The approach indicates that more detailed study of taphonomic processes can further clarify the relationship of animal bone to other materials, and aid understanding of how contexts came into being.

Introduction

The excavation of part of an extensive Middle to Late Iron Age site at Sigwells, Somerset (part of the South Cadbury Environs Project), comprising a partly enclosed concentration of pits (Tabor 2004, 43-55), produced amongst other material associated bone groups (ABGs) and human remains which suggested highly patterned deposition. The question arose whether apparent concentrations of disarticulated bone and other materials were as 'special' as ABGs and other 'special finds'. It was realized that if the bone deposition was structured, it would inevitably affect any socio-economic inferences that could be drawn from it, but that it could also assist in site interpretation. A strategy was needed to address the issue. This paper reflects the methodology used in that study. Further discussion and interpretation of the findings are discussed in Randall (prep, a), and the site will be considered as a whole in a South Cadbury Environs Project monograph.

Pits, animal bones and special deposits

The general understanding of pits is that they were mainly constructed for grain storage (Cunliffe and Poole 1991, 161-2), and experimental pits have been found effective for bulk storage (Reynolds 1983, 15), although at Winklebury it was suggested that pits were dug to contain rubbish (Smith 1977, 42). While early interpretations of articulated animals in pits as ritual were superseded by functional explanations of food waste (e.g. Bersu 1940, 53), incorporation of human remains was explained as convenience of disposal or inclusion in 'general rubbish' (Ellison and Drewett 1971, 183,192). However, pit contents can become regarded as divorced from their original function (Reynolds 1979, 71). Cunliffe (1992) postulated that deposition of this type relates to propitiation of chthonic deities, with pit digging a ritual activity (Cunliffe and Poole 1991, 162). It may be part of a wider regenerative cycle (Fitzpatrick 1997, 83). Pit distribution at Wakerley suggests digging pits was a structured activity, an arena for communal activities (Gwilt 1997, 161-2). Therefore interpretation of the contents of the Sigwells pits is regarded as crucial to understanding the site as a whole.

Some material within pits has become widely regarded as constituting 'special deposits'. Complete and partial animal skeletons (ABGs) are common on British Iron Age sites (Maltby 1996, 19), and the concept of 'special deposits' developed from attempts to understand them (Poole 1995, 249). ABGs can include the major domestic food species, dogs, horses and wild species. The species deposited do not necessarily reflect the make up of the overall assemblage (Grant 1984, 222-223; 1991, 536, 538, 542). ABGs are interpreted as occurring due to a range of causes (e.g. Maltby 1996, 19; Stallibrass 2000, 160, 162; O'Connor 2004, 439-440), including ritual practices, which are commonly suggested for prehistoric and especially Iron Age contexts (e.g. Jones 1977, 59; Millett and Russell 1982, 73-74; Armour-Chelu 1991, 145-146; Wilson 1999, 59). Some ABGs may have multiple meaning (Hill 1995, 14) and therefore need to be considered in their own context, as discussed by Morris (2008).

Statistically significant relationships between human remains and ABGs in the same pit, have been noted (Grant 1991, 539-41), and disarticulated human remains occur commonly on Iron Age sites (indicating secondary burial after the remains have decayed, suggesting an 'invisible' mortuary rite) (Whimster 1977, 317). Where deposited with material regarded as refuse, this may have connotations of regeneration (Carr and Knüsel 1997). Additionally, special deposits have also been recognized as including whole, or largely whole, pots or closely associated large sherds, although how these are defined is problematic. Deliberate breakage may indicate ritual destruction (Poole 1995, 249,260). Given this apparent

Table 8.1 The incidence of deposits in pit thirds in Hill's study. Quern fragments occur throughout fills but there is an increase in middle and especially bottom fills (Hill 1995:46-8).

	Human Remains	ABGs	All Small Finds	Loom Weights	Iron Object	Unusual Objects	Quern	Brooches
Upper	X		X		X		X	X
Middle	X	X	X	X	X	X	X	
Lower		X	X	X		X	X	

Table 8.2 Taphonomic processes and other factors affecting animal bone assemblages.

Process	Affects	Reference
Butchery and carcase utilisation	Preference for elements, method and degree of dismemberment affects size and element deposited.	Maltby 1985a, 49-56; Gilchrist and Mytum 1996, 36; Cain 2005, 881
Burning	Colour change, shrinkage, warping and fragmentation. Dogs prefer roasted bone.	Pearce and Luff 1994; Stiner and Kuhn 1995, 224, 234-5;
Gnawing	Canid gnawing preferentially destroys articulations, and small elements are swallowed.	Gifford 1981, 406; Maltby 1985a, 41; Pickering 2001, 407
Mechanical breakage -element density	Element frequency recovered affected by differential destruction and selective transportation for less dense elements and zones.	Gifford 1981, 400; Horwitz and Smith 1990, 655,663; Ioannidou 2003, 355, 361, 364
Mechanical breakage -juvenile bone	Element frequency recovered affected by differential destruction and selective transportation of porous elements and epiphyses.	Horwitz and Smith 1990, 655, 663; Munson 2000, 391
Sub-aerial weathering and trampling	Breakage and surface changes including cracking and delamination. Varies according to length of time exposed.	Gifford 1981, 415-6; Villa and Courtin 1983, 273; Olsen and Shipman 1988, 536-7
Post-depositional chemical/pH	Low soil pH (acid soils) attacks bone. Effects lower density elements and small fragments.	Endt and Ortner 1984, 247-8, 252; Marean 1991, 678, 691
Post-depositional microbial	Affected by soil pH and related to water content and percolation; microbial activity attacks bone.	Hedges and Millard 1995, 155; Nicholson 1996, 523, 529
Recovery bias	Hand collection differentially recovers larger and more identifiable material.	Casteel 1972, 386; Payne 1972; Cannon 1999, 206, 210-212; Shaffer and Sanchez 1994, 528

propensity for breakage, concentrations of all sorts of materials could be similarly defined as 'special'. This introduces issues about where the line between the 'special' and 'ordinary' is to be drawn. However, deliberate fragmentation may apply to other classes of material such as animal bone and the brokenness of an assemblage may be part of the point.

Ritual and Rubbish in the Iron Age of Wessex J. D. Hill 1995

Examining records from several Wessex sites, Hill (1995, 33) established patterns of material within 'layers' (contexts), pit 'thirds' (lower, middle and upper thirds of fills) and whole pits, and compared them to the presence/absence of human remains, ABGs and 'small' finds recovered from them. He identified different incidences of pottery and bone deposition. If contexts originated in generally mixed midden deposits, the majority of contexts should be homogenous. However, the concentrations were patterned and therefore interpreted as curated refuse, deposited similarly to ABGs, human remains and 'special' items (Hill 1995, 39-40, 125-6). Patterns were identified in the position of certain items within pit fills that are reproduced in Table 8.1. Post-depositional processes were only briefly examined. Bone fragmentation was greater with depth, with elevated numbers of loose teeth in upper fills.

However, bone condition varied between species (i.e. well preserved dog and human bone in upper fills), so the more fragmented material in upper fills was interpreted as having a different history rather than having degraded *in situ* (Hill 1995, 46-50). Acts of deposition were not frequent, probably separated by years. Hill regarded structuration of deposits as ritual (1995, 74-75, 86-114). Hill identified a number of shortcomings in his study including mismatches in units of measure between different classes of data, and the 'crude' designation of pit thirds. He suggested consideration of regional variations, and application of additional techniques from soil science, wet sieving, and examining whether plant remains also show structuration (Hill 1995, 41,45, 126-127). This study has sought to replicate Hill's approach and address some of his suggestions. Also, as taphonomic and other factors affect interpretation of animal bone assemblages (Maltby 1996, 18) (Table 8.2), these issues needed to be addressed.

Methods

Overview

The site examined in this study consists of an extensive scatter of pits, mainly unenclosed, overlooking South Cadbury hillfort, at Sigwells, Charleton Horethorne, Somerset (Figure 8.1). Situated on a ridge, referencing earlier landscape features, the site developed from the early to mid 3rd century BC and developed throughout the Middle to the very end of the Late Iron Age. It was partly enclosed towards the end of the sequence (Tabor 2004, 47). Calculations based on the density of excavated features compared with the magnetic anomalies shown in Figure 8.2 suggest the possibility of the presence of upward of 5,000 pits with some considerable intercutting. Given the lack of evident settlement on or immediately adjacent to the locale, understanding the context and content of the pits as the predominant feature of the site was crucial to understanding how and why such an extensive group of pits came into existence.

The aim of this study was to integrate all the available lines of evidence from the inception of the post-excavation analysis, be they contextual, artefactual or ecofactual, and carry out the types of comparisons which were employed by Hill (1995). This included analysis of the animal bone assemblage, disarticulated human remains, pottery, other ceramics (e.g. daub), vitrified materials, a range of other worked objects ('small finds' including metal objects, querns and slingstones), plant macrofossils and microartefacts (including additional bone) from wet-sieved soil samples. This was supplemented with data from pH and magnetic susceptibility tests on soil samples. It was possible to co-ordinate and undertake analyses on the different classes of material in parallel.

Relational databases were constructed to record animal bone and bulk soil sample contents, and enable cross-comparisons. Concentrations of material were identified using the same methods as Hill (1995, 34) by calculating the mean values and standard deviations of various variables, adding these to produce '+SD' values (values in excess of one standard deviation above the mean). Context groups of material with these '+SD' values were identified as outliers. The incidence of these concentrations were compared with the presence/absence of human remains, ABGs, 'small finds' and other items using a variety of scatter plots and histograms. The apparent associations were then, where possible, tested using χ^2 to determine if associations were statistically significant.

Site Records

Feature and context information was available from site records, plans, section drawings and photographs. These were employed in producing a typology of fills for use in the analysis, as described below, and used to consider whether material quantity was an effect of the excavated volume. For calculation purposes pits were assumed to be cylindrical, and adjustments made to the depth of deposits to account for lensing of contexts. Whilst volume calculations were approximate, they were considered to be of sufficient accuracy for the purposes

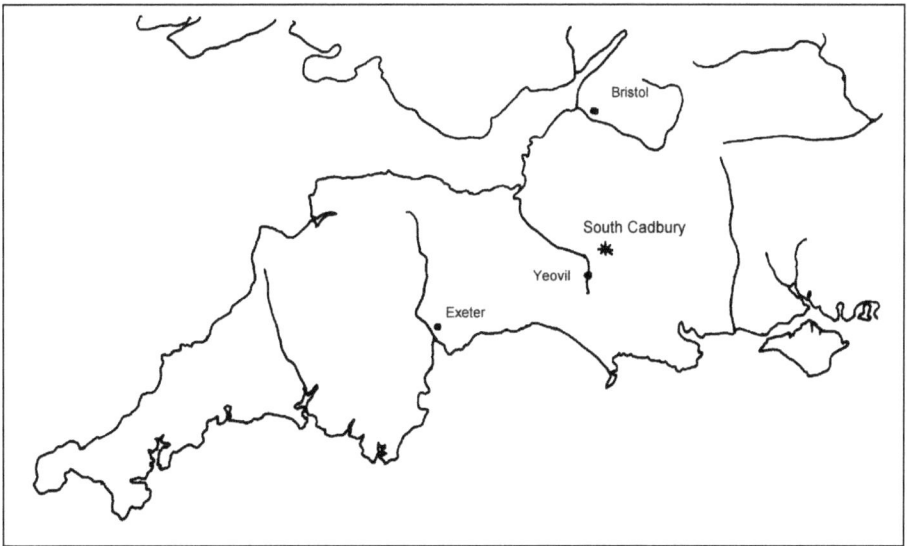

Figure 8.1 Location of Cadbury Castle, South Cadbury, Somerset

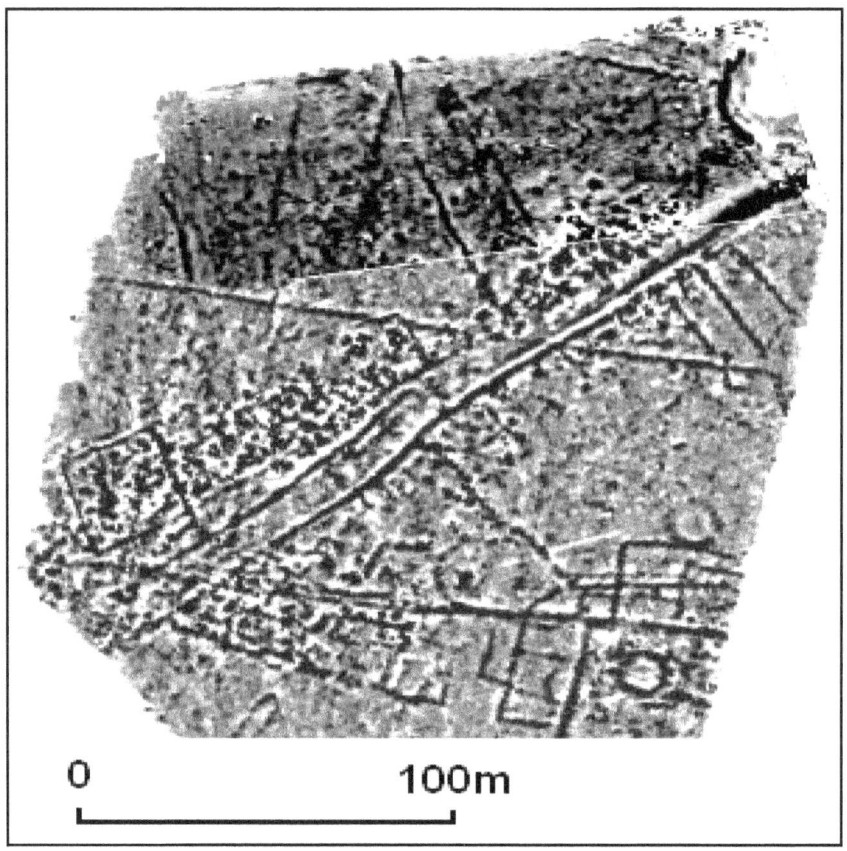

Figure 8.2 Fluxgate gradiometer survey of the west end of Sigwells carried out in 1993 (Tabor 2002:57). North is at the top of the plot. A double-ditched track runs diagonally intersecting with Bronze Age and Romano-British boundaries to the south. The rectangular enclosure is visible to the north west of the track. Note the dense scatter of anomalies within the enclosure and spreading along the north side of the track which runs from near an extant Early Bronze Age barrow at the north east end. Most of these anomalies have, on excavation, been shown to be pits. Source: South Cadbury Environs Project.

of this assessment. Bioturbation was also assessed from original context records and photographs and recorded on a descriptive basis.

Recording and analysis of the animal and disarticulated human bone

Each bone fragment, in both the main bone assemblage and material from soil samples that was >6mm and/or identifiable, was identified where possible to element and species, and where this was not possible, it was assigned to Large Mammal (e.g. cattle sized), Medium Mammal (e.g. sheep sized) and Unidentified categories, in a similar fashion to Maiden Castle (Armour-Chelu 1991, 140). While breakage patterns are important as fragmentation may occur due to marrow and fat processing (Outram 2001, 401), or as a result of canid gnawing (Maltby 1985a, 41), breakage patterns were not recorded. Metrical data were recorded using the measurements in von den Driesch (1976). Toothwear was recorded for cattle, pig and sheep/goat following Grant (1982) and for sheep/goat, Deniz and Payne (1982).

Fusion status was recorded for all epiphyseal areas present. Bone porosity was recorded for all fragments. To further consider fragmentation, the percentage of the element present was estimated and recorded to the nearest 5% for all identified fragments. Additionally, the greatest diameter of each fragment was measured using digital calipers to the nearest tenth of a millimetre to enable direct comparison with the pottery assemblage. Taphonomic indicators were recorded for all fragments. Gnawing was recorded where possible by severity (Minimal, Moderate and Severe) and location on the bone; weathering was recorded by severity on the same scale, as was eroded bone; burnt bone was recorded by colour (Buff, Brown, Black and Calcined). Although Munsell charts are advocated for recording the colour of burnt bone (Cain 2005, 874; Shipman et al 1984, 309), colour as a temperature indicator is unreliable (Shipman et al 1984, 320) and so they were not used. The condition of all fragments was assessed on a five-point scale from Poor to Good.

ABGs were treated as described above, but noted as being part of an ABG, and excluded from frequency counts (cf Armour-Chelu 1991, 140). Unidentified bone fragments from the <6mm soil residue were counted and weighed and burnt bone identified to colour category. The disarticulated human material was recorded by anatomical area and side by zones present (Knüsel and Outram 2004), whilst condition was assessed using the same five point system as the animal bone for comparability. In all cases there was insufficient information to determine age or sex or consider any other anthropological analysis.

Recording and analysis of the pottery

Analysis of form and fabric was carried out using the SCEP typology outlined in Tabor (2002, 34-50) and refined in Tabor (2004, 7-16). Maximum dimension, sherd thickness (mm) and weight (g) were recorded to provide comparison to the animal bone assemblage. Abrasion occurs when sherds are moved, trampled and redeposited (Schiffer 1983, 683). Therefore abrasion and sherd condition were examined in shell-tempered fabrics from two pits in order to provide condition comparison with the bone. Study of residuality and redeposition of pottery can elucidate the origin of other material, which cannot be so easily dated (Evans and Millett 1992, 225). Estimated vessel equivalents (EVEs) (Orton *et al* 1993, 171) were checked for efficacy against a small sample but did not prove of use due to the small number of diagnostic sherds. Refitting sherds, may indicate low levels of disturbance and these have been used to examine the relationships of sherds spread across surfaces (Bollong 1994, 16, 25) (e.g. late Bronze Age middens at Runnymede (Stig Sörensen 1996, 62-67). Associated sherds were therefore looked for within context collections and recorded where observed (recent breaks were reunited and counted as one sherd). The association of sherds within the wider assemblage could not be undertaken due to the scale of the task. These methods could inform reconstruction of context formation, especially when considered in conjunction with other materials. The leaching of shell in some pottery also affected the weight. The normal assumption in pottery analysis is that all ceramic types weigh the same (Orton 1993, 179), but this is patently not the case with these ceramics. This needs to be taken into account, especially when making comparisons with bone weights, which themselves may be variably affected by taphonomic processes.

Recording of other materials

A variety of other artefactual and ecofactual material was examined. Ceramics other than pottery, small lithics, metals, vitrified materials and other lithics (e.g. querns, slingstones etc) were recorded, including weight and number of pieces for all materials and fragment size for metals and non-pottery ceramics.

Soil samples

Bulk soil samples were taken systematically for large portions of the site. These were normally restricted to *c.*10 litres. Contexts of less than 10 litres were retained in their entirety. Excavators were directed not to extract finds that they noticed whilst taking samples. Samples were processed using a water only separation tank using a 1mm gauze for the main tank, and a 0.25mm gauze for the flot sieve. Whilst 'froth' separation is recommended (Jarman *et al* 1972), denser particles were recovered by hand-sorting residues avoiding a more complicated, expensive, and potentially contaminating method. Data for plant macrofossils from flots (Blenman 2006) were incorporated with other classes of material in establishing the presence of patterning. The residue (stones and gravels, charcoal, bone, pot, ceramic, slag, flint etc) was washed clean and air dried. Squeezing and rubbing was discouraged to minimise fragmentation of delicate material.

Microartefacts (0.25-2mm) are potentially useful as they are less affected by deliberate actions, so they furnish information about sediment origins and formation processes; poor sorting indicates local origin whilst well-sorted distributions imply greater transportation (Miller Kosen 1993, 141-147). Microartefacts can be moved upward and downward in soil profiles by trampling (Gé *et al* 1993, 149-50), and this may be responsible for some pre-depositional mixing. This supplies a background against which larger finds can be considered. Finds of all types were therefore retained, weighed and recorded. The lithic component was separated, sorted and recorded by weight and degrees of angularity for >600mm, >6mm and <6mm portions. For larger samples producing >80g of <6mm residue, one quarter was sorted and weights adjusted to reflect extrapolated values. The geological type and proportion of the sample as a whole was estimated and recorded. Burnt and unburnt stone was recorded separately for each size category. For burnt stones the weight, size, shape and colour were recorded. All of this information was then used in characterizing fills.

Magnetic Susceptibility

A variety of activities can result in magnetic enhancement of soils. The level of enhancement varies but is increased by burning and organic decay (Tite 1972, 229; Cole *et al* 1995, 144). Consequently this was of interest in considering bone presence and condition and relationship to the presence of other materials. Sub-samples of *c.*100ml were taken from bulk soil samples. These were subjected to laboratory based magnetic susceptibility testing, being air dried and ground down to pass through a 2mm sieve. Each sample was weighed and recorded. Using a Bartington MS2-B, samples were examined at frequencies of 0.43 hHz (Low frequency - LF) and 4.3kHz (High Frequency – HF). Each sample

Table 8.3 Sigwells fill types

Process	Broad Description	Fill Type
1. Weathering/ environmental processes	1.1. Fine, pale silts and grits with few inclusions	1.1.1. Grey or greenish- grey thin deposits. **Type 1**
		1.1.2. Pale yellow or buff fine sandy silts. **Type 2**
	1.2. Pale yellow-brown fine to coarse grits with varying degrees of inclusions/ clasts	1.2.1. Pale yellow to yellow-brown fine to coarse grits. Smaller and fewer clasts normally rounded to angular. **Type 3**
		1.2.2. Pale yellow to yellow-brown fine to coarse grits. Smaller and fewer clasts normally subangular to angular. **Type 4**
2. Intentional	2.1. Heterogeneous deposits of sorted fine-gritty sands and silts, ranging from thin lenses of material, localized dumps to thick evenly distributed layers.	2.1.1. Dark/very dark brown sandy silts with a range of materials and variety of clast inclusions, often including burnt stone. **Type 5**
		2.1.2. Yellow brown sandy silts with a variety of materials and clast inclusions, often including burnt stone. **Type 6**
	2.2. Bulky deposits of small to very large stones, with sparse fine infilling silts.	2.2.1. Dense accumulations of subrounded to angular gravels with brown/dark brown sandy silts. Variable amounts of burnt stone. **Type 7**
		2.2.2. Densely packed subangular to subrounded medium to large stones, normally limestone. Variable amounts of burnt stone. **Type 8**
3. Accumulation	3.1. Mottled or laminated yellow-dark brown sediments with a wide range of possible inclusions.	3.1.1 Diverse possible range of soil colours and rate and form of clasts, but homogenous within each deposit. **Type 9**
	3.2. Deep deposits of brown sandy silts with varying quantities of small to medium subrounded to subangular gravels.	3.2.1 Variable heterogeneous soils covering the width of the feature or occurring in localised areas. **Type 10**

was measured three times at the low frequency and the average reading logged. This was then repeated for each sample at high frequency.

pH Tests

Soil acidity has a considerable effect on bone preservation (Gordon and Buikstra 1981, 566), and determines a range of other soil characteristics including microbial activity, which is increased by organic matter (Ashman and Puri 2002, 58). It is useful as a crude marker of organic content and to compare with bone condition. Using the sub-samples retained for magnetic susceptibility, pH tests were carried out. 2-3g of sediment was placed in a beaker and mixed with 1.5-2 times analytical reagent grade water, stirred and left for 15 minutes. The pH was then measured with a Camlab ISFET pH meter zeroed to 6.9.

Recording context formation processes – Fill Type and Fill Character

Fill formation and the rapidity and nature of the filling process will have affected bone distribution and condition. In order to move beyond Hill's pit 'thirds', which are merely a measure of depth, categorization of contexts was required to group data. These groups ('Fill Types' Table 8.3) were determined by consideration of the local soils and geology and encompass a range of silts and sediments, and a range of types and sizes of clast inclusion. These were arranged for manageability and interpretive reasons by broad formation process; weathering and environmental processes; intentional (anthropogenic) deposits; and accumulation (a combination of environmental and anthropogenic action). Often context formation processes have been described in terms of the cultural and ecofactual material that they contain but for this study it was necessary to attempt a

Table 8.4 Sigwells fill characters

Process	Broad Description	Fill Type
1. Weathering/ environmental processes	1.1. Very low proportions (<5% by volume) of clast	1.1.1. Virtually no clast residue, mainly small and very small stones, rounded to sub-rounded sandstone. **Type 1**
		1.1.2. Virtually no clast residue, mainly small and very small stones, sub-rounded to angular sandstone or limestone. **Type 2**
	1.2. Low proportions of clast (5-10%)	1.2.1. Small amounts of clast normally small and very small stones rounded to angular sandstone. **Type 3**
		1.2.2. Small amounts of clast normally small and very small stones subangular to angular sandstone with occasional large stones and limestones (<20%). **Type 4**
2. Intentional	2.1. Low proportions of clast (5-10%)	2.1.1. A range of clast inclusions veering the range of sizes and shapes, but generally heterogeneous within that range. **Type 5**
		2.1.2. A range of clast inclusions veering the range of sizes and shapes, but generally homogenous within that range (i.e. small angular). **Type 6**
	2.2. Moderate to high proportions of clast (10-30%, 30%+).	2.2.1. High proportions of subrounded to angular small and very small sandstones with few limestones. **Type 7**
		2.2.2. High proportions of subangular to subrounded medium to large stones, normally limestone. **Type 8**
3. Accumulation	3.1. Moderate incidence of clasts (10-30%).	3.1.1 Generally small and very small clasts ranging from rounded to angular and generally homogenous within that range (i.e. mainly sun-rounded, mainly angular). **Type 9**
	3.2. Moderate incidence of clasts (10-30%).	3.2.1 Generally small and very small clasts, generally rounded to subangular, and heterogeneous within that range. **Type 10**

Table 8.5 NISP counts and percentages for domestic species and unidentified material by feature type for the Sigwells hand collected main assemblage (total Iron Age). ABGs were removed before calculation. Note the generally increased amount of material in pits as opposed to ditches.

	Ditch	Pits	Postholes and gullies	Bank, floor and general layers	Other	Total
Cow	139/ 1.31 %	201/ 1.89%	28/ 0.26%	59/ 0.56%	31/ 0.29%	458/ 4.31%
Pig	111/ 1.04%	214/ 2.01%	15/ 0.14%	48/ 0.45%	9/ 0.08%	397/ 3.74%
Sheep/Goat	275/ 2.59 %	1054/ 9.92%	95/ 0.89%	214/ 2.01%	117/ 1.10%	1755/ 16.52%
Horse	40/ 0.38%	37/ 0.35%	2/ 0.02%	13/ 0.12%	12/ 0.11%	104/ 0.98%
Dog	8/ 0.08%	17/ 0.16%	2/ 0.02%	2/ 0.02%	2/ 0.02%	31/ 0.29%
Unidentified	1502/ 14.14%	4308/ 40.55%	448/ 4.22%	953/ 8.97%	668/ 6.29%	7879/ 74.16%
Total	2075/ 19.53%	5831/ 54.89%	590/ 5.55%	1289/ 12.13%	839/ 7.90%	**10624/ 100%**

consideration of how artifacts relate to the formation processes, so as far as possible contexts have been described and categorized without reference to cultural material. This enabled clear comparison with the fill's 'contents'. These types are site specific, but there is no reason why this could not be adapted for different features, fills and geologies. The system used includes a range of silts and sediments and range of types and sizes of clast inclusions. A separate series of categories was also developed for application to soil samples ('Fill Characters' Table 8.4).

Results

Statistical approaches

Histograms and scatter plots indicated patterns, but testing statistical significance was difficult due to very low values for certain attributes rendering χ^2 testing inappropriate for most data. However it showed significance at the 1% level in the incidence of concentration of bone by weight with the incidence of 'small' finds, and at the 5% level for bone weight and ABGs. Other categories could not be merged as this would have made comparisons archaeologically meaningless. There will be problems in applying statistical procedures to smaller sites such as the excavated area of Sigwells due to the generally small numbers of special deposits and concentrations of bone and other materials. Small sample size was also a problem for Hill (1995, 35). Other tests such as correspondence analysis (Moreno-García 1996, 439), which suits abundance type data sets (Bølviken *et al* 1982, 41; Ringrose 1992, 615), and is useful in comparing taphonomic variables (Bar-Oz and Dayan 2003, 885, 898), could be used in future to compare bone condition, volume and ABG incidence. These methods themselves may however have the same limitations as χ^2, and cluster analysis should be considered (Baxter 1994, 101, 149), as this might be useful for presence/absence data such as comparing ABGs with bone concentrations.

Site level analysis

The full results of this project will be detailed in a SCEP monograph, but some findings are presented here to illustrate the efficacy of the approach. Nor will this paper discuss the diachronic differences found in detail, although analysis revealed an increase in the intensity of activity, ABGs and metalwork inclusion toward the end of the Iron Age. Having taken account of features excavated, there was a bias toward deposition in pits at Sigwells, especially for sheep (Table 8.5), although it should be noted that the assemblage was very fragmented and the identified material dominated by sheep/goat. While deposition may relate to carcase size and location of utilization (Maltby 1985b, 101, 105), the spatial relationship with settlement is currently impossible to interpret for Sigwells. The proportion of weathered bone, and less distinctly, gnawed bone, within pits, was less than in other features (Figure 8.3) with generally even percentages of burnt material throughout feature types, implying a background level on the site, with increasing proportion in general layers, possibly relating to occupation. However the decrease in proportions of weathered bone in pits suggests more rapid burial; bias to pit deposition and decreased weathering also occurred at Danebury (Grant 1991, 447) and Winnall Down (Maltby 1985b, 97-8, 104, 108). ABG deposition at Sigwells is

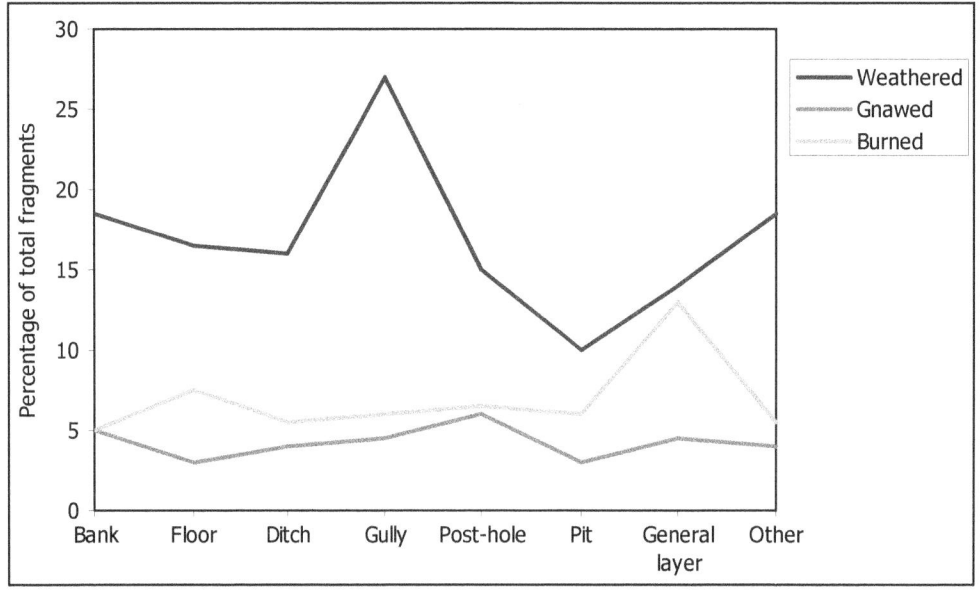

Figure 8.3 Distribution of weathered, gnawed and burnt bone by feature types by percentage of total fragments for that feature type.

Table 8.6 Details of all ABGs identified in the Sigwells site assemblage.

Feature	Context	Feature type	Associated Bone Group details	Period
TR12/F004	130	Pit	Cow skull with stones in sockets	LIA
TR12/F011	186	Pit	Articulated juvenile sheep	LIA
TR12/F018	076	Pit	Horse skull, jaws and daub 'tongue'	LIA
TR12/F042	231	Pit	Articulated adult male dog	LIA
TR12/F059	272	Pit	Articulated neonatal dog	LIA
TR12/F014	127	Pit	Articulated corvid under stones	LIA
TR12/F031	225	Pit	Sheep skull and vertebrae	LIA
TR12/F058	262	Pit	Adjoining pig vertebrae	MIA
TR12/F002	051	Pit	Articulated cow hind leg and pelvis	MIA
TR12/F008	053	Posthole in pit	Dog skull and mandible	MIA

Table 8.7 Bone condition by species for pits (Total Iron Age). There are broad similarities between the three main domestic species, but the better and narrower range of condition of dog and particularly horse bone is notable, and much increased for the human bone.

	Good	Average-Good	Average	Poor-Average	Poor	Median	Mode
Cow	2%	23%	41%	26%	7%	A	A
Sheep/Goat	5%	33%	39%	17%	5%	A	A
Pig	7%	30%	33%	25%	5%	A	A
Dog	23%	23%	31%	23%	0%	A	A
Horse	22%	47%	19%	12%	0%	AG	AG
Human	62.5%	12.5%	25%	0%	0%	G	G

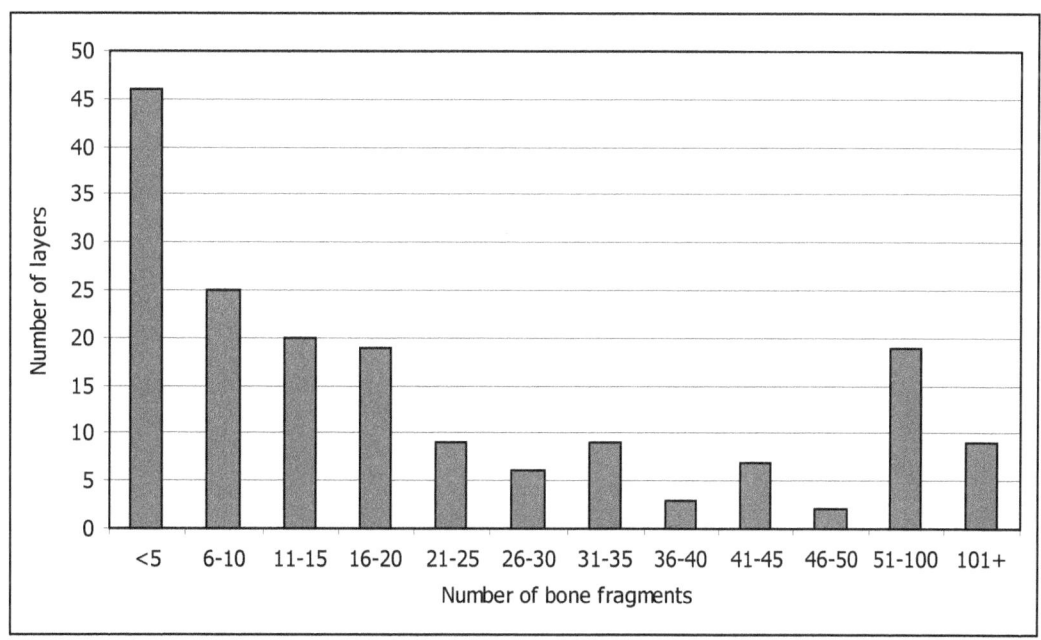

Figure 8.4 Histogram showing the incidence of animal bone fragments in layers in pits. Note the large number of layers with very few fragments but the significant number of layers with more than 50 fragments. The profile for pottery is almost identical.

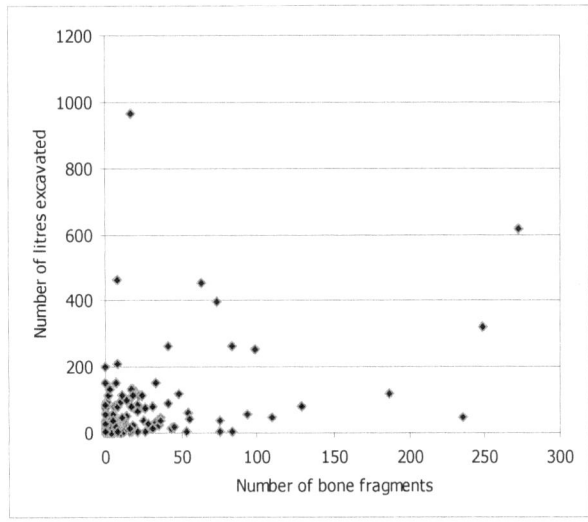

Figure 8.5 Comparison of total bone number recovered by the number of excavated litres per context. Note the clustering of low recovery to smaller volumes excavated. Some large contexts however produce low numbers of bone fragments and vice versa.

also biased towards pits (Table 8.6). Whilst only a small proportion of the total site has been excavated and this may introduce a bias, there is no immediately obvious difference between enclosed and unenclosed areas. However, there is an apparent difference in volume of material and number of ABGs between the middle and late Iron Age and the way in which later pits cut earlier ones.

Layers within pits

Material from pits was considered by looking first at individual layers (in Hill's terminology). Most Sigwells bone and pot came from contexts (layers) containing few fragments. A few contexts had large concentrations of material (*cf* Hill 1995, 42), although there is the full range of incidences (Figure 8.4), replicating data elsewhere (*cf* Maltby 1985b, 102). The maximum dimensions for pot and bone, produced similar sizes in the same contexts, with more smaller fragments and fewer large ones, implying similar treatment of the two assemblages (*contra* Hill 1995, 44). Poole (1995, 255) postulated that patterning probably occurred across a range of perishable and non-perishable materials. At Sigwells, comparison of contexts with large amounts of bone and other materials indicated that outlying quantities (above '+SD' as outlined above) of bone were also characterised by increased concentrations of non-pottery ceramics (e.g. daub) and vitrified materials confirming the positive relationship of those other items to deposition of animal bone.

The disarticulated human remains were generally in better condition than the animal bone assemblage (Table 8.7), and displayed no cut marks or gnawing. Comparative studies of human and animal bone fragmentation have shown different dismemberment practices employed for human disarticulated material and animal bones (e.g. Outram *et al.* 2005, 1705), and this is evident at Sigwells. Good bone condition for dog and horse implies special treatment for these species as well, and agrees with Hill's findings (1995, 41). The lack of gnawing of the Sigwells human remains may argue against some indicators of exposure (Carr and Knüsel 1997, 169-70), and contrasts with an articulated cow leg which had been seriously gnawed.

Context volume versus quantity of finds was not fully considered by Hill. The Sigwells contexts were highly variable in size, and there is a relationship between context volume and recovered finds, which holds true for bone (Figure 8.5), pottery, other ceramics and vitrified materials. Nevertheless, there are still outlying contexts, where small excavated volumes produced high concentrations. There is also no strong correlation between context volume and the presence of human bone, which appears to indicate that deposition of human remains occurs independently of high volume deposition; it is therefore less likely to be randomly incorporated but implies deliberate thought in deposition. However, few contexts identified this way match those identified via the Hill method. This study therefore demonstrates serious implications, if volume is not taken into account. Also, comparison of bone from the main assemblage with that from soil samples showed no real correlation between the presence or amount of bone in one with the other. This may imply that at Sigwells most bone was combined with the sediment as they entered the pit rather than in middens, supporting deliberate choice in deposition, and indicating how highly structured that activity may have been.

Pit Thirds

Hill (1995, 45) admitted that division of pits into thirds was simplistic. The methodological problems became clear when assigning contexts for Sigwells with uneven distribution of fills, and their variable thickness. Consequently, calculations on this basis should be regarded only in general terms. Nevertheless, Sigwells shows discernable patterns in the distribution of animal bone and pottery, although these could not be tested statistically. The mean number of bone fragments and pottery sherds both decrease with depth in an extremely similar fashion (Table 8.6 and 8.7). This seems to run contrary in some respects to the admittedly slight patterns in vertical distribution of ABGs and human remains shown in figures 8.9 and 8.10. This should be compared with Hill's findings in Table 8.1 and implies that there are some site specific or regional differences in the habits of deposition of ABGs and human remains. Small finds (Table 8.8) and charred plant material however showed a marked preference for the upper fills, the former at least agreeing with Hill's findings (*cf* 1995, 47), but contrary to the location of metalwork and grain noted at

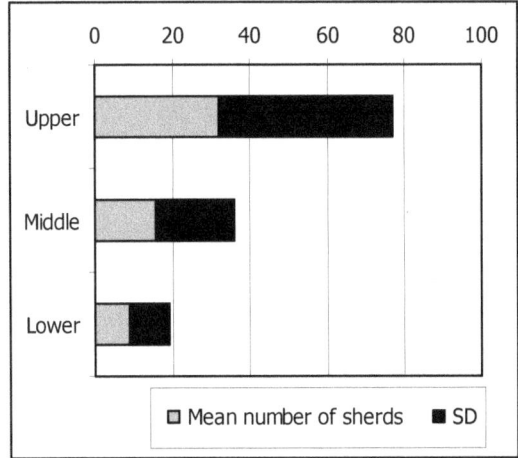 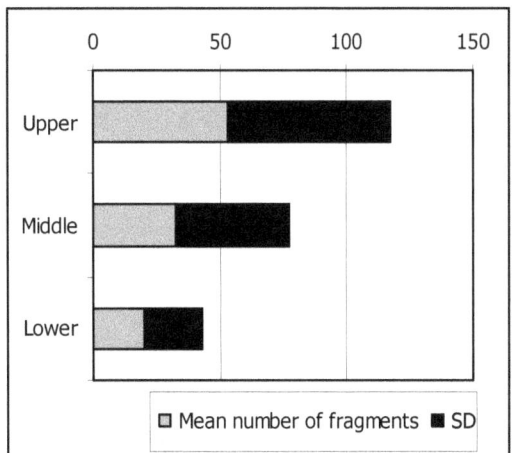

Figures 8.6 and 8.7 Distribution of pottery sherd numbers (left) and bone fragments (right) within each pit third for total Iron Age. Note the correlation of both materials having a preponderance of numbers in upper fills, although this is less pronounced for bone.

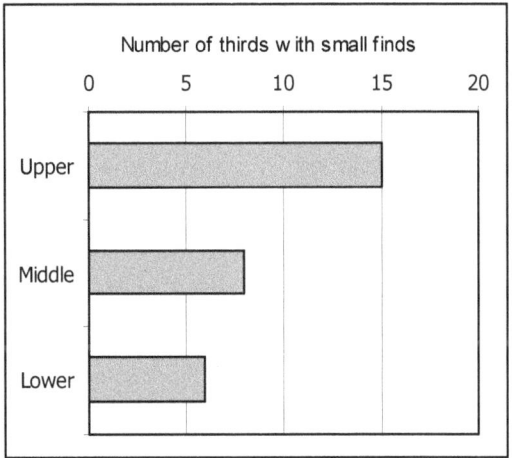

Figure 8.8 Distribution of small/special finds within each third for total Iron Age. Note the considerable increase of finds in the uppermost fills, many of which are items of metalwork.

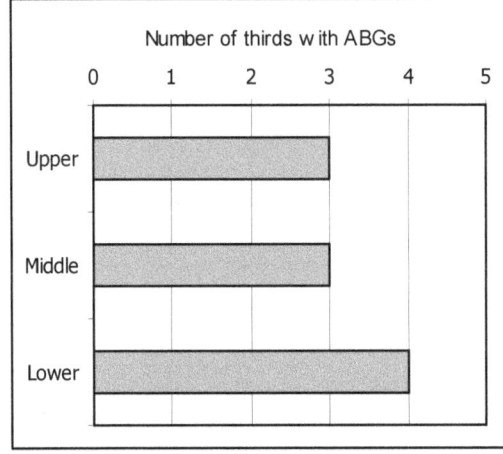 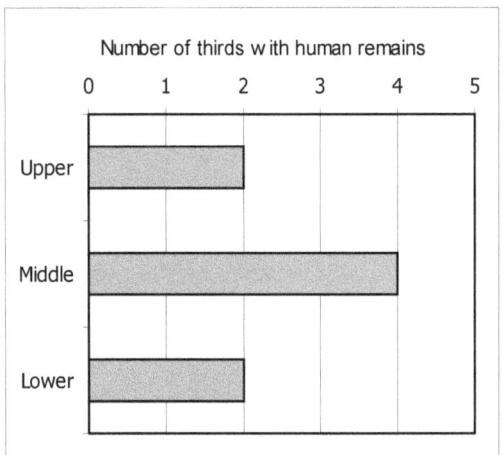

Figures 8.9 and 8.10 Distribution of ABGs (left) and human remains (right) within each pit third (Total Iron Age). Note the even distribution of ABGs through the thirds, and the increase in human remains in the middle thirds but also the small numbers involved.

Danebury, which tended to occur in basal silts (Poole 1995, 263). At Sigwells, grain and charcoal occurred only in middle and upper fills, with some significant concentrations. Whilst charred rachis fragments and straw, which tend not to survive (Boardman and Jones 1990, 9) did not often occur, concentrations of grains and weed seeds were found in a number of pits (Blenman 2006).

Fill Type

Given the problems with 'thirds', the Sigwells data was assessed against ten 'fill types' outlined above and based on criteria independent of the finds and material they contained. The approach should be tested against a larger data set, but there appears to be positive correlation between fill types and bone condition and fragmentation (Table 8.8). For example, natural slow silts have lower proportions of unidentified material, less loose teeth, and generally better bone condition, compared to fills in the deliberate deposition or long-term cultural accumulation categories. This is interesting as it implies that materials were not necessarily available to fall into open features of their own accord. Deliberately deposited fills unsurprisingly show larger total numbers of bone fragments, which supports their designation. Although the proportion of weathered bone in some anthropogenic contexts may seem surprising it has been affected by small numbers, although it may indicate redeposition from a previously stockpiled source. This is an initial test of the approach, but appears useful as an alternative to pit thirds and could contribute to understanding individual fills and assemblage formation.

Whole pits

The study found similarities in patterning of deposited material within whole pits to those noted by Hill (1995, 54, 61-3) and this will be explored further in Randall (in prep, a). Positive correlations of vitrified material and ceramic concentrations in pits with ABGs, and human remains were demonstrated. Some ABGs were closely associated with post settings dug into the centre of pits, probably marking deposits, indicating the importance of noting structural elements. Piles of stones occurred in bases of pits, with ABGs placed under, within and over them, at Danebury (Poole 1995, 262, 274). This is reflected in two Sigwells cases, with evidence from the fill types and contextual information indicating that these and other deposited objects were allowed to silt over naturally. In addition, some Sigwells pits show a range of geological components and sediment types originating from a variety of locations in the immediate and further landscape. Some burnt bone may relate to the widespread presence within fills of vitrified materials. The extensive quantities of burnt stone at Sigwells, beyond that which is usually related to settlement or occupation debris, seem to imply a concentrated pyrotechnic activity. The broadness of included components may support the idea that these types of deposits had ritual meaning (as defined by Hill (1995, 95-101), but the individual complexity and variation indicates a breadth of possible meaning.

Bone Taphonomy - *In situ* degeneration or depositional choice?

Hill saw patterning of bone deposition as suggesting choice rather than post-depositional factors (1995, 48), but more unidentifiable material and loose teeth in upper pit fills at Sigwells fits with previous discussions of fragmentation caused by percolation of water, crushing and root action (Maltby 1996, 18-19). Bone condition and fragmentation at Sigwells were therefore compared by depth (pit thirds), with the degree of leaching displayed by a sample of shell-tempered pottery. This method will be considered in detail in Randall (in prep, b), but the initial findings (Figure 8.11) indicate that shell- and limestone-tempered wares can be used as a control for the effects of water percolation on bone in the same deposits. It may also provide an indication of the level of residuality. There was some evidence of improved bone quality with depth, supporting the contention that some weathering was due to its proximity to the surface.

Consideration of bone condition compared to fill types, show that differences were unlikely to be related to the soil that bone was deposited in. Neither weathering nor bone condition scores were fully predictable by depth, and in all contexts a mixture of conditions and degrees of weathering was present. This implied that the bone had been combined from different sources before deposition. However, robust elements survived well in upper fills, whilst others predominated in middle fills. Whether this reflects the original pattern of deposition, or degradation needs further consideration, as density of bone varies with species, element, sex, diet and age (Gifford 1981, 400; Horwitz and Smith 1990, 655, 663; Nicholson 1996, 528; Ioannidou 2003, 355, 361, 364). As this is also affected by preferential canid gnawing of articulations (Gifford 1981, 406), it should be considered in the light of the recovery of extensive gnawed fragments and a dog coprolite full of gnawed bone. Bone survival of porous and unfused (juvenile) bone needs further study. This is normally under-represented (Munson 2000, 391, 399) although the age profiles of domestic species at Sigwells show the youngest animals were present. Completeness of selected elements at different depths could be considered, but this data set was too small, especially when accounting for size differences between domestic species.

The comparison between taphonomic markers in the main hand-collected and sieved assemblage was enlightening. One would expect that if the bone and soil was combined before deposition and degradation occurred in situ, the material in the two assemblages would be proportionally similar, but in several cases this did not occur, as indicated in Figure 8.14. The >6mm and <6mm burnt bone also has opposite distributions with the former increasing in upper fills and the latter in bottom thirds (Figure 8.15 and 8.16). In addition, there is a marked difference in the pattern of burnt bone deposition between the Middle and Late Iron Age contexts (Figures 8.17 and 8.18); percolation or bioturbation do not seem to offer feasible explanations. However, these taphonomic processes demonstrate subtleties in fill formation that have not previously been accounted for.

When using data from soil samples, the effects of bioturbation in particular need to be considered. Any assemblage is altered considerably by soil fauna which will change, mask or produce patterns, and this is particularly true for microartefacts. However, the maximum particle size ingested by *Lumbricus terrestris* earthworms is c2mm and charred plant remains are unpalatable (Canti 2003, 136, 141).

Table 8.8 Mean percentages and numbers of fragments for various taphonomic indicators by fill type. Fill types 1-4 relate to weathering processes, 5-8 to deliberate deposition and 9-10 to gradual accumulation. Lowest values are indicated in italics and highest in bold.

FT	Unidentified %	Loose teeth %	Bone No.	Burnt %	Weathered %	Gnawed %	Mean Bone portion %
1	60.5	*0*	16	7	39	*0*	37.5
2	*36*	*0*	123	**19.2**	*5.2*	**9.5**	58
3	77	2.4	268	5.6	8.3	5.3	50
4	74	9.8	266	8.9	9.1	4.3	48
5	76.5	6.6	701	14.3	13.9	4.6	44
6	74	13.3	**847**	10.1	13.8	3.4	43
7	**95**	4.7	*9*	*0*	**52.3**	4.7	**70**
8	70.5	7.2	333	5.7	13.3	4.8	41
9	88	*0.2*	115	10	47.8	*0*	*35*
10	74	**14.1**	441	7.3	15.7	1.1	50.3

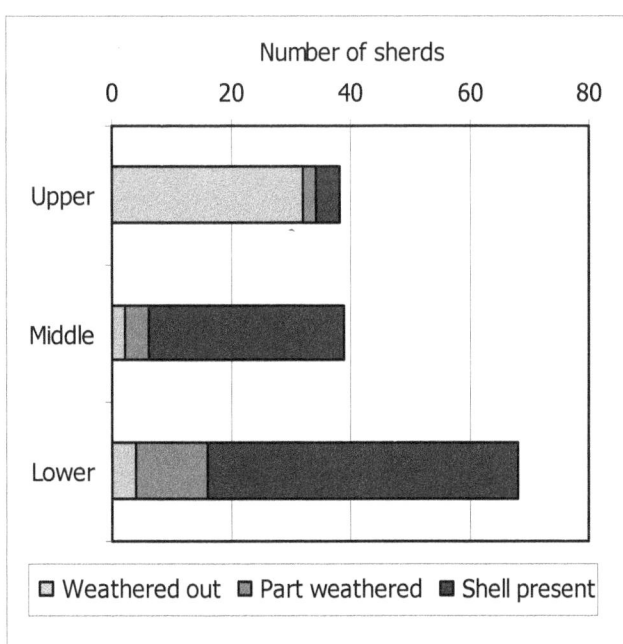

Figure 8.11 The presence of shell in shell-tempered pottery from a selection of contexts from three pits arranged by pit thirds. Note the large predominance of weathered sherds in the top fills.

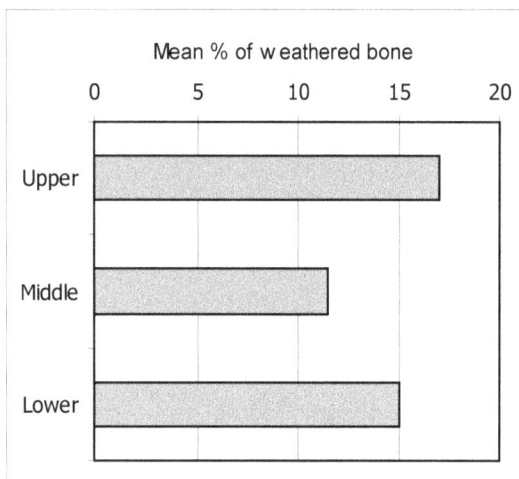 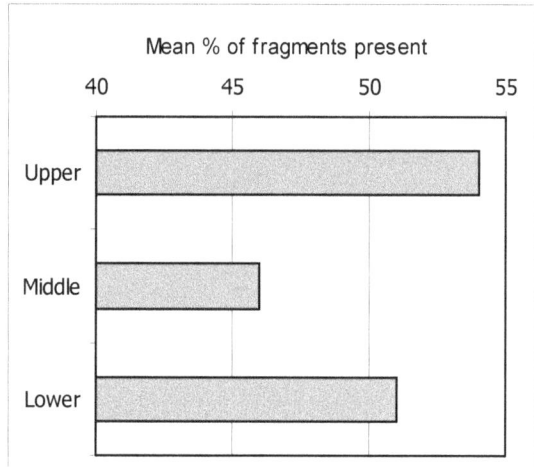

Figures 8.12 and 8.13 Mean percentage of weathered (left) and bone portion (right), for identified bone by depth in pit thirds. Note the increased weathering percentages in the upper thirds and less strongly in the bottom thirds, and the increased size of identified bone in the upper fills, which is difficult to explain. The overall bone quality improves slightly with depth.

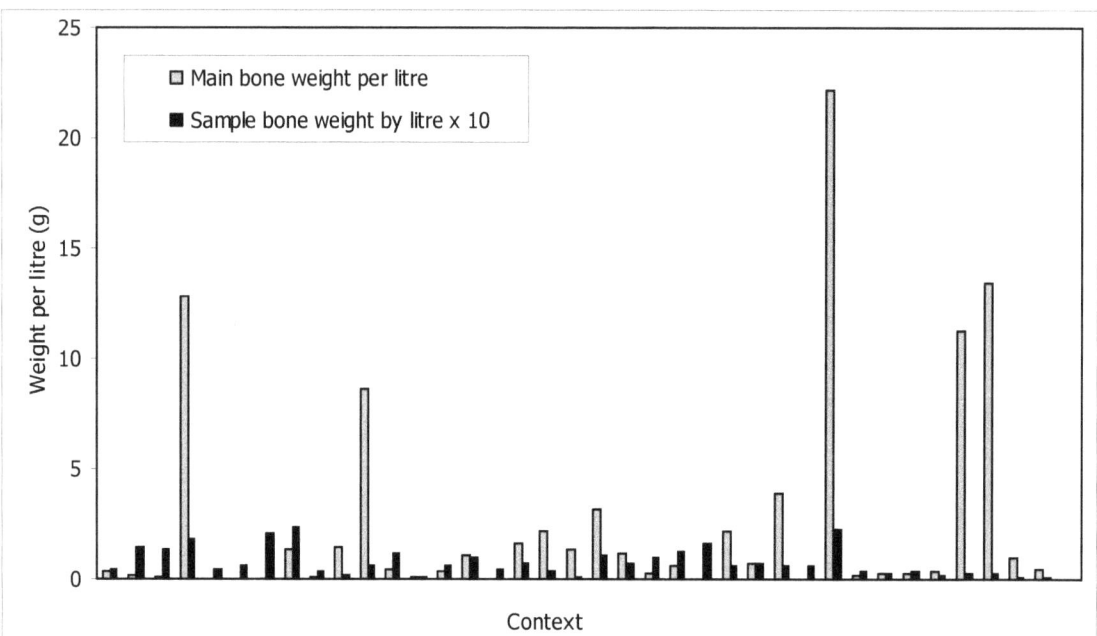

Figure 8.14 Histogram showing the proportions of bone recovered by hand and via soil samples by volume of excavated context for a selection of five pits. The soil sample figures have been multiplied by 10 for comparison purposes. Bone from soil samples occurs in some contexts, from which there is no hand collected material whereas amounts of bone from soil samples is not particularly elevated in contexts where there is a large amount of hand recovered bone.

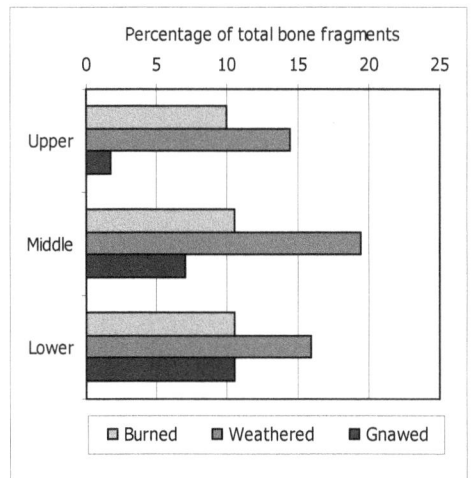 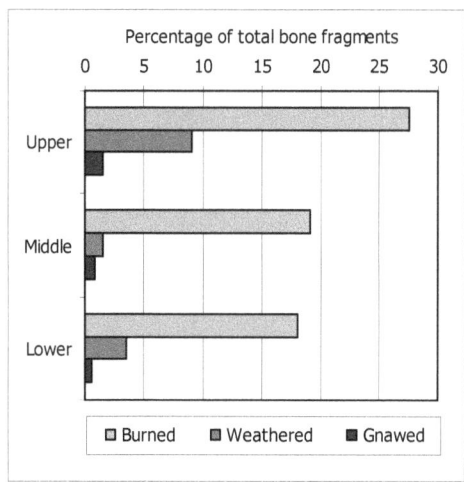

Figures 8.15 and 8.16 Comparison of burnt, weathered and gnawed bone as a percentage of the total bone fragment count in the main bone (left) and >6mm soil sample residue (right) assemblages for Trench 14 pits by pit third. Note the similar proportion of burnt bone and weathered bone in the main sample. The increase in gnawed bone by depth is interesting. In the soil sample assemblage there is a higher proportion of burnt bone in the top thirds and a dramatic decrease in the weathered and gnawed bone in lower thirds.

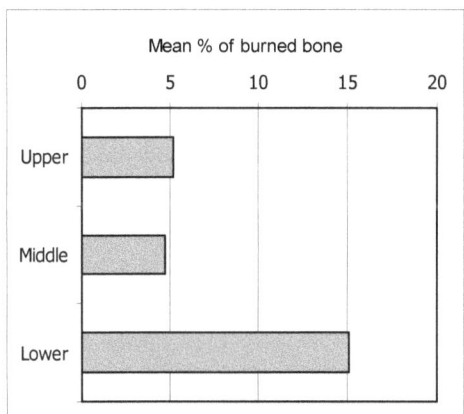 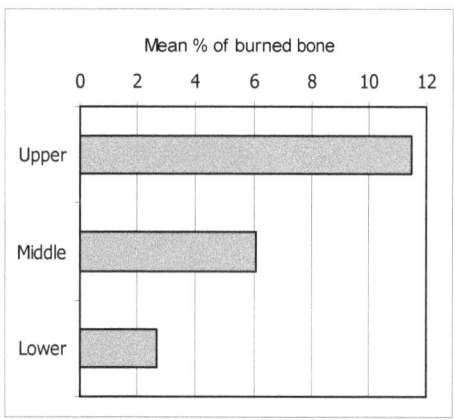

Figures 8.17 and 8.18 Mean percentage of burnt bone in pit thirds split into middle Iron Age (left) and late Iron Age (right). Note the change in distribution in LIA upper fills from MIA lower thirds.

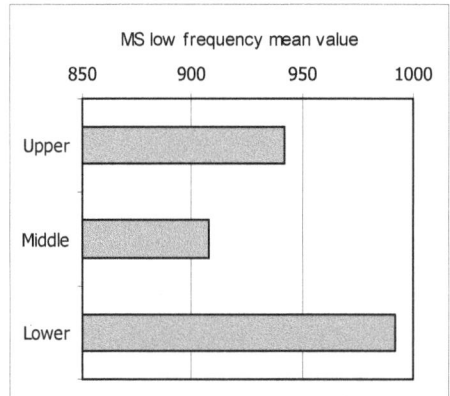 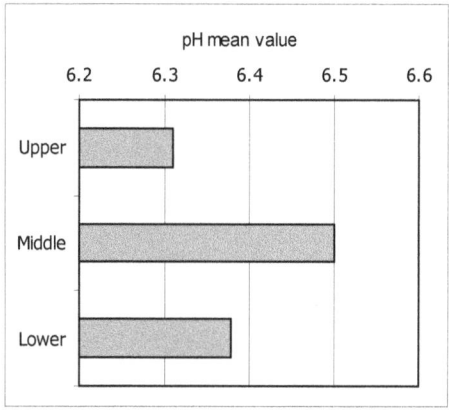

Figures 8.19 and 8.20 Comparison of Magnetic Susceptibility (left) and pH values (right) by depth using pit thirds for five pits. Note the lower MS readings for middle thirds and the increase in pH (decrease in acidity) in middle thirds. This is the reverse of the pattern of the MS

This implies most bone and other microartefacts would not be displaced by worms. Given the acid soils at

Sigwells, and low observed numbers of worms, disturbance was probably limited. Whilst small animal burrowing can be very destructive, at Sigwells little disturbance was detected, although burrows were noted and field voles observed. The presence of modern seeds in the Sigwells plant macrofossil assemblages was employed as a marker of intrusion. It occurs in samples due to poor sampling method, aerial transport, washing into cracks and earthworm action. At Winnall Down, (Monk and Fasham 1980, 322), and Winklebury, contamination occurred in the upper layers, whilst at Blackstone there was a less definable pattern (Keepax 1977, 223-4) explained as aerial contamination. At Sigwells, most intrusive seeds occurred in the top and middle fills, but comparisons of concentrations with observed bioturbation produced no strong correlation.

Sigwells fills were probably contaminated aerially, with upper and some larger middle fills exposed longer prior to and during excavation. Variety and diversity in the finds and microartefacts may be an indicator of fill origins. The examination of the bone content of soil samples discussed above has provided a range of information, but the findings for other microartefacts show that the various types of material are almost ubiquitous, occurring in some quantity and variety in most contexts. This mixing indicates redeposition and is probably indicative of secondary refuse. Studies of the Sigwells microartefacts were very labour intensive and the need to have high precision recognition skills limited the available workforce. The development of estimation algorithms (Kontogiorgos and Leontitsis 2005, 1275, 1280-1281) should extend the possibilities for future use. Fine silty soils with low clast density and large amounts of artifacts were identified as midden material at Danebury (Poole 1995, 261). Some of the Sigwells fills are similar and this may account for contexts with elevated MS and reduced pH readings, which do not contain charred material or burnt bone.

Poole (1995, 255) regarded 'lost' organic deposits as undetectable, but magnetic enhancement can be produced both by burning or as a by-product of microbial activity in organic material (Weston 2002, 208-9). The MS and pH readings for Sigwells pits suggest changes in organic content with depth (Figures 8.19 and 8.20), which correlate only occasionally with burnt bone and charred plant material in contexts. Weathering of bone relates to low soil pH, although this relationship is complex (Gordon and Buikstra 1981, 566; Nicholson 1996, 523, 529; White and Hannus 1983, 321). The reduction of weathered bone in middle thirds, where soils appear less acidic, may be related, but this needs exploration in a larger sample.

It is evident that whilst individual methods supply limited information, they are considerably more powerful in combination and lead us towards far more detailed and meaningful interpretations. MS and pH could be used alongside soil chemistry to further explore this. Both horizontal and vertical spatial analysis, using a combination of MS and phosphate analysis mapped deposition of organic material at the Iron Age enclosure at Guiting Power. The incidence of phosphates did not relate to the incidence of bone but indicated deposition of manure (Marshall 2001, 83, 89, 92-93) which could be a feasible component in the Sigwells fills. Micromorphology and microstratigraphy can also identify single depositional events including organic material (Matthews *et al.* 1997, 303) and this could also be used in future in conjunction with further studies of bone condition and microartefacts.

Time, small animals and open pits

Examination of site records and consideration of fill types indicated punctuated filling of pits, in some cases accumulating long-term wind-blown silts. The profile of some pits indicates that some were subject to long-term erosion. In considering these processes, the presence of small vertebrates seemed to offer elucidation. Some Sigwells small mammal bone is probably intrusive but it is unlikely that all animals dying in burrows did so in the same contexts. A range of species with differing burrowing habits were present. The site produced extensive and widespread burnt small mammal bone with some contexts containing numerous fragments and diverse species. Concentrations, against a generally low incidence background, have been noted previously (Brothwell and Jones 1978, 48). These factors and lack of evidence for disturbance implies the small mammal bone was not intrusive. Most accumulations probably represent predation or pit falls, especially as the majority of Sigwells accumulations occurred in lower fills. Hill (1995, 64) regarded associated small mammal and amphibian bone as pit fall victims; accumulation by pit fall or buzzard pellets was the preferred explanation for concentrations at Danebury (Grant 1984, 526). Both mechanisms require pits to be open long enough for accumulation to happen. Therefore, amphibians and small mammals have been shown to be useful indicators of pauses in pit filling. This, in combination with other contents of pits, allows us to approach questions of timescale and memory, which are further explored in Randall (in prep, a).

Pulling together the threads

The wide range of data and methods used enables the construction of detailed pit biographies, leading to new insights into the complexity of Iron Age behaviour. It became evident that although some patterns were visible across the site, each pit showed a considerable degree of individuality within those patterns in the sequence of filling, the components, and volumes of material. Common themes in these pit biographies include the pit being left open early in the fill sequence, often for a long period, numerous episodes of deliberate deposition punctuated by pauses, ABGs and metal objects being left to silt over gradually and the combination of ABGs and structural elements such as posts, that imply marking or making the location visible. The opportunity to understand the elements of behaviour involved in the creation of this large agglomeration of pits directly relates to interpreting its landscape location and development, which will be explored further in Randall (in prep, a).

This study demonstrates the need to understand the circumstances of deposition before seeking to interpret it. The Sigwells animal bone assemblage was not purely a by-product of economic activity. It also demonstrates the value of assemblages in providing wider interpretations of site use. Analysis of the Sigwells animal bone indicates the validity of Hill's findings and his general method. Extending analysis to taphonomic processes and soil sample assemblages revealed additional information, including extending the likelihood of structured deposition to other materials such as vitrified materials, other ceramics and some plant macrofossils. Taphonomic information indicated that the main bone assemblage probably originated separately from that in the soil matrix, and accumulated from a variety of sources. Complexities were indicated by bone taphonomy that deserves future exploration, and the results support the efficacy of an integrated approach in providing much richer possibilities in interpretation.

A range of additional studies could further clarify depositional practice. Replication of some of the tests used here (particularly using fill types and taking context volume into account) should be carried out against larger data sets. Long bone fragmentation, recent breaks, and especially butchery would further enhance understanding of context formation. Soil chemistry might elucidate the source of sediments, organic content and bone condition, whilst distribution by bone element and species could be further compared with other pottery analysis, including refitting and study of decorated pot and vessel-type distribution. Multivariate statistical methods and correspondence analysis would test significance in the relationships between bone condition, species distribution and other factors. Additionally, the use of small mammal bone to elucidate speed and type of fill formation could be applied to other sites. The key is however the use of these methods in tandem rather than in isolation and use a holistic approach in interpretation.

Acknowledgements

Thanks are due to Richard Tabor, director of the South Cadbury Environs Project (funded by an AHRC grant), for enabling me to have access to the Sigwells finds and site records, and Liz Caldwell for her determined work on the soil samples. Gratitude also goes to the SCEP volunteers especially Duncan Black for prioritizing the Sigwells MS samples, and to Kate Blenman for her work on the plant macrofossils. What I have done with their data is entirely my own fault. Mark Maltby, James Morris and Ellen Hambleton also need my thanks for their helpful comments at various points along the way.

Bibliography

Armour-Chelu, M. (1991) The faunal remains In. N. Sharples (ed.) *Maiden Castle: Excavation and Field Survey 1985-6*, 139-151. London, English Heritage.

Ashman, M. R. and Puri, G. (2002) *Essential Soil Science: a Clear and Concise Introduction to Soil Science*. Oxford, Blackwell.

Bar-Oz, G. and Dayan, T. (2003) Testing the use of multivariate inter-site taphonomic comparisons: the faunal analysis of Hefzibah in its Epipalaeolithic cultural context *Journal of Archaeological Science* 30, 885-900.

Baxter, M. J. (1994) *Exploratory Multivariate Analysis in Archaeology*. Edinburgh, Edinburgh University Press.

Bersu, G. (1940) Excavations at Little Woodbury, Wiltshire. *Proceedings of the Prehistoric Society* 6, 30-107.

Blenman, K. (2006) An Environmental Study of Middle and Late Iron Age Pits at Sigwells, Looking to Further the Understanding of Palaeoenvironment and Palaeodiet : A study of Carbonized Plant Remains. University of Bristol, BA Dissertation.

Boardman, S. and Jones, G. (1990) Experiments on the effects of charring on cereal components *Journal of Archaeological Science* 17, 1-11.

Bollong, C. A. (1994) Analysis of site stratigraphy and formation processes using patterns of pottery sherd dispersion. *Journal of Field Archaeology* 21, 15-28.

Bølviken, E., Helskog, E., Helskog, K., Holm-Olsen, I. M., Solheim, L. and Bertelsen, R. (1982) Correspondence analysis: an alternative to principal components. *World Archaeology* 14, 41-60.

Brothwell, D. and Jones, R. (1978) The relevance of small mammal studies to Archaeology. In. D. Brothwell, K. Thomas and J. Clutton-Brock (eds.) *Research Problems in Zooarchaeology*, 47-57. London, Institute of archaeology Occasional Paper No 3 University of London.

Cain, C. R. (2005) Using burnt animal bone to look at Middle Stone Age occupation and behaviour *Journal of Archaeological Science* 32, 873-884.

Cannon, M. D. (1999) A mathematical model of the effects of screen size on zooarchaeological relative abundance measures. *Journal of Archaeological Science* 26, 205-214.

Canti, M. G. (2003) Earthworm activity and archaeological stratigraphy: a review of products and processes. *Journal of Archaeological Science* 30, 135-148.

Carr, G. and Knüsel, C. (1997) The ritual framework of excarnation by exposure as the mortuary practice of the early and middle Iron Ages of central southern Britain. In. A. Gwilt and C. Haselgrove (eds.) *Reconstructing Iron Age Societies*, 167-173. Oxford, Oxbow Monograph 71.

Casteel, R. W. (1972) Some biases in the recovery of archaeological faunal remains. *Proceedings of the Prehistoric Society* 38, 382-388.

Cole, M. A., Linford, N. T., Payne, A. W. and Linford, P. K. (1995) Soil magnetic susceptibility measurements and their application to archaeological site investigation. In. J. Beavis and K. Barker (eds.) *Science and Site: Evaluation and Conservation*, 144-162. Bournemouth. Bournemouth University School of Conservation Sciences Occasional Paper 1.

Cunliffe, B. (1992) Pits, preconceptions and propitiation in the British Iron Age. *Oxford Journal of Archaeology* 11, 69-83.

Cunliffe, B. and Poole, C. (1991) *Danebury: an Iron Age Hillfort in Hampshire. Volume 5. The Excavations, 1979-88: the Finds*. London, Council for British Archaeology Research Report 73.

Deniz, E. and Payne, S. (1982) Eruption and wear in the mandibular dentition as a guide to ageing Turkish Angora goats In. B. Wilson, C. Grigson and S. Payne (eds.) *Ageing and Sexing Animal Bones from Archaeological Sites*, 155-206. Oxford, British Archaeological Report British Series 109.

Ellison, A. and Drewett, P. (1971) Pits and post holes in the British early Iron Age: some alternative explanations *Proceedings of the Prehistoric Society* 37, 183-194.

Endt, D. W. and Ortner, D. J. (1984) Experimental effects in bone size and temperature on bone diagenesis. *Journal of Archaeological Science* 11, 247-253.

Evans, J. and Millett, M. (1992) Residuality revisited. *Oxford Journal of Archaeology* 11, 225-240.

Fitzpatrick, A. P. (1997) Everyday life in Iron Age Wessex. In. A. Gwilt and C. Haselgrove (eds.) *Reconstructing Iron Age Societies*, 73-86. Oxford, Oxbow Monograph 71.

Gé, T., Courty, M-A., Matthews, W. and Wattez, J. (1993) Sedimentary formation processes of occupation surfaces. In. P. Goldberg, D. T. Nash and M. D. Petraglia (eds.) *Formation Processes in Archaeological Context*, 149-163. Madison Wisconsin, Prehistoric Press Monographs in World Archaeology 17.

Gifford, D. P. (1981) Taphonomy and palaeoecology: a critical review of archaeology's sister disciplines In M. B. Schiffer (ed.) *Advances in Archaeological Method and Theory Volume 4*, 365-438. New York, Academic Press.

Gilchrist, R. and Mytum, H. C. (1986) Experimental archaeology and burnt animal bone from archaeological sites. *Circaea* 4, 29-38.

Gordon, C. C. and Buikstra, J. E. (1981) Soil pH, bone preservation and sampling bias at mortuary sites. *American Antiquity* 46, 566-571.

Grant, A. (1982) The use of tooth wear as a guide to the age of domestic ungulates. In. B. Wilson, C. Grigson and S. Payne (eds.) *Ageing and Sexing Animal Bones from Archaeological Sites*, 91-108. Oxford, British Archaeological Report British Series 109.

Grant, A. (1984) Animal husbandry. In. B. Cunliffe (ed.) *Danebury: an Iron Age Hillfort in Hampshire. Volume 2. The Excavations 1969-1978: the Finds*, 496-548. London, Council for British Archaeology Research Report 52.

Grant, A. (1991) Animal husbandry. In. B. Cunliffe and C. Poole (eds.) *Danebury: an Iron Age hillfort in Hampshire, Volume 5, 1979-1988: the Finds*, 447-487. London, Council for British Archaeology Research Report 73.

Gwilt, A. (1997) Popular practices from material culture: a case study of the Iron Age settlement at Wakerley. In. A. Gwilt and C. Haselgrove (eds.) *Reconstructing Iron Age Societies*, 153-166. Oxford, Oxbow Monograph 71.

Hedges, R. E. M. and Millard, A. R. (1995) Bones and groundwater: towards modeling of diagenetic processes. *Journal of Archaeological Science* 22, 155-164.

Hill, J. D. (1995) *Ritual and Rubbish in the Iron Age of Wessex*. Oxford, British Archaeological Report British Series 242.

Horwitz, L. K. Smith, P. (1990) A radiographic study of the extent of variation of cortical bone thickness in Soay Sheep. *Journal of Archaeological Science* 17, 655-664.

Ioannidou, E. (2003) Taphonomy of animal bones: species, sex, age and breed variability of sheep, cattle and pig bone density. *Journal of Archaeological Science* 30, 355-365.

Jarman, H. N., Legge, A. J. and Charles, J. A. (1972) Retrieval of plant remains from archaeological sites by froth flotation. In. E. S. Higgs (ed) *Papers in Economic Prehistory*, 39-48. Cambridge, Cambridge University Press.

Jones, R. (1977) Animal bones. In. K. Smith. The excavation of Winklebury Camp, Basingstoke, Hampshire. *Proceedings of the Prehistoric Society*, 43, 58-66.

Keepax, C. (1977) Contamination of archaeological deposits by seeds of modern origin with particular reference to the use of flotation machines. *Journal of Archaeological Science* 4, 221-229.

Kontogiorgos, D. and Leonstitsis, A (2005) Microartefacts' weight estimation by genetic algorithm minimization. *Journal of Archaeological Science* 32, 1275-1282.

Knüsel, C. J. and Outram, A. K. (2004) Fragmentation: the zonation method applied to fragmented human remains from archaeological and forensic contexts. *Environmental Archaeology* 9, 85-97.

Maltby, M. (1985a) Patterns in faunal assemblage variability. In. G. Barker and C. Gamble (eds.) *Beyond Domestication in Prehistoric Europe*, 33-74. London, Academic Press.

Maltby, M. (1985b) The Animal bones. In. P. J. Fasham (ed.) *The Prehistoric Settlement at Winnall Down, Winchester*, 97-112. Winchester, Hampshire Field Club Monograph 12.

Maltby, M. (1996) The exploitation of animals in the Iron Age; the archaeozoological evidence. In. T. C. Champion and J. R. Collis (eds.) *The Iron Age of Britain and Ireland: Recent Trends*, 17-27. Sheffield, University of Sheffield J. R. Collis Publications..

Marean, C. W. (1991) Measuring the post-depositional destruction of bone in archaeological assemblages. *Journal of Archaeological Science* 18, 677-694.

Marshall, A. (2001) Functional analysis of settlement areas: prospection over a defended enclosure of Iron Age date at The Bowsings, Guiting Power, Gloucestershire, UK. *Archaeological Prospection* 8, 79-106.

Matthews, W., French, C. A. I., Lawrence, T., Cutler, D. F and Jones, M. K. (1997) Microstratigraphic traces of site formation processes and human activities. *World Archaeology* 29, 281-308.

Miller Kosen, A. (1993) Microartefacts as a reflection of cultural factors in site formation. In. P. Goldberg, D. T. Nash and M. D. Petraglia (eds.) *Formation Processes in Archaeological Context*, 141-148. Madison Wisconsin, Prehistoric Press Monographs in World Archaeology 17.

Millett, M. and Russell, D. (1982) An Iron Age burial from Viables Farm, Basingstoke. *Archaeological Journal* 139, 69-90.

Monk, M. A. and Fasham, P. J. (1980) Carbonised plant remains from two Iron Age sites in Central Hampshire. *Proceedings of the Prehistoric Society* 46, 321-344.

Moreno-García, M. (1996) A new statistical tool for comparing animal bone assemblages. *Journal of Archaeological Science* 23, 437-453.

Morris, J. (2008) Associated bone groups; one archaeologist's rubbish is another's ritual. In. O. Davis, N. Sharples and K. Waddington (eds.) *Changing Perspectives on the First Millennium BC*, 83-98. Oxford, Oxbow.

Munson, P. J. (2000) Age-correlated differential destruction of bones and its effect on archaeological mortality profiles of domestic sheep and goats. *Journal of Archaeological Science* 27, 391-407.

Nicholson, R. A. (1996) Bone degradation, burial medium and species representation: debunking the myths, an experiment-based approach. *Journal of Archaeological Science* 23, 513-533.

O'Connor, T. P. (2004) Animals bones from Anglo-Scandinavian York. In. R. A. Hall, D. W. Rollason, M. Backburn, D. N. Parsons, G. Fellows-Jensen, T. P. O'Connor, D. Tweddle, A. J. Mainman and N. S. H. Rogers *Aspects of Anglo-Scandinavian York*, 427-445. York, Council of British Archaeology and York Archaeological Trust, The Archaeology of York 8/4.

Olsen, S. L. and Shipman, P. (1988) Surface modification on bone: trampling versus butchery. *Journal of Archaeological Science* 15, 535-553.

Orton, C. (1993) How many pots make five? An historical review of pottery quantification. *Archaeometry* 35, 169-184.

Orton, C., Tyers, P. and Vince, A. (1993) *Pottery in Archaeology*. Cambridge, Cambridge University Press.

Outram, A. K. (2001) A new approach to identifying bone marrow and grease exploitation: why the 'indeterminate' fragments should not be ignored. *Journal of Archaeological Science* 28, 401-410.

Outram, A. K., Knüsel, C. J., Knight, S. and Harding, A. F. (2005) Understanding complex fragmented assemblages of human and animal remains: a fully integrated approach. *Journal of Archaeological Science* 32, 1699-1710.

Payne, S. (1972) Partial recovery and sample bias: the results of some sieving experiments. In. E. S. Higgs (ed.) *Papers in Economic Prehistory*, 49-63. Cambridge, Cambridge University Press.

Pearce, J. and Luff, R. (1994) The taphonomy of cooked bone. In. R. Luff and P. Rowley-Conwy (eds.) *Whither Environmental Archaeology?*, 51-56. Oxford, Oxbow Monograph 38.

Pickering, T. R. (2001) Carnivore voiding: a taphonomic process with the potential for the deposition of forensic evidence. *Journal of Forensic Science* 46, 406-411.

Poole, C. (1995) Pits and propitiation. In. B. Cunliffe (ed.) *Danebury an Iron Age Hillfort in Hampshire Volume 6. A Hillfort Community in Perspective*, 249-275. London, Council for British Archaeology Research Report 102.

Randall, C. E. (in prep a) Recycling 'Ritual and Rubbish': a study of deposition in Iron Age pits at Sigwells, Somerset. In. M, Lally and J, Joy. (eds.). Proceedings of the Iron Age Student Seminar, Southampton, 2007.

Randall, C. E. (in prep b) A technique for testing effects of sub-aerial weathering on bone: a comparison of leaching in limestone tempered pottery with bone condition at Sigwells, Somerset.

Reynolds, P. J. (1979) *Iron Age Farm: the Butser Experiment*. London, Colonnade Books.

Reynolds, P. J. (1985) *Iron Age Agriculture Reviewed*. Wessex Lecture No 1. London, Council for British Archaeology Group 12.

Ringrose, T. J. (1992) Bootstrapping and correspondence analysis in archaeology. *Journal of Archaeological Science* 19, 615-629.

Schiffer, M. B. (1983) Toward the identification of formation processes. *American Antiquity* 48, 675-706.

Shaffer, B. S. and Sanchez, J. L. J. (1994) Comparison of ⅛" and ¼" mesh recovery of controlled samples of small-to-medium-sized mammals. *American Antiquity* 59, 525-530.

Shipman, P., Foster, G. and Schoeninger, M. (1984) Burnt bones and teeth: an experimental study of color, morphology, crystal structure and shrinkage. *Journal of Archaeological Science* 11, 307-325.

Smith, K. (1977) The excavation of Winklebury Camp Basingstoke Hampshire. *Proceedings of the Prehistoric Society* 43, 31-129.

Stallibrass, S. (2000) Dead dogs, dead horses: site formation processes at Ribchester Roman fort. In. P. Rowley–Conwy (ed.) *Animals Bones, Human Societies*, 158-165. Oxford, Oxbow.

Stig Sørensen, M-L. (1996) Sherds and pot groups as keys to site formation processes. In. S. Needham and T. Spence (eds.) *Refuse and Disposal at Area 16 East Runnymede Runnymede Bridge Research Excavations Volume 2*, 61-73. London, British Museum Press.

Stiner, M. C. and Kuhn, S. L. (1995) Differential burning, recrystallization and fragmentation of archaeological bone. *Journal of Archaeological Science* 22, 223-237.

Tabor, R. (2002) A prehistoric series. In. R. Tabor (ed.) *South Cadbury Environs Project Interim Fieldwork Report 1998-2001*, 34-50. Bristol, University of Bristol.

Tabor, R. (2004) Prehistoric pottery update. In. R. Tabor (ed.) *South Cadbury Environs Project Interim Fieldwork Report 2002-2003*, 7-16. Bristol, University of Bristol.

Tite, M. S. (1972) The influence of geology on the magnetic susceptibility of soils on archaeological sits. *Archaeometry* 14, 229-236.

Villa, P. and Courtin, L. (1983) The interpretation of stratified sites: a view from underground. *Journal of Archaeological Science* 10, 267-281.

Von den Driesch, A. (1976) *A Guide to the Measurement of Animal Bones from Archaeological Sites*. Cambridge Massachusetts, Peabody Museum Bulletin 1.

Weston, D. G. (2002) Soil and susceptibility: aspects of thermally induced magnetism within the dynamic pedological system. *Archaeological Prospection* 9, 207-215.

Whimster, R. (1977) Iron Age burial in southern Britain. *Proceedings of the Prehistoric Society* 43, 317-327.

White, E. M. and Hannus, L. A. (1983) Chemical weathering of bone in archaeological soils. *American Antiquity* 48, 316-322.

Wilson, B. (1999) The animal bone. In. J. Muir and M. R. Roberts (eds.) *Excavations at Wyndyke Furlong, Abingdon, Oxfordshire, 1994*, 58-60. Oxford, Oxford Archaeological Unit.

Authors' Affiliations

Clare Randall
School of Conservation Sciences
Bournemouth University
Christchurch House
Talbot Campus
Poole
Dorset
BH12 5BB
UK

9. The politics of the everyday: exploring 'midden' space in Late Bronze Age Wiltshire

Kate Waddington

Abstract

This paper addresses a range of performances that took place at the sites of East Chisenbury and All Cannings Cross in Late Bronze Age Wiltshire. The sites are referred to in the archaeological literature as 'midden' complexes, and they consist of mass surface-spreads of artefacts and organic accumulations, with post-built structures, pits, hearths and stone surfaces dispersed throughout the sequences. Activities relating to farming, feasting, 'ritual', artefact production and exchange are largely associated with these complexes. This paper provides a critique of some current approaches and interpretations, discussing the problems inherent in employing the term 'ritual' when referring to archaeological deposits and monuments. Drawing from a range of performance theory and practice, I propose some more dynamic ways for considering the formation and experience of these sites, and consider the concept of social display in the creation of particular structures and deposits. I focus on a series of structures where such displays may have been focussed – the chalk platforms. Some of the platforms seal large quantities of pottery sherds, animal bones and artefacts, suggesting they were the focus for a range of depositional activities and performances. I argue that the luminosity and surface quality of the chalk provided a vehicle for display in itself at these sites, and I consider how some of the performances carried out there may have taken shape.

Introduction

Faunal and flora remains from midden deposits have traditionally provided a useful resource for archaeologists and ethnoarchaeologists who wish to study the economy of a given site, its subsistence strategies, and the diets and habits of its inhabitants (Miracle and Milner 2002, 1). Although these approaches are extremely important in understanding some elements within past societies, they lack a range of important questions which address some aspects of human experience, and in particular, the ways in which animals and plants are conceptualised. A number of studies have recently attempted to address this imbalance in bio-archaeological approaches by drawing on a range of anthropological literature (Whittle 2003, 78-87). For instance, the recent edited volume by Miracle and Milner (2002) sought to refocus debates away from production activities to consumption activities, highlighting the role of food consumption and feasts as providing important arenas '…for the highly condensed symbolic representation of social relations…' (Dietler 1996, 89; cited in Miracle 2002, 65).

Attention has also been given to animals as performing important roles in the negotiation of people's belief systems and their identities, and depositional patterns have invariably been interpreted as feeding into wider cosmological schemes (e.g. Parker Pearson 2000; Sharples 2000; Tilley 1996). In discussing some of the merits and drawbacks of these approaches, Whittle recently argued that too much attention is given 'to the definition of social relationships and the workings of sacred imperatives, and relatively little to the flow of life as constituted in part by animals and their behaviour' (2003, 87). Indeed humans are not self-contained individuals who go about their daily lives tackling their environments, but rather through interaction and dwelling, people become enmeshed with the various elements *within* their environments (Ingold 2000, 173). In other words, the environment is not a passive backdrop for actors to play out their daily lives. Therefore people's conceptualisation of plants and animals are multiple and become 'part of a considerable diversity' of understanding and identity when experienced within different contexts and settings in the world (Whittle 2003, 87). Moreover, the social practices of production and consumption are integral to daily life, and rather than understand them as opposing entities, both should be considered simultaneously, if we are to create richer narratives of past action and thought. This relates to a general tendency in environmental archaeology to separate and classify particular bodies, materials, and social practices, with each being analysed and presented as distinct. This ultimately derives from a Platonic or Cartesian worldview, which separates different essences of the world and it is much more helpful to view these elements as entangled in a continual process of being.

This paper will address the 'flow of life' during the Late Bronze Age and Early Iron Age transition in southern Britain by considering a range of performances that took place at the monumental complexes of All Cannings Cross (Cunnington 1923; Barrett and McOmish 2004) and East Chisenbury (McOmish 1996; McOmish *et al* 2002; Brown *et al* forthcoming) in Wiltshire. The sites are referred to in the archaeological literature as 'midden' complexes, and they consist of mass surface-spreads of artefacts and organic accumulations, with post-built structures, pits, hearths and stone surfaces dispersed throughout. Activities related to farming, feasting and artefact production and exchange are largely associated with these complexes. Whilst the artefact and environmental assemblages, alongside the various soil analyses, support these interpretations, there has been a tendency by many analysts to seek various *meanings* behind the creation of these residues. These interpretations are often defined in either economic or symbolic ways, and the deposits are invariably viewed as representing mounds of rubbish that accumulated through farming practices (e.g. Lawson 2000, 32), or as monuments which symbolise the 'conspicuous consumption of the product of the agricultural cycle' and 'ceremonial feasting places...' (McOmish 1996, 75).

Whilst providing invaluable insights into the formation of these deposits, these current interpretations raise a number of theoretical issues. Firstly, many ethnographic approaches have demonstrated that organic accumulations are often conceptualised not as rubbish but as politically charged residues which are intimately associated with the social fabric of the community (Fowler 2004, 118; Luby and Gruber 1999, 95; Needham and Spence 1997). Secondly, disposal practices in the Late Bronze Age indicate different practices, perceptions and beliefs to many contemporary Western ones, and they often involve the manipulation of materials and their careful mixing and remixing over periods of time. Thirdly, employing the terms 'refuse' and 'rubbish' unfortunately reduces the importance of discarded materials and diminishes 'the significance of the means of disposal' (Chapman 2000, 4), and even the term 'midden' itself denotes economic connotations and agricultural activities. And fourthly, and perhaps most importantly, the interpretations are ultimately structured in ways which emphasise dichotomies and dialectical relationships between different forms of social practice, and ultimately different elements and beings; between the domestic and the ritual, between the economic and the symbolic, and between the human and the non-human. Drawing polarisations between different entities and concepts is limiting when attempting to understand what it means to be human, and how humans in turn relate to their worlds (Latour 1993, 55-6).

This paper will overcome these imbalances by broadening discussion on the complexities of social interaction within these particular environments. The research was initially presented at the Archaeological Environmental Association 2006, in a session which sought to tackle the issue of 'ritual deposits', and before going any further I will briefly introduce the sites and discuss some of the problems inherent in using the term 'ritual' and it's separation from the 'everyday' in archaeological narratives.[1]

The 'midden' phenomena

The emergence of 'midden' sites is increasingly recognised as an important phenomenon in southern Britain at the end of the Bronze Age, and these sites represent a period of agricultural and artefact deposition on an unusually massive scale (Figure 9.1).[2] The monumental accumulations form over relatively short periods of time at the end of the Late Bronze Age, between the ninth and seventh centuries cal. BC (Needham 1996, 137). Their formation undoubtedly results from a wide range of daily practices involving large numbers of people and animals, and they can broadly be characterised as consisting of four elements (after Lawson et al 2000, 264):

1. The rapid accumulation of dark anthropogenic soil resulting from large numbers of animals and people carrying out activities on the sites. The soil micromorphology demonstrates that large numbers of domestic animals were actually kept and maintained at these locations and that crops were sometimes processed and materials burned.
2. The high density of artefacts and ecofacts suggesting intensive depositional activities. Masses of butchered animal bones and fragmented pots were moved around and discarded in different places within the sites, and they demonstrate the preparation and consumption of food on a large scale. The presence of many artefacts and the residues from their creation suggests that the sites were focal places for artefact creation, the working of materials and gift exchange.
3. The evidence for buildings and features demonstrating an array of architectures associated with the formation of these deposits. They are most visible at the base of these deposits where the stratigraphy is more defined, although features do recur in all layers in the sequences.
4. The continuity of practice which enabled the accumulation to reach monumental proportions.

It is unlikely that the dark earths accumulated in a homogeneous way, and we should comprehend the residues as forming via discrete depositional events, with a range of activity areas and buildings situated within. These areas should not be regarded as static, but rather as unfixed and transitory locales which moved around the site as and when groups of people became involved, and during different times in the agricultural cycle. The scale of deposition, material accumulation and fragmentation mark these complexes as unique and important, and they were undoubtedly regarded as significant places in the landscapes of the southern British Late Bronze Age.

Problems with the term 'ritual'

The term 'ritual' is an increasingly cited phenomenon within archaeological interpretations of past social action and events. A number of scholars have sought to differentiate a range of activities in the past which separate practical functional acts from non-functional and 'irrational' pursuits. These latter actions, which often take the form of 'special' deposits such as human bone, articulated animal bone, or complete and high quality artefacts, are often described as 'ritual'. The use of this term, however, is problematic, as the social practices and activities that constitute 'ritual' action transforms across space, time and within different social contexts (Goody 1977, 28; Lewis 1980, 17). Not surprisingly then, the

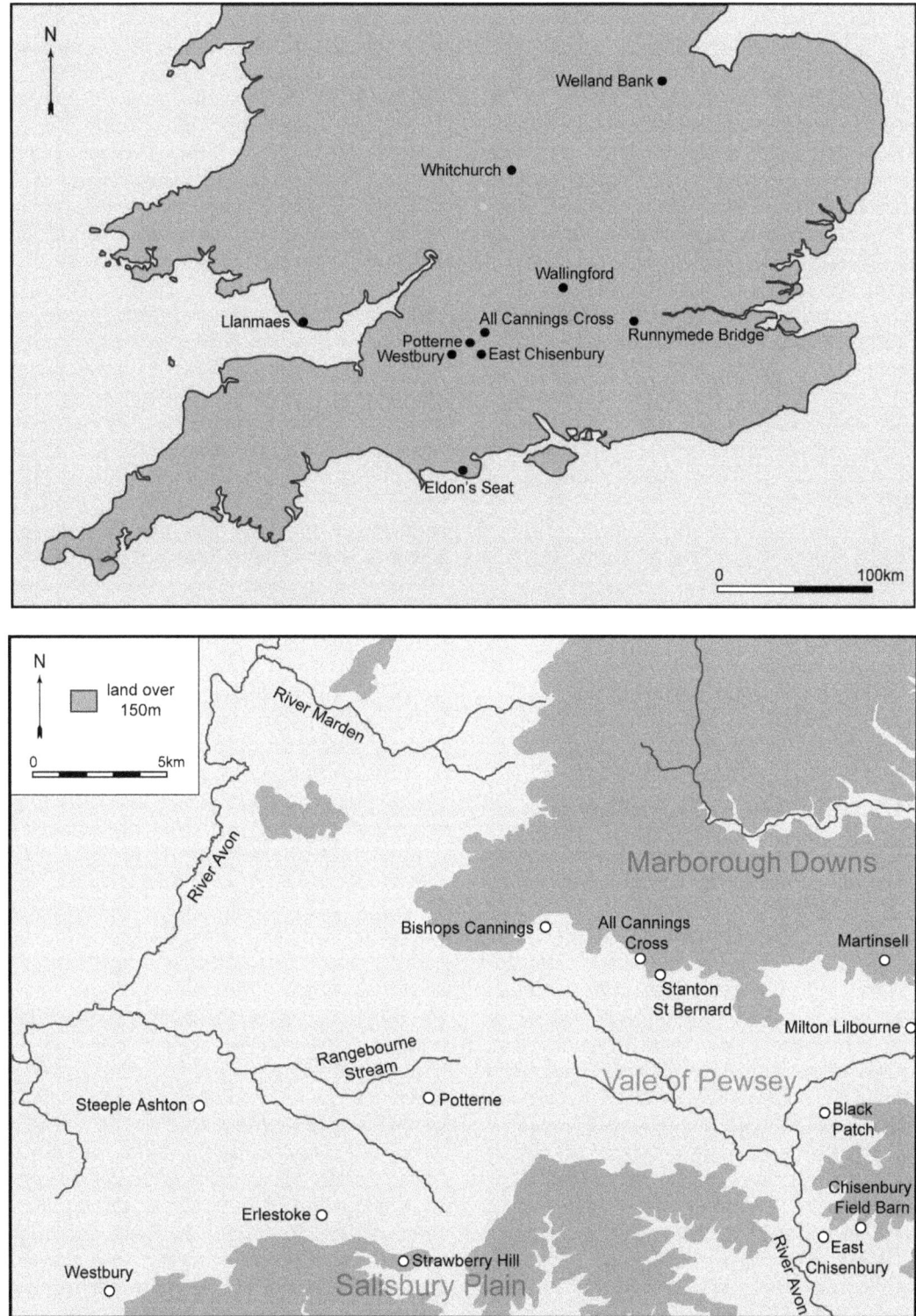

Figure 9.1 Top; Location plan showing a selection of excavated midden sites in southern Britain. Bottom; Distribution of the excavated sites in Wiltshire (adapted from Lawson 2000, Figure 99).

topic has been widely debated within the archaeological (e.g. Bradley 2005; Brück 1999b, Hill 1995; Richards and Thomas 1984) and anthropological (e.g. Bell 1992; 1997; Bourdieu 1977; Goody 1977; Lewis 1989; Turner 1982) literatures within recent years. Much of the problem lies in the assumption that ritual is a symbolic and religious activity, and that these practices were also largely separated from the everyday in the past (Bradley 2005, 20; Brück 1999b, 314). As many scholars have asserted, these interpretations are more a commentary on some Western thought and belief systems, rather than a universal norm *per se* (e.g. Bell 1992, 16-17; Latour 1993, 33, 47). A traditional pursuit of the ethnographer was in the identification of ritual and 'the symbolically charged practices which bridge the ordinary and the extraordinary' (Moran 2005, 9), further reiterating a distinction in daily practices between the 'ordinary' (functional) and 'extraordinary' (symbolic). This point is emphasised within the anthropological writings of Catherine Bell (1997, xi);

> 'Today we think of "ritual" as a complex sociocultural medium variously constructed of tradition, exigency, and self-expression... For the most part, ritual is the medium chosen to invoke those ordered relationships that are thought to obtain between human beings in the here-and-now and non-immediate sources of power, authority and value'...

This particular worldview has therefore had a dramatic effect on the way some people conceptualise 'ritual' activity across space and time, not only defining it in terms of religious activity, but also by separating this action from daily practices and routines (Bell 1992, 16-17). For instance, in highly secularised societies such as Britain today, religious practice is often carried out at very specific places and times, such as in churches, temples and synagogues. These events are set aside from the daily routine and are relatively exclusive to religious members (Bell 1997, 201). This is not a universal practice, and in contrast, religious practices and rites in 'non-secular' societies have been characterised by ethnographers as more fluid and public affairs, which seek to express the collective concerns of the social group and being deeply embedded within daily life and dwelling architectures (Bell 1997, 201; Bloch 1992, 10-11; van Gennep 1960, 24).[3]

Recent research analysing depositional practice in later prehistory has considered these perspectives and sought to emphasise that ceremonial activities were deeply embedded within daily life in the past. Studies surrounding settlement deposits in the Bronze and Iron Ages have demonstrated that many interesting patterns were indeed visible in the deposition of materials (e.g. Bowden and McOmish 1987; Brück 1995; 1999a; 2001; 2006; Fitzpatrick 1997; Hill 1995; Hingley 1990; 1992; 1995; Parker Pearson 1996). A range of analyses have shown that these events were relatively transient but were consistent over long periods of time. Similarly, whilst inhumation burials are uncommon in later prehistory, worn or manipulated fragments of human bone are sometimes deposited within dwelling space or incorporated within 'midden' residues deriving from the day-to-day existence of life (Brück 1995; Carr and Knüsel 1997; Whimster 1981). The incorporation of these materials within dwelling contexts suggests that 'ritual' activity was deeply embedded within 'domestic' life, thereby removing or at least blurring the modern dichotomy between the two (Brück 1999b).

Many of the characteristics of 'ritual', however, identified as structured, formalised, and expressive forms of behaviour, are equally shared by a number of activities traditionally defined as 'secular' or everyday routine practices. Such practices may include something as 'mundane' as eating a meal, attending a business meeting or waiting for a bus at a bus stop (Brück 1999b, 314-316; Moran 2005, 3). In this sense we should regard the performance of many everyday practices and routine activities as ritual as well (Moran 2005, 9). For instance, we know from both ethnographic and archaeological studies that the way 'refuse' is classified and disposed of will eventually lead to its deposition in a structured and formalised manner (Needham and Spence 1997). The term 'structured deposition' has become popular in archaeology in the definition of such deposits, although this has also been critiqued recently for carrying many connotations for religious action. For instance, Hill (1995, 95-96) carefully argued that although 'structured deposition' may well result from particular performances, it should not automatically be equated with religious activity. No universal set of rules governed the formation of deposits and the placement of materials in the ground, but rather they came about through the experiences of daily life and the negotiation of people's social norms and values. Although the formal placement of materials in prehistory may have sometimes affirmed or subverted people's belief systems, they may also have occasionally been linked with 'the identity of places, the definition of different kinds of personhood or being, or the working of relations and obligations' (Pollard 2001, 316). We should therefore regard ritual as a performative practice; one that cannot simply be categorised or defined in a spiritual sense and one that permeates all aspects and settings of daily life (Bradley 2005, 33). Ritual is not simply about symbolising and communicating meanings and values; it is a way of constructing particular types of meanings and values in specific ways (Bell 1997, 82).

Judith Butler (1990) took the concept of 'ritual' in the modern everyday to stress normative processes of socialisation. She cites the sociological concepts of gender and identity as forms of 'performative practices', being a sequence of constructs and acts through which the fabric of a person is created or reiterated within a social setting (Butler 1990; Salih 2002, 63). Personhood is not static or predetermined, but is instead constantly shaped and negotiated, maintained or subverted through performative acts and citations; 'in this sense, gender is always a doing', it is a 'doing' rather than a 'being' (Salih

2002, 62). Gender is understood to be a set of repeated performances, and it is through such repeated action that people's norms are shaped and lived up to (Shepherd and Wallis 2004, 221). Butler's concept of citation and performativity has been important within recent archaeological discourses, enabling various depositional practices to be interpreted as citing different genders or identities (see Harris 2005). Performance theory therefore allows people to comment on what a ritual *does* rather than what it is supposed to *mean*.

A 'practice approach' seeks to examine the performance of ritual as an activity of differentiation, a concept others have termed *ritualisation* (after Bell 1992, 74-83). Here the context of action and the performance of the body are considered as integral in the creation of social norms and values (Bell 1997, 81-82; Bradley 2005, 33). In many writings, however, a basic binary opposition between thought and action is asserted, and moreover, the very construction of this boundary is considered to be an integral process *of* ritualisation (see for example Bell 1992, 78; Bourdieu 1977; Shepherd and Wallis 2004, 121-122). Such a dialectic only asserts a further polarisation in ritual theory; between the mind and the body. This ultimately derives from a Cartesian worldview, which in practice divides the mind and its various thought processes from the actions of the body and practice. As cognitive studies have shown, minds, bodies and objects may appear on the surface to be bounded entities, but on closer analysis these boundaries become blurred, with each mixing with the other (Knappett 2005, 85). If we take the position that ritual is a performance, an embodied act that takes on varied concerns and actions in different contexts and settings, then it may be possible to overcome some of these problems in our understanding of people and their experiences in the past.

Platforms for performance and display

Similar to 'ritual', social display is a type of behaviour which serves to single out and accentuate particular events, people, identities and things in life for consideration and contemplation (Gosden 2004, 35). Pearson and Shanks (2001, 69) argue that social display is a similar concept to 'ostension' – the most basic element of performance and common to all parts of life and in all settings. This was undoubtedly a powerful force in prehistoric life as well, and in British archaeology, monuments such as Neolithic chambered tombs, stone and timber avenues and circles, and causewayed camps are regularly cited as highly appropriate contexts for performance, social display and ritualisation (e.g. Barrett 1994, 17-19; Gosden 2004, 41; Parker Pearson and Shanks 2001, 68-69; Thomas 1991, 34). In this paper I argue that the monumental accumulations at East Chisenbury and All Cannings Cross formed through complex entanglements of social practice, and that the sites were centres for social display. I focus on a series of structures where such displays may have been focussed – the chalk platforms.[4] The surfaces are constructed out of compacted chalk and stone and interspersed throughout the sequences, providing clear stratigraphic horizons and marking distinctive temporal spaces. Similar laid surfaces have also been identified at the nearby sites of Potterne (Lawson *et al* 2000, 255-256) and Westbury (Wessex Archaeology 2004), indicating that they held special significances at the sites. Some of the platforms seal large quantities of pottery sherds, animal bones and artefacts, suggesting they related to consumption and depositional activities, marking and sealing earlier events that took place there. I argue that the hard, white, chalk surfaces created conspicuous spaces or 'stages', which provided a vehicle for display and where a series of acts were performed. Drawing from the discussion above on performance theory and practice, I will consider how some of these acts may have taken shape, looking at the emotive, physical and sensual aspects. First I shall discuss the sites of All Cannings Cross and East Chisenbury, drawing attention to particular structures and deposits.

All Cannings Cross

All Cannings Cross was excavated between 1911 and 1922 by Maud Cunnington (Cunnington 1923), and more recently by John Barrett and Dave McOmish in 2003 and 2004. The recent investigations have shown there to be a substantial mound spread over 15,000m² of lower chalk with deposits up to 0.60m deep (Brown *et al* forthcoming). Survey and subsequent excavations have revealed the presence of two further sites in the immediate environs, one at Stanton St Bernard, 600m to the east, and a smaller and discrete spread of dark earth and ceramics in the field of Heather Coombe, where the original site is located (Barrett and McOmish 2004). The deposits at Stanton St Bernard are more extensive, covering an area of 25,000m² and reaching a depth of 1.4m, and this still survives as a visible mound today. As the results from the recent excavations are currently awaiting publication, I shall focus most of my attention in this paper to a range of features excavated and published by Cunnington (1923).

This complex of sites lies on a gently sloping valley floor at the northern edge of the Vale of Pewsey in Wiltshire, and despite being only 1km apart, they are physically separated by the chalk spur of Cliffords Hill (Tullett 2008). The location is particularly dramatic, boasting excellent views across the Vale of Pewsey to the south, and framed to the north by the dramatic backdrop of the chalk escarpments, Tan and Clifford's Hill (Figures 9.1 and 9.2).

Figure 9.2 All Cannings Cross sits within the gently sloping valley floor, framed to the north by Clifford's Hill and Rybury hillfort (photo: author).

Rybury hillfort is located directly above the site on Clifford's Hill, and a short climb to the top and along to Tan Hill is very rewarding providing one with impressive views; looking across to the Cotswolds and Mendips in the northwest and southwest, the Marlborough Downs to the north, across the Vale of Pewsey to Salisbury Plain in the south, and northeast along the escarpment towards Avebury. This location was presumably extremely important and it seems likely that the locality was chosen for its position on a major routeway through the landscape and into the Vale of Pewsey.

The site was brought to Cunnington's attention in 1911 by the presence of large numbers of quern fragments and hammerstones scattered within the ploughsoil of Heather Coombe (Cunnington 1923, 13). The first trenches opened in 1911 produced a large quantity of broken pottery vessels, fragmented animal and human bone, bronze and iron fragments and objects, and large quantities of worked bone and stone. With the exception of the pits, postholes and chalk floors, most of the material came from 'a layer of dark soil, or humus, that varies in thickness from three to four inches up to one foot ten inches' (up to 0.56 cm thick) (Cunnington 1923, 14). The discovery of this site was very important in the early twentieth century, and the large pottery assemblage has provided the archetypal ceramic sequence for the Late Bronze Age and Early Iron Age period in southern England. This classic assemblage represents the emergence of new repertoires of ceramic styles, and stylistic innovations are apparent through the innovative decorative motifs and vessel forms, suggesting an increased desire for the public display and the communal consumption of food (Brown *et al* forthcoming). Recent excavations and ceramic analyses suggest the materials accumulated between the ninth and seventh centuries BC, with the main phase of deposition occurring during the eighth century BC (Brown *et al* forthcoming).

A series of nine rectangular laid chalk surfaces were identified and excavated across the site. They appear to have been kept clean and some sealed thick dark humic soils containing spreads of fragmented pottery and animal bone. These platforms were carefully constructed in a mixture of compacted chalk, flint and broken sarsen stones, forming a thickness of about 0.20m and encompassing relatively small areas, with the largest being roughly 9m by 6m. Some of the adjoining surfaces were burnt or fire-reddened, being constructed from compacted burnt clay, flints and chalk and containing reddened ash and charcoal fragments (Figure 9.3). It appears that some were related to consumption and depositional activities; for instance, platform F sealed a large deposit of pottery, described in publication as being 'packed tightly together in a large dump' (Cunnington 1923, 58).[5] Platform E also produced an interesting assemblage of artefacts, incorporating a chalk loomweight within its surface, and three saddle querns and 14 hammerstones were discovered resting on the surface (Cunnington 1923, 58). The other half of the platform had been burnt and this structure also sealed a pit (Pit 19), which contained four hammerstones, alongside worked clay, a serrated rib bone, and fragments of pottery and animal bone (Cunnington 1923, 64). We may draw some correlations between both the pit and platform assemblages, considering the quantities of hammerstones recovered. It is possible to establish from the published section sketches that these structures recur sporadically throughout the sequence, and in some instances there is a cyclical sequence of chalk platform, material accumulations, and chalk platform (Cunnington 1923; Figure 9.4). With the exception of the burnt platforms, this is a sequence recognised at East Chisenbury also (see below), suggesting these structures were important in the formation of the deposits and in the experience of the sites. The burnt platforms appeared to suffer very high temperatures and it may be possible in one sense to describe them as massive hearths where activities relating to food production and pottery and metalwork creation took place.

The chalk platforms were originally thought to represent the floors of rectangular houses, which had beendismantled and sometimes burnt during abandonment (Cunnington 1923, 14, 57). In the recent excavations at All Cannings Cross a sequence of pits and two overlying chalk platforms were excavated on the southeast corner of the site amongst the deepest deposits of 'dark humus', and some postholes were visibly associated with one of the structures (Barrett and McOmish 2004). That the structures represent houses is not, however, an interpretation preferred by the excavators, in that they appear to have been exposed to the elements and to trampling for periods of time (Brown *et al* forthcoming). Due to the association of some floors with large spreads of fragmented pottery and articulated animal bone, it has instead been proposed that they functioned as feasting structures (Barrett and McOmish 2004; Figure 9.5). Although some appear to have formed the focus for a range of acts relating to feasting, others

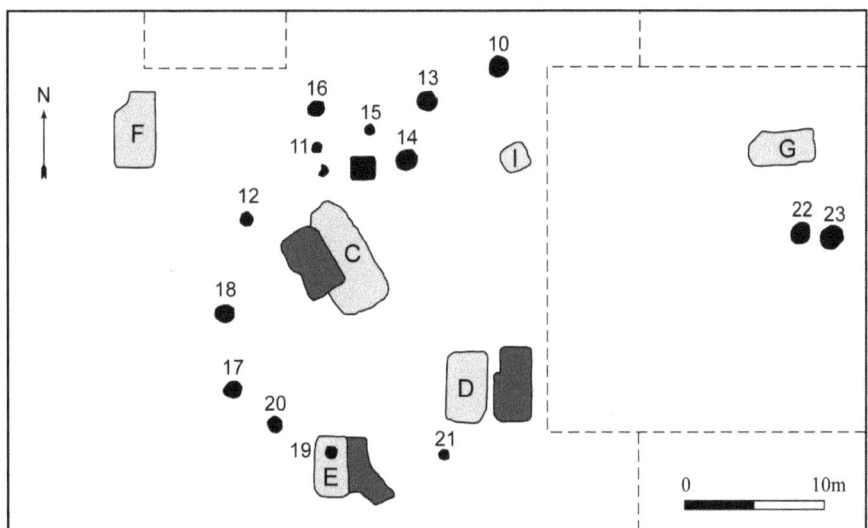

Figure 9.3 Plan of an area excavated by Cunnington at All Cannings Cross showing the position of various features; pits and post-holes are indicated in black, chalk platforms in light grey, and fire-reddened platforms in dark grey (adapted from Cunnington 1923, plate 2).

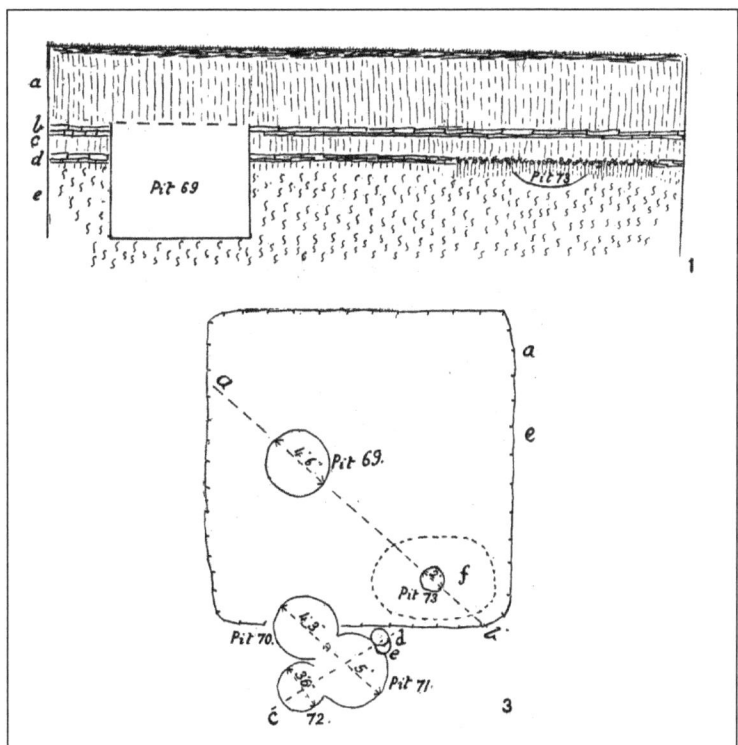

Figure 9.4 Top; Sketch of a section at All Cannings Cross showing a sequence of dark humic soils and chalk platforms (B and D show the location of the chalk platforms). Bottom; Plan of platform H (indicated as D in the section drawing), showing associated pits (adapted from Cunnington 1923, Plate 4).

Figure 9.5 Planning one of the irregular chalk platforms or floors at All Cannings Cross, during the recent excavations carried out by John Barrett and Dave McOmish. The surfaces incorporate and seal substantial deposits of material culture – animal bone and pottery can be seen along the nearest edge of the platform (Barrett and McOmish 2004; photograph courtesy of John Barrett and Dave McOmish).

appear to have been kept clean, and hence we may argue that they were incorporated within other performances taking place as well. Certainly it does appear that this material was repeatedly utilised to mark specific horizons and localities within the site; a series of five pits excavated by Cunnington were also capped with similar chalk and burnt clay surfaces (Pits 39, 40, 45, 46, 51; Cunnington 1923, 61). The surface sealing Pit 46 contained slabs of shaped chalk, which had been laid within a soft clay surface before it was fired *in situ*. Likewise, the fills of Pit 39 were sealed by a fired clay surface which contained fragmented pottery sherds (Cunnington 1923, 61). The dome-shaped profile of these features led Cunnington to interpret the structures as roofing for storage pits.[6] In contrast, I would argue that parallels can be drawn between the pit capping and the use of the chalk platforms discussed above, and the significance of these features is described below.

East Chisenbury

East Chisenbury is situated to the southeast of All Cannings Cross on Salisbury Plain, near the northern end of the Avon Valley where the river flows out of the Vale of Pewsey. The site is positioned on top of a chalk spur which looks down on to lower ground and possesses wide and extensive views from all directions; south-eastwards across Salisbury Plain, westwards towards the Late Bronze Age enclosures of Casterley Camp and Widdington Farm, with outstanding views of the Plain and a long stretch of the Avon, and northwards into the Vale of Pewsey (Figure 9.6). The Marlborough Downs are visible in the distance to the north, where the contemporary enclosure and midden complex of Martinsell Hill and Adam's Grave are visible (Brown *et al* forthcoming). When standing on this hilltop, it becomes strikingly clear that the site may have been chosen for these spectacular views, possessing uninterrupted horizons in all directions, including views of All Cannings Cross and Stanton St Bernard in the north (Brown *et al* forthcoming). Again we may argue that it was positioned along a routeway into the Vale, defined in part by the River Avon nearby. This evidently became a focal place in the landscape where people and animals repeatedly came together.

The mound was discovered in the 1990s when the military authorities were planning the construction of a new road cutting across the top of the hilltop, which was at first assumed to be completely natural. Following survey and the excavation of two small trenches, it became clear that the hilltop had been physically enhanced in the Late Bronze Age, when massive quantities of materials were accumulated. The mound at East Chisenbury is 25,000m² in size and remains nearly 3m high in the landscape despite compaction, erosion, cultivation and tree planting (McOmish *et al* 2002, 73). Augur survey reveals this mound is 200m in diameter, and a staggering *c.* 65,000 cubic metres of the original mound survives despite centuries of erosion (McOmish 1996, 70; McOmish *et al* 2002, 73; Brown *et al* forthcoming). It is argued that a substantial, and as yet undated prehistoric enclosure, is located immediately to the east of the midden mound (Brown *et al* forthcoming). It is suggested that this is an earlier construct and survey has indicated the material accumulations partially overlie this feature (McOmish *et al* 2002, 73; Brown *et al* forthcoming).[7]

Three seasons of excavation took place in the years 1992-4, when two small trenches were opened to examine the nature and depths of the deposits. Trench A was 2m by 1m and located in the centre of the mound (Brown *et al* forthcoming). The trench was excavated in 1m sample squares and 0.10m spits, but due to the quantity of material, only one square was completely excavated. Trench B was 3m by 2m, and located on the southern perimeter of the mound (Brown *et al* forthcoming). The deposits in this trench reached a depth of 1.67m and a sequence of postholes and a hearth were discovered at the base of the sequence.

The depths of the stratigraphy and the volume of finds produced made the excavation of these small areas incredibly slow and cumbersome. A staggering 10,000 pottery sherds were recovered from these small excavations, many of which are similar in style to the ceramics of Potterne and All Cannings Cross (Raymond forthcoming).[7] At the base of the midden there are vessel

Figure 9.6 View from the top of the mound at East Chisenbury, with All Cannings Cross in the distance to the north (photo: author).

fragments of post Deverel-Rimbury plain wares, whilst the main accumulations contained vessel forms of post Deverel-Rimbury decorated wares (Raymond forthcoming). This provisionally places the main depositional phase between the ninth and seventh centuries BC, with activity diminishing by the end of the seventh century BC, although the analysts do suggest that the deposits belong mostly to the eighth century BC (Brown *et al* forthcoming). The presence of adjoining potsherds within different layers, alongside the occurrence of earlier and later styles of pottery within the primary layers of the sequences, also demonstrate the repeated mixing of residues prior to their final deposition on this part of the site (Raymond forthcoming). At Potterne, the incomplete nature of the pottery spreads led Morris to interpret the residues as secondary acts of deposition, deriving originally from settlement middens

Figure 9.7 Top left; Grave digging at the cemetery of Potterne, August 2005. Right; animal bone and pottery collected from the spoil heap of the grave. Bottom; The section of the grave, showing a deep sequence of deposits and a laid stone surface (greensand) running horizontally through the section. (photos: author).

(2000, 177). Given the extensive nature of these sites it seems more likely that the residues were manipulated and moved around internally, possibly during transitional times when different spaces became restructured (Waddington 2008). This section will briefly discuss the sequence of chalk platforms from the excavated areas, and will present some preliminary interpretations offered by the analysts (Brown *et al* forthcoming).

The sequence in both the trenches is a complex layering of dark humic material accumulations, which are interweaved with laid chalk surfaces. Similar to All Cannings Cross, some of the chalk surfaces had the appearance of being deliberately rammed to create a floor which had been kept clean and exposed, and they included fragments of charcoal, pottery and animal bone. For example, a chalk layer in trench B (context 22) contained 377g of animal bone and 898g of pottery sherds. This surface was constructed upon another (context 23), which produced similar quantities of materials, and directly beneath this was a large deposit of chalk rubble (context 24). This latter deposit does not represent a laid surface as such, but rather a compact spread of chalk rubble with substantial quantities of materials intermingled within; 5,639g of animal bone, 5,616g of pottery sherds and one human bone (see below). There are at least 18 events of chalk deposition within the sequences in the trenches, and these vary in size and depth within the excavated areas, with some being only 1m wide (David Field pers. comm.).

Although the small size of the trenches make it impossible to discuss overall dimensions, it may be possible to argue that the patchy chalk surfaces originally covered larger areas of the site than has previously been imagined. More recent investigations reiterate the regular occurrence of these surfaces across the mound; an augur hole in another area produced two distinct chalk surfaces within the sequence, one at 0.40-0.60m deep and a further one at 1.15-1.40m deep (Norcott 2006, 39).

At East Chisenbury, the chalk surfaces were viewed as playing an important role in the formation of the mound, and their clean appearance has led to some provisional interpretations relating to site management strategies; as either providing routeways for people and animals, providing 'tipping' platforms for depositional events, or as a mechanism for sealing the noxious gases produced by the decaying organic residues (Brown *et al* forthcoming). Another interpretation is that the structures acted as end points in the various sequences of deposition, and certainly it does appear that the deposition of chalk played an important role in the formation of the mound. A large manmade chalk hollow discovered during survey, 20m in diameter and 3m deep, is located some 40m to the northeast of the mound, possibly indicating the location where this material was quarried (McOmish *et al* 2002, 73). The act of quarrying chalk and spreading this material to enhance and monumentalise manmade features is noted later on in the British Iron Age. For instance, hillfort ramparts are often faced in white chalk to stand out against green grassy landscapes, as demonstrated at Segsbury Camp on the Berkshire Downs for instance. Such acts may be viewed as 'forms of display in its own right' (Gosden 2004, 42), and it may be possible to view the chalk structures at East Chisenbury and All Cannings Cross in a similar way too.

Recently, Wessex Archaeology excavated some evaluation trenches at a midden discovered at Westbury in Wiltshire, situated on the cusp of greensand and chalk, just south of Potterne (Wessex Archaeology 2004). This evaluation identified a large site comparable to All Cannings Cross and East Chisenbury, and although smaller at 3,800m^2, Westbury produced comparative artefact-rich dark soils and structures (Wessex Archaeology 2004). A chalk surface excavated in one the evaluation trenches also sealed deposits of pottery and animal bone. Similar chalk surfaces were identified in the excavations at the greensand site of Potterne (Lawson *et al* 2000, 255-256), and although they occur less frequently than the other sites discussed in this paper, their very appearance is noteworthy as this material had to be imported. More recently a stone surface was observed within the four sections of a grave cut in the modern cemetery at Potterne, although this surface appeared to be constructed out of greensand, rather than chalk (Figure 9.7).[9] The recurrence of these features at a number of complexes in Wiltshire suggests they had particular functions and significances, being appropriate locations for display and forming a series of 'stages' where different performances occurred. Some of these acts of display involved the manipulation, fragmentation, mixing and accumulation of various materials and substances. Drawing from a range of performance theory and practice, let us now consider how some of these events may have been played out and experienced.

Narratives of performance and action

In performance theory it has been argued that as soon as a stage is created, a new social dynamic is produced, and performance is amplified by the attention and gaze of the spectators or participants and the special quality of the situation (Benjamin 1977, 156; Pearson and Shanks 2001, 67). Performance may be signalled, at least in part, by a way of speaking, moving and acting that contrasts the conduct of everyday routine with more formalised or special styles of behaviour (Bell 1997, 74). We should not assume that performance is 'restricted to any such social or cultural locale as a theatre or ritual' (Pearson and Shanks 2001, 69). Today this may include a wide range of activities, genres and localities; theatre, sporting events, dance, carnivals, festivals, music concerts, funerals, play, public spectacles or more private engagements.

As briefly discussed above, the theory of performativity is integral here, being an important and crucial dimension in everyday life (Butler 1990; Harris 2005; Pearson and Shanks 2001, 69). Whilst performativity and performance should not be mistaken as being the same process, some of the concepts are fairly similar, in that both involve social display on some level. When we think of a performance today, we generally think of a separation between the actors and players and the collective audience (e.g. Benjamin 1970, 149, 156). We should not assume that there is always a separation between 'performers' and those who observe as an 'audience', as in some instances 'the spectacle is bound up with the scene' (Baudrillard 2003, 27). In carnivalesque environments, for example, there are no real spectators as everyone present is immersed to one degree or another (Bailey 2005, 190-195; Cochrane 2005, 8). In these contexts, status quo and power relations are often overturned, and gender and status roles are subverted; it is a time for social affirmation, liberation, subversion, colourful displays, fantasy, consumption, surrealism, intoxication, and debauchery (Bailey 2005, 191).

Butler (1990, 136) articulates this point in her discussion of contemporary drag; such displays are often most appropriate in the context of the carnival or show, seeking to subvert gender roles through processes of parody and ostentation. Indeed, the carnivalesque plays an important political and social role in many societies across the world, 'loudly proclaiming alternate worldviews in which existing norms and values (are) inverted' (Bailey 2005, 190). A consideration of these perspectives enables one to consider the complex layering of the social within the residues at the sites discussed here. Rather than comprehend the residues as forming through symbolic or economic action, we may instead consider the ways in which certain spaces, materials and architectures came to matter through the daily negotiation of people's lives, and through the construction and performance of the 'self' within the communal events which took place there.

I first wish to consider the conspicuous materiality of the stone platforms whose luminosity and surface quality provided a vehicle for display in itself. At a very basic level, and perhaps for only a short time span, the visual contrast between the clean white chalk and the surrounding deposits must have been incredibly striking. At East Chisenbury, for example, the sequences of chalk layers may suggest that large parts of the mound became covered in a patchy layer of chalk for a period of time. If this were the case, then we may envisage substantial parts of the hilltop becoming illuminated in white on particular occasions in the agricultural cycle; the visual display, not only from the hilltop, but further afield, must have been dramatic. Such displays would have been relatively transient affairs, however, as chalk not only develops a green mouldy surface on decay, but also the rapid accumulation of deposits suggests these surfaces became concealed fairly quickly. The act of quarrying the chalk, creating and standing on the surfaces would be experienced very differently depending on the time of year. In summer, during dry, hot weather, this material would be concreted and dusty, whereas in cooler and wetter climes such as winter, it would become wet, slippery and sticky, caking bodies and things in a white chalky substance. Chalk is utilised in other contexts at East Chisenbury as a vehicle for expression and display. The presence of chalk inlays on a number of decorated potsherds suggests that the curation of this material was also associated with the creation of some pottery vessels (Figure 9.8).

The sense of interruption provided by the chalk surfaces created a series of arenas where both intimate and communal performances took place. This would have been amplified by the lighting of fires on or adjacent to the platforms, and even through the chalk material itself, which would have occasionally become illuminated in sunshine, moonlight and firelight. The individual platforms may have been associated with different family or social groups, providing visual markers and commemorating the location of earlier episodes of deposition. Their creation may have enabled people to orientate themselves through the complex and to delineate particular spaces or establish future meeting places. This is particularly explicit when we consider the chalk domed surfaces which sealed a range of pits at All Cannings Cross (see above). They effectively created a series of miniature monuments which were visible throughout the site and possibly cited the actions and identities of specific persons. The act of digging a pit, deliberately back-filling it with earth and materials, followed by the final capping with a stone surface, undoubtedly played important roles in the negotiation of some people's social values. By physically sealing some of the pits with carefully constructed chalk and fired clay surfaces, people were not only limiting the possibility of later disturbance, they were also ensuring that the locations became observed, if only for a time, within some future activities at the site. Thus processes of

Figure 9.8 A decorated pottery sherd with chalk inlay from trench B, context 22, at East Chisenbury (photo: author).

remembering *and* forgetting became inextricably shaped by the actions of displaying and concealing materials. Although the features were not permanent fixtures, in that they too became concealed by the residues from later activities, they articulate a desire for innovative displays, which referenced a range of events, concerns and knowledge.

On the chalk platforms themselves, we can envisage people engaging in various activities, sometimes evoking the carnivalesque through colourful and debauched displays of singing, dancing, speaking and shouting. Food may have been prepared, animals killed for sacrifice and consumption, and then roasted on the fire-reddened surfaces. They may have provided adequate surfaces where cups and bowls and plates were smashed and fragmented, artefacts destroyed, creating noise and disruption, social affirmation, and again creating a display. The structures may even have served a funerary role, where bodies of the dead were laid out for funerary rites (e.g. Parker Pearson 1999, 49). For instance at East Chisenbury, the fragmented and manipulated bones from at least ten people were recovered from the excavation trenches, and this suggests that hundreds, possibly thousands of human bones, were deposited within the mound (Brown *et al* forthcoming). The incorporation of a human phalange within a chalk rubble layer in trench B (context 24; see above) may be an explicit indicator that human bodies were excarnated and fragmented here, as the small bones from hands and feet are rarely curated during such practices. Alongside the visual display of bodies of the dead, materials with complex lifecycles were assembled, displayed, manipulated and fragmented on these platforms. We should remember here the combination of materials placed on platform E at All Cannings Cross, which included hammerstones, saddle querns, a chalk loomweight and fragments of pottery and animal bone. The small dimensions of the platforms at All Cannings Cross suggests that only limited numbers of people could be present on them at any one time, and hence they may have provided arenas where people greeted one another on intimate occasions, (re)establishing relations through the flow of substances and artefacts (e.g. Chapman 2000).

At night we can envisage roaring fires warming the skin, bringing people together, transfixing the gaze, and creating colourful, flickering lights and exciting, sensual pleasures. Acrid smoke may have permeated eyes and nostrils, creating tension and discomfort, singeing flesh, hair and clothing. All these moments would be 'framed' by differences in dress, ornamentation, language, speech and movement (Bauman 1975, 295), and the presence of old and new faces, both local and perhaps from afar, would further accentuate these different atmospheres. These performances would have brought about transformations of some kind, bringing about certain shifts and changes, both emotive and physical, and new situations and experiences (Bauman 1975, 302-304; Bell 1997, 74-75; Turner 1982, 89-101). The processes of burning at these platforms, at All Cannings Cross at least, would have provided an appropriate and necessary means for display and transformation. We have no reason in assuming that a single and consistent meaning was derived from the use of these settings, or the creation and performance of acts.

Conclusion

This paper has sought to demonstrate that human experience is dynamic, complex and fluid, and we should endeavour to accentuate this in archaeology by utilising multidisciplinary approaches and by creating multiple narratives. Peoples, animals, places, substances and things should not be interpreted as separate actors with a set of prescribed roles in the world, but rather they should be understood as entangled elements within a continual process of understanding and being. The sites discussed in this paper are structured through a range of transitory and localised settings and stages, represented by hearths, platforms, large deposits of materials, and timber post structures. These locales are both architectural and depositional, and they were places for events and offerings, and for the social dynamics of performance and display. A fluid cycle of comings and goings, exchange and consumption, involving peoples, animals and things all contributed to the accumulation of materials at these sites. The processes of material fragmentation, burning, decay and mixing were important, creating regeneration and renewal in the community (Waddington 2008). These acts of creative rememberings and forgettings produced locales through which the politics of the everyday could be negotiated, and where identities and relationships could be cited, improvised and publicly displayed.

Acknowledgements

I am grateful to Dave McOmish, Dave Field and Graham Brown for granting me access to the forthcoming publication on the East Chisenbury excavations and for allowing me to discuss some of the results and analyses in this paper. Discussions with Dave Field on East Chisenbury were invaluable. Many thanks are also extended to John Barrett for discussing the All Cannings Cross excavations with me and for allowing me to use a photograph of a chalk platform from the recent excavations. I wish to thank Niall Sharples for his support and supervision in my doctoral research, and for his critical comments on this paper. Andrew Cochrane and Penny Bickle provided numerous insightful comments on this paper, and Alasdair Whittle's suggestions on an earlier version were of tremendous help. Funding for this doctoral research is provided by the Arts and Humanities Research Council. I am grateful to Mark Maltby and James Morris for allowing me to contribute this paper to the publication. Any errors remaining in this paper are entirely my own.

Additional Notes

[1] The session was entitled 'The role of environmental analysis in integrated investigations of ritual deposits', Archaeological Environmental Association, Exeter University, 30 March 2006.

[2] The excavated 'midden' complexes are All Cannings Cross and Stanton St Bernard (Cunnington 1923; Barrett and McOmish 2004), Potterne (Lawson 2000), East Chisenbury (McOmish 1996; Brown et al forthcoming) and Westbury (Wessex Archaeology 2004) in Wiltshire, the Thames Valley site of Runnymede Bridge in Berkshire (Needham 1991, Needham and Spence 1997), Whitchurch in Warwickshire (Waddington and Sharples forthcoming), Llanmaes in the Vale of Glamorgan (Lodwick and Gwilt 2004; 2005), and Welland Bank in Peterborough (Pryor 1998, 116-212). This list is not exhaustive (see Figure 9.1 for the location of others), and does not include sites provisionally identified through fieldwalking.

[3] The festa of the Madonna on 115th St, the Mukanda initiation among the Ndembu and the potlatch among the Kwakiutl are good examples of these activities (Bell 1997, 201). The initiation rites of the Orokaiva in Papua New Guinea involve all parts of settlement space (Bloch 1992, 22). Rites of exit and entry into dwelling structures in some societies are documented by van Gennep (1960, 23-25).

[4] I employ the term 'platform' to describe a surface or area on which something may stand, rather than a raised level surface, which is so often associated with this term.

[5] Due to the way it was excavated and subsequently analysed, no quantitative information is available for analysis and it is therefore difficult to establish the phasing of these platforms.

[6] Cunnington also describes the features as containing 'entrance passages leading down to the level of the base of the pit' (Cunnington 1923, 61). The description and section sketches are slightly confusing and it is difficult to establish whether these 'entrance passages' were associated with these features, or whether earlier linear-shaped features were being recognised, which were simply cut by these later pits.

[7] Further excavations are required in order to validate the claim that an enclosure exists on the site, and future investigations should attempt to explore the relationship between the earthworks and midden.

[8] A recent analysis carried out by the author has demonstrated that the total pottery assemblage weighs 77,237g, a staggering quantity of material given the small size of the excavation trenches.

[9] In contrast, the Berkshire site of Runnymede Bridge did not produce chalk surfaces, although this may be due to the natural geology of the site, rather than major differences in formation processes. Runnymede did produce floors consisting of compacted fragments of pottery, fired clay and burnt flint, and also a cobbled burnt flint surface, and these may have performed similar roles (Needham 1991; pers. comm.).

Bibliography

Bailey, D. W. (2005) *Prehistoric Figurines: Representation and Corporeality in the Neolithic*. London, Routledge.

Barrett, J.C. (1994) *Fragments from Antiquity*. Oxford, Blackwell.

Barrett, J.C., and McOmish, D. (2004) *All Cannings Cross*. http://www.kennet.gov.uk/planservices/AveburyW.nsf/AllCanningsdiary accessed March 2006.

Baudrillard, J. (2003) *Passwords*. London, Verso Books.

Bauman, R. (1975) Verbal art as performance. *American Anthropologist*, 77, 290-311.

Benjamin, W. (1977) What is epic theatre? In. H. Arendt (ed.) *Illuminations*, 148-56. London, Fontana.

Bell, C. (1992) *Ritual Theory, Ritual Practice*. Oxford, Oxford University Press.

Bell, C. (1997). *Ritual: Perspectives and Dimensions*. Oxford, Oxford University Press.

Bloch, M. E. F. (1992) *Prey into Hunter: the Politics of Religious Experience*. Cambridge, Cambridge University Press.

Bloch, M. E. F. (1995) Questions not to ask of Malagasy carvings. In. I. Hodder, M. Shanks, A. Alexandri, V. Buchli, J. Carmen, J. Last and G. Lucus (eds.) *Interpreting Archaeology: Finding Meaning in the Past*, 212-215. London, Routledge.

Bloch, M. E. F. and Parry, J. (1982) Introduction: death and the regeneration of life. In. M. E. F. Bloch and J. Parry (eds.) *Death and the Regeneration of Life*, 1-44. Cambridge, Cambridge University Press.

Bourdieu, P. (1977) *Outline of a Theory of Practice*. Cambridge, Cambridge University Press.

Bowden, M., and McOmish, D. (1987) The required barrier. *Scottish Archaeological Review* 4, 76-84.

Bradley, R. (2005) *Ritual and Domestic Life*. London, Routledge.

Brown, G., Field, D. and McOmish, D. (1994) East Chisenbury midden complex, Wiltshire. In. A. P. Fitzpatrick and E. L. Morris (eds.) *The Iron Age in Wessex: Recent Work*, 46-49. Salisbury, Trust for Wessex Archaeology.

Brown, G., Field, D. and McOmish, D. (Forthcoming) *The Late Bronze Age – Early Iron Age Site at East Chisenbury, Wiltshire*.

Brück, J. (1995) A place for the dead: the role of human remains in late Bronze Age Britain. *Proceedings of the Prehistoric Society* 61, 245-277.

Brück, J. (1999a) Houses, lifecycles and deposition on middle Bronze Age settlements in Southern

England. *Proceedings of the Prehistoric Society* 65, 145-166.

Brück, J. (1999b) Rituals and rationality: some problems of interpretation in European archaeology. *European Journal of Archaeology*, 2, 313-344.

Brück, J. (2001) Body metaphors and technologies of transformation in the English middle and late Bronze Age. In. J. Brück (ed.) *Bronze Age Landscapes: Tradition and Transformation*, 149-160. Oxford, Oxbow.

Brück, J. (2006) Fragmentation, personhood and the social construction of technology in middle and late Bronze Age Britain. *Cambridge Archaeological Journal*, 16, 297-315.

Butler, J. (1990) *Gender Trouble: Feminism and the Subversion of Identity*. New York, Routledge.

Carr, G. and Knüsel, C. (1997) The ritual framework of excarnation by exposure as the mortuary practice of the early and middle Iron Ages of central southern Britain. In. A. Gwilt and C. Haselgrove (eds.) *Reconstructing Iron Age Societies*, 167-73. Oxford, Oxbow.

Chapman, J. (2000) *Fragmentation in Archaeology: People, Places and Broken Objects in the Prehistory of South-Eastern Europe*. London, Routledge.

Cochrane, A. (2005) A taste of the unexpected: subverting *mentalités* through the motifs and settings of Irish passage tombs. In. D. Hofmann, J. Mills and A. Cochrane (eds.) *Elements of Being: Mentalities, Identities and Movements*, 5-19. Oxford, British Archaeological Report International Series 1437.

Cunnington, M. E. (1923) *The Early Iron Age Inhabited Site at All Cannings Cross Farm, Wiltshire*. Devizes, G. Simpson.

Dietler, M. (1996) Feasts and commensal politics in the political economy: food, power and status in prehistoric Europe. In. P. Wiessner and W. Schiefenhövel (eds.) *Food and the Status Quest: an Interdisciplinary Perspective*, 87-125. Providence, Berghahn.

Fitzpatrick, A. (1997) Everyday life in the Iron Age of Wessex. In. A. Gwilt and C. Haselgrove (eds.) *Reconstructing Iron Age Societies*, 73-86. Oxford, Oxbow.

Fowler, C. (2004) *The Archaeology of Personhood: an Anthropological Approach*. London, Routledge.

Goody, J. R. (1977) Against ritual: loosely structured thoughts on a loosely defined topic. In. S. F. Moore and B. G. Myerhoff (eds.) *Secular Ritual*, 25-35. Amsterdam, Van Gorcum.

Gosden, C. (2004) Making and display: our aesthetic appreciation of things and objects. In. C. Renfrew, C. Gosden and E. DeMarrais (eds.) *Substance, Memory, Display: Archaeology and Art*, 35-46. Cambridge, McDonald Institute for Archaeological Research.

Harris, O. (2005) Agents of identity: performative practice at the Etton causeway enclosure. In. D. Hofmann, J. Mills and A. Cochrane (eds.) *Elements of Being: Mentalities, Identities and Movements*, 40-49. Oxford, British Archaeological Report International Series 1437.

Hill, J. D. (1995) *Ritual and Rubbish in the Iron Age of Wessex*. Oxford, British Archaeological Report British Series 242.

Hingley, R. (1990) Boundaries surrounding Iron Age and Romano-British settlements. *Scottish Archaeological Review* 7, 96-103.

Hingley, R. (1992) Society of Scotland from 700 BC to AD 200. *Proceedings of the Society of Antiquaries of Scotland* 122, 7-53.

Hingley, R. (1995) The Iron Age in Atlantic Scotland: searching for the meaning of the substantial house. In. J. D. Hill and C. G. Cumberpatch (eds.) *Different Iron Ages: Studies on the Iron Age in Temperate Europe*, 185-194. Oxford, British Archaeological Report British Series 602.

Ingold, T. (2000) *The Perception of the Environment: Essays in Livelihood, Dwelling and Skill*. London, Routledge.

Knappett, C. (2005) *Thinking through Material Culture: an Interdisciplinary Perspective*. Philadelphia, University of Philadelphia Press.

Latour, B. (1993) *We have never been Modern*. Hertfordshire, Harvester Wheatsheaf.

Latour, B. (2000) The Berlin key or how to do words with things. In. P. M. Graves-Brown (ed.) *Matter, Materiality, and Modern Culture*, 10-21. London, Routledge.

Lawson, A. J. (2000) *Potterne 1982-5: Animal Husbandry in Later Prehistoric Wiltshire*. Salisbury, Trust for Wessex Archaeology 17.

Lawson, A., Powell, A. and Thomas, R. (2000) Discussion. In. A. J. Lawson (ed.) *Potterne 1982-5: Animal Husbandry in Later Prehistoric Wiltshire*, 250-272. Salisbury, Trust for Wessex Archaeology 17.

Lewis, G. (1980) *Day of Shining Red: an Essay on Understanding Ritual*. Cambridge, Cambridge University Press.

Lodwick, M. and Gwilt. A. (2004) Cauldrons and consumption: Llanmaes and Llyn Fawr. *Archaeology in Wales* 44, 77-81.

Lodwick, M. and Gwilt, A. (2005) Continuing excavation at Llanmaes, Vale of Glamorgan. *Archaeology in Wales* 45, 91-92.

Luby, E. M. and Gruber, M. F. (1999) The dead must be fed: symbolic meanings of the shellmounds of the San Francisco Bay area. *Cambridge Archaeological Journal* 9, 95-108.

McOmish, D. (1996) East Chisenbury: ritual and rubbish at the British Bronze Age-Iron Age transition. *Antiquity* 70, 68-76.

McOmish, D., Field, D. and Brown, G. (2002) *The Field Archaeology of the Salisbury Plain Training Area*. London, English Heritage.

Miracle, P. (2002) Mesolithic Meals from Mesolithic Middens. In. P. Miracle and N. Milner (eds.) *Consuming Passions and Patterns of Consumption*, 65-88. Oxford, Oxbow.

Miracle, P., and Milner, N. (2002) (eds.) *Consuming Passions and Patterns of Consumption*. Oxford, Oxbow.

Moran, J. (2005) *Reading the Everyday*. London, Routledge.

Mulville, J., Parker Pearson, M., Sharples, N. M., Smith, H. and Chamberlain, A. (2003) Quarters, arcs and squares: human and animal remains in the Hebridean Late Iron Age. In. J. Downes and A. Ritchie (eds.) *Sea Change: Orkney and Northern Europe in the later Iron Age AD 300-800*, 20-34. Balgavies, Angus, Pinkfoot Press.

Needham, S. P. (1991) *Excavation and Salvage at Runnymede Bridge, 1978: the Late Bronze Age Waterfront Site*. London, British Museum Press.

Needham, S. P. (1993) The Structure of settlement and ritual in the late Bronze Age of south-east Britain. In. C. Mordant and A. Richard (eds.) *L'Habitat et L'Occupation du Sol á L'Âge du Bronze en Europe: Actes du Colloque International de Lons-le-Saunier, 16-19 Mai 1990*, 49-69. Paris, Éditions du Comité des Travaux historique et scientifique. Documents Préhistoriques 4.

Needham, S. P. (1996) Chronology and periodization in the British Bronze Age. *Acta Archaeologica* 67, 121-140.

Needham, S. P. and Spence, T. (1997) Refuse and the formation of middens. *Antiquity* 71, 77-90.

Needham, S. P. and Stig-Sørensen, M. L. (1988) Runnymede refuse tip: a consideration of midden deposits and their formation. In. J. C. Barrett and I. A. Kinnes (eds.) *The Archaeology of Context in the Neolithic and Bronze Age: Recent Trends*, 113-126. Sheffield, University of Sheffield.

Norcott, D. (2006) Later prehistoric midden sites in the Vale of Pewsey: a multi-proxi geoarchaeological study. University of Reading, Unpublished M.A. Thesis.

Parker Pearson, M. (1996) Food, fertility and front doors in the first millennium BC. In. T. C. Champion and J. R. Collis (eds.) *The Iron Age in Britain and Ireland: Recent Trends*, 117-132. Sheffield, J.R. Collis Publications.

Parker Pearson, M. (1999) *The Archaeology of Death and Burial*. Stroud, Sutton.

Parker Pearson, M. (2000) Eating money: a study in the ethnoarchaeology of food. *Archaeological Dialogues* 7, 217-232.

Parker Pearson, M. and Richards, C. (1994) Ordering the world: perceptions of architecture, space and time. In. M. Parker Pearson and C. Richards (eds.) *Architecture and Order: Approaches to Social Space*, 1-37. London, Routledge.

Pearson, M. (2006) *In Comes I: Performance, Memory and Landscape*. Exeter, University of Exeter Press.

Pearson, M. and Shanks, M. (2001) *Theatre/Archaeology*. London, Routledge.

Pollard, J. (2001) The aesthetics of depositional practice. *World Archaeology* 33, 315-333.

Pollard, J. (2004) The art of decay and the transformation of substance. In. C. Renfrew, C. Gosden and E. DeMarrais (eds.) *Substance, Memory, Display: Archaeology and Art*, 47-62. Cambridge, McDonald Institute for Archaeological Research.

Pollard, J. (2005) Memory, monuments and middens in the Neolithic landscape. In. G. Brown, D. Field and D. McOmish (eds.) *The Avebury Landscape: Aspects of the Field Archaeology of the Marlborough Downs*, 103-14. Oxford, Oxbow.

Pryor, F. (1998) *Farmers in Prehistoric Britain*. Stroud, Tempus.

Raftery, B. (1996) *Trackway Excavations in the Mount Dillon Bogs, Co. Longford 1985-1991*. Dublin, Irish Archaeological Wetland Unit Transactions 3.

Raymond, F. (Forthcoming) Note on the Ceramics from East Chisenbury. In. G. Brown, D. Field and D. McOmish (eds.) *The Late Bronze Age – Early Iron Age Site at East Chisenbury, Wiltshire*.

Richards, C. and Thomas, J. (1984) Ritual activity and structured deposition in later Neolithic Wessex. In. R. Bradley and J. Gardiner (eds.) *Neolithic Studies, a Review of Some Current Research*, 189-218. Oxford, British Archaeological Report British Series 133.

Salih, S. (2002) *Judith Butler*. London, Routledge.

Sharples, N. M. (2000) Antlers and Orcadian rituals: an ambiguous role for red deer in the Neolithic. In. A. Ritchie (ed.) *Neolithic Orkney in its European Context*, 107-116. Cambridge, MacDonald Institute for Archaeological Research.

Shepherd, S. and Wallis, M. (2004) *Drama/Theatre/Performance: a New Critical Idiom*, London, Routledge.

Thomas, J. (1991) *Rethinking the Neolithic*. Cambridge, Cambridge University Press.

Tilley, C. (1996) *An Ethnography of the Neolithic: early Prehistoric Societies in Southern Scandinavia*. Cambridge, Cambridge University Press.

Tullett, A. (2008) Black earth, bone and bits of old pot: the Pewsey middens. Recent work by the University of Sheffield. In. O. Davis, N. Sharples and K. Waddington (eds.) *Changing Perspectives on the First Millennium BC*, 11-20. Oxford, Oxbow.

Turner, V. (1969) *The Ritual Process: Structure and Anti-structure*. Chicago, Aldine.

Turner, V. (1982) *From Ritual to Theatre: the Human Seriousness of Play*. New York, PAJ Publications.

van Gennep, A. (1960) *The Rites of Passage*. London, Routledge and Kegan Paul.

Waddington, K. E. (2008) Topographies of accumulation at late Bronze Age Potterne. In. O. P. Davis, N. M. Sharples and K. E. Waddington (eds.) *Changing Perspectives on the First Millennium BC*, 161-84. Oxford, Oxbow.

Waddington, K. E., and Sharples, N. M. (Forthcoming) *The Whitchurch Excavations 2006: an Interim*

Report. Cardiff, Cardiff University Archaeological Reports.

Wessex Archaeology, (2004) Proposed Westbury Eastern By-pass, Wiltshire: Archaeological Evaluation Report. Salisbury, unpublished client report (54100.03).

Whimster, R. (1981) *Burial Practices in Iron Age Britain*. Oxford, British Archaeological Report British Series 90.

Whittle, A. (2003) *The Archaeology of People: Dimensions of Neolithic life*. London, Routledge.

Author's affiliation

Kate Waddington
Cardiff School of Archaeology and History
Cardiff University
Humanities building
Colum Drive
Cardiff
CF10 3EU
UK

www.ingramcontent.com/pod-product-compliance
Lightning Source LLC
Chambersburg PA
CBHW050941010526
44108CB00060B/2855